Thomas Bulfinch

Oregon and Eldorado

Or, Romance of the Rivers

Thomas Bulfinch

Oregon and Eldorado

Or, Romance of the Rivers

ISBN/EAN: 9783744770002

Printed in Europe, USA, Canada, Australia, Japan

Cover: Foto ©Andreas Hilbeck / pixelio.de

More available books at **www.hansebooks.com**

OREGON AND ELDORADO;

OR,

ROMANCE OF THE RIVERS.

BY
THOMAS BULFINCH,
AUTHOR OF "THE AGE OF FABLE," "THE AGE OF CHIVALRY," ETC.

BOSTON:
J. E. TILTON AND COMPANY.
1866.

PREFACE.

WHEN one observes attentively the maps of South and North America, no feature appears more striking than the provision which Nature seems to have made, in both continents, for water-communication across the breadth of each. In the Northern continent, this channel of communication is formed by the Missouri and Columbia Rivers, which stretch over an extent of three thousand miles, interrupted only by the ridge of the Rocky Mountains. In the Southern continent, the River Amazon, in its path from the Andes to the sea, traverses a course of thirty-three hundred miles. In both cases, a few hundred miles of land-carriage will complete the transit from ocean to ocean. The analogy presented in the length and direction of these magnificent water-pathways is preserved in their history. A series of romantic adventures attaches to each. I indulge the hope, that young readers who have so favorably received my former attempts to amuse and instruct them, in my several works reviving the fabulous legends of remote ages, will find equally attractive these true narratives of bold adventure, whose date is comparatively recent. Moreover, their scenes are laid, in the one instance, in our own country; and, in the other, in that great and rising empire of Brazil to which our distinguished naturalist, Prof. Agassiz, has gone on a pilgrimage of science. It will enable us better to appreciate the discoveries and observations which the professor will lay before us on his return, to know something beforehand of the history and peculiarities of the region which is the scene of his labors; and, on the other hand, the route across the North-American continent, to which the first part of the volume relates, derives increased interest, at this time, from the fact that it nearly corresponds to the route of the contemplated Northern Pacific Railroad.

BOSTON, June, 1866. T. B.

CONTENTS.

OREGON.

CHAPTER I.
DISCOVERY OF COLUMBIA RIVER . . . . .

CHAPTER II.
LEWIS AND CLARKE . . . .

CHAPTER III.
THE SIOUX . . . .

CHAPTER IV.
SUMMARY OF TRAVEL TO WINTER-QUARTERS . . .

CHAPTER V.
INDIAN TRIBES . . . .

CHAPTER VI.
THE MARCH RESUMED . . . .

CHAPTER VII.
THE JOURNEY CONTINUED . . . .

CONTENTS.

CHAPTER VIII.
The Sources of the Missouri and Columbia 97

CHAPTER IX.
The Party in the Boats 107

CHAPTER X.
The Descent of the Columbia 120

CHAPTER XI.
Clarke's River 131

CHAPTER XII.
Kooskooskee River 147

CHAPTER XIII.
Winter-Quarters 176

CHAPTER XIV.
A New Year 187

CHAPTER XV.
Winter Life 197

CHAPTER XVI.
The Return 210

CHAPTER XVII.
The Rocky Mountains 230

CHAPTER XVIII.
Capt. Clarke's Route down the Yellowstone . . . 241

ELDORADO.

CHAPTER I.
THE DISCOVERY 255

CHAPTER II.
ORELLANA DESCENDS THE RIVER 265

CHAPTER III.
ORELLANA'S ADVENTURE CONTINUED 275

CHAPTER IV.
SIR WALTER RALEIGH 285

CHAPTER V.
RALEIGH'S FIRST EXPEDITION 293

CHAPTER VI.
RALEIGH'S ADVENTURES CONTINUED 307

CHAPTER VII.
RALEIGH'S SECOND EXPEDITION 316

CHAPTER VIII.
THE FRENCH PHILOSOPHERS 326

CHAPTER IX.
Madame Godin's Voyage down the Amazon

CHAPTER X.
Madame Godin's Voyage continued . .

CHAPTER XI.
Herndon's Expedition . . . . .

CHAPTER XII.
Herndon's Expedition continued . . .

CHAPTER XIII.
Herndon's Expedition continued . . .

CHAPTER XIV.
Herndon's Expedition concluded . . .

CHAPTER XV.
Latest Explorations . . . . .

CHAPTER XVI.
The Naturalist on the Amazon . . .

CHAPTER XVII.
Animated Nature . . . . . .

OREGON.

OREGON.

CHAPTER I.

DISCOVERY OF COLUMBIA RIVER.

A FEW years ago, there was still standing in Bowdoin Square, Boston, opposite the Revere House, an ancient mansion, since removed to make room for the granite range called the Coolidge Building. In that mansion, then neither old nor inelegant, but, on the contrary, having good pretensions to rank among the principal residences of the place, was assembled, in the year 1787, a group, consisting of the master of the mansion, Dr. Bulfinch, his only son Charles, and Joseph Barrell, their neighbor, an eminent merchant of Boston. The conversation turned upon the topic of the day, — the voyages and discoveries of Capt. Cook, the account of which had lately been published. The brilliant achievements of Capt. Cook, his admirable qualities, and his sad fate (slain by the chance stroke of a Sandwich-Islander, in a sudden brawl which arose between the sailors and the natives), — these formed the current of the conversation; till at last it changed, and turned more upon the commercial aspects of the subject. Mr. Barrell was particularly struck with what Cook relates of the abundance of valuable furs offered by the natives of the country in exchange for beads, knives, and other trifling commodities valued by them. The remark of Capt. Cook respecting the sea-otter was cited: —

"This animal abounds here: the fur is softer and finer than that of any other we know of; and therefore the discovery of this part of the continent, where so valuable an article of commerce may be met with, cannot be a matter of indifference." He adds in a note, "The sea-otter skins are sold by the Russians to the Chinese at from sixteen to twenty pounds each."

Mr. Barrell remarked, "There is a rich harvest to be reaped there by those who shall first go in." The idea thus suggested was followed out in future conversations at the doctor's fireside, admitting other congenial spirits to the discussion, and resulted in the equipping of an expedition consisting of two vessels, the ship "Columbia" and sloop "Washington," to make the proposed adventure. The partners in the enterprise were Joseph Barrell, Samuel Brown, Charles Bulfinch, John Derby, Crowell Hatch, and J. M. Pintard. So important was the expedition deemed by the adventurers themselves, that they caused a medal to be struck, bearing on one side a representation of the two vessels under sail, and on the other the names of the parties to the enterprise. Several copies of this medal were made both in bronze and silver, and distributed to public bodies and distinguished individuals. One of these medals lies before the writer as he pens these lines. A representation is subjoined: —

The expedition was also provided with sea-letters, issued by the Federal Government agreeably to a resolution of Congress, and with passports from the State of Massachusetts; and they received letters from the Spanish minister plenipotentiary in the United States, recommending them to the attention of the authorities of his nation on the Pacific coast.

The "Columbia" was commanded by John Kendrick, to whom was intrusted the general control of the expedition. The master of the "Washington" was Robert Gray.

The two vessels sailed together from Boston on the 30th of September, 1787: thence they proceeded to the Cape Verde Islands, and thence to the Falkland Islands, in each of which groups they procured refreshments. In January, 1788, they doubled Cape Horn; immediately after which they were separated during a violent gale. The "Washington," continuing her course through the Pacific, made the north-west coast in August, near the 46th degree of latitude. Here Capt. Gray thought he perceived indications of the mouth of a river; but he was unable to ascertain the fact, in consequence of his vessel having grounded, and been attacked by the savages, who killed one of his men, and wounded the mate. But she escaped without further injury, and, on the 17th of September, reached Nootka Sound, which had been agreed upon as the port of re-union in case of separation. The "Columbia" did not enter the sound until some days afterward.

The two vessels spent their winter in the sound; where the "Columbia" also lay during the following summer, collecting furs, while Capt. Gray, in the "Washington," explored the adjacent waters. On his return to Nootka, it was agreed upon between the two captains that Kendrick should take command of the sloop, and remain on the coast, while Gray, in the "Columbia," should carry to Canton all the furs which had been collected by both vessels. This was accordingly done; and Gray arrived on the 6th of December at Canton, where he sold his furs, and took in a cargo of tea, with which he entered Boston on the 10th of August, 1790, having carried the flag of the United States for the first time round the world.

Kendrick, immediately on parting with the "Columbia," proceeded with the "Washington" to the Strait of Fuca, through which he sailed, in its whole length, to its issue in the Pacific, in lat. 51. To him belongs the credit of ascertaining that Nootka and the parts adjacent are an island, to which the name of Vancouver's Island has since been given, which it now retains. Vancouver was a British commander who followed in the track of the Americans a year later. The injustice done to Kendrick by thus robbing him of the credit of his discovery is but one of many similar instances; the greatest of all being that by which our continent itself bears the name, not of Columbus, but of a subsequent navigator.

Capt. Kendrick, during the time occupied by Gray in his return voyage, besides collecting furs, engaged in various speculations; one of which was the collection, and transportation to China, of the odoriferous wood called "sandal," which grows in many of the tropical islands of the Pacific, and is in great demand throughout the Celestial Empire, for ornamental fabrics, and also for medicinal purposes. Vancouver pronounced this scheme chimerical; but experience has shown that it was founded on just calculations, and the business has ever since been prosecuted with advantage, especially by Americans.

Another of Kendrick's speculations has not hitherto produced any fruit. In the summer of 1791, he purchased from Maquinna, Wicanish, and other Indian chiefs, several large tracts of land near Nootka Sound, for which he obtained deeds, duly *marked* by those personages, and witnessed by the officers and men of the "Washington." Attempts were afterwards made by the owners of the vessel to sell these lands in London, but no purchasers were found; and applications have since been addressed by the legal representatives of the owners to the Government of the

United States for a confirmation of the title, but hitherto without success.

Capt. Kendrick lost his life by a singular accident. In exchanging salutes with a Spanish vessel which they met at the Sandwich Islands, the wad of the gun of the Spaniard struck Capt. Kendrick as he stood on the deck of his vessel, conspicuous in his dress-coat and cocked hat as commander of the expedition. It was instantly fatal.

The ship "Columbia" returned to Boston from Canton under the command of Gray, as already stated, arriving on the 10th of August, 1790; but the cargo of Chinese articles brought by her was insufficient to cover the expenses of her voyage: nevertheless her owners determined to persevere in the enterprise, and refitted the ship for a new voyage of the same kind.

The "Columbia," under her former captain, Gray, left Boston, on her second voyage, on the 28th of September, 1790, and, without the occurrence of any thing worthy of note, arrived at Clyoquot, near the entrance of Fuca's Strait, on the 5th of June, 1791. There, and in the neighboring waters, she remained through the summer and winter following, engaged in trading and exploring. In the spring of 1792, Gray took his departure in the ship, on a cruise southward, along the coast, bent on ascertaining the truth of appearances which had led him in the former voyage to suspect the existence of a river discharging its waters at or about the latitude of 46 degrees. During his cruise, he met the English vessels commanded by Commodore Vancouver. "On the 29th of April," Vancouver writes in his journal, "at four o'clock, a sail was discovered to the westward, standing in shore. This was a very great novelty, not having seen any vessel but our consort during the last eight months. She soon hoisted American colors, and fired a gun to leeward. At six, we spoke her. She proved to be the ship 'Columbia,' commanded by Capt. Robert Gray, belonging to Boston, whence she had been absent nineteen months. I sent two of my officers on board to acquire such information as might be serviceable in our future operations. Capt. Gray informed them of his having been off the mouth of a river, in the latitude of 46 degrees 10 minutes, for nine days; but the outset or reflux was so strong as to prevent his entering."

To this statement of Capt. Gray, Vancouver gave little credit. He remarks, "I was thoroughly persuaded, as were also most persons of observation on board, that we could not have passed any safe navigable opening, harbor, or place of security for shipping, from Cape Mendocino to Fuca's Strait."

After parting with the English ships, Gray sailed along the coast of the continent southward; and on the 7th of May, 1792, he " saw an entrance which had a very good appearance of a harbor." Passing through this entrance, he found himself in a bay, "well sheltered from the sea by long sand-bars and spits," where he remained three days trading with the natives, and then resumed his voyage, bestowing on the place thus discovered the name of Bulfinch's Harbor, in honor of one of the owners of his ship. This is now known as Gray's Harbor.

At daybreak on the 11th, after leaving Bulfinch's Harbor, Gray observed " the entrance of his desired port, bearing east-south-east, distant six leagues; and running into it with all sails set, between the breakers, he anchored at one o'clock in a large river of fresh water, ten miles above its mouth. At this spot he remained three days, engaged in trading with the natives, and filling his casks with water; and then sailed up the river about twelve miles along its northern shore, where, finding that he could proceed no farther from having taken the wrong channel, he again came to anchor. On the 20th, he recrossed the bar at the mouth of the river, and regained the Pacific.

On leaving the river, Gray gave it the name of his ship, the Columbia, which it still bears. He called the southern point of land, at the entrance, Cape Adams; and the northern, Cape Hancock. The former of these names retains its place in the maps, the latter does not; the promontory being known as Cape Disappointment,—a name it received from Lieut. Meares, an English navigator, who, like Capt. Gray, judged from appearances that there was the outlet of a river at that point, but failed to find it, and recorded his failure in the name he assigned to the conspicuous headland which marked the place of his fruitless search.

NOTE.

As the discovery of Columbia River was an event of historical importance, the reader will perhaps be gratified to see it as recorded in the words of Capt. Gray himself, copied from his log-book as follows:—

"May 11 (1792), at eight, P.M., the entrance of Bulfinch's Harbor bore north, distance four miles. Sent up the main-topgallant yard, and set all sail. At four, A.M., saw the entrance of our desired port, bearing east-south-east, distance six leagues; in steering sails, and hauled our wind in shore. At eight, A.M., being a little to windward of the entrance of the harbor,

From the mouth of Columbia River, Gray sailed to Nootka Sound, where he communicated his recent discoveries to the Spanish commandant, Quadra; to whom he also gave charts and descriptions of Bulfinch's Harbor, and of the mouth of the Columbia. He departed for Canton in September, and thence sailed to the United States.

The voyages of Kendrick and Gray were not profitable to the adventurers, yet not fruitless of benefit to their country. They opened the way to subsequent enterprises in the same region, which were eminently successful. And, in another point of view, these expeditions were fraught with consequences of the ut-

---

bore away, and ran in east-north-east between the breakers, having from five to seven fathoms of water. When we were over the bar, we found this to be a large river of fresh water, up which we steered. Many canoes came alongside. At one, P.M., came to, with the small bower in ten fathoms black and white sand. The entrance between the bars bore west-south-west, distant ten miles; the north side of the river a half-mile distant from the ship, the south side of the same two and a half miles distance; a village on the north side of the river, west by north, distant three-quarters of a mile. Vast numbers of natives came alongside. People employed in pumping the salt water out of our water-casks, in order to fill with fresh, while the ship floated in. So ends."

most importance. Gray's discovery of Columbia River was the point most relied upon by our negotiators in a subsequent era for establishing the claim of the United States to the part of the continent through which that river flows; and it is in a great measure owing to that discovery that the growing State of Oregon is now a part of the American Republic.

From the date of the discovery of Columbia River to the war of 1812, the direct trade between the American coast and China was almost entirely in the hands of the citizens of the United States. The British merchants were restrained from pursuing it by the opposition of their East-India Company; the Russians were not admitted into Chinese ports; and few ships of any other nation were seen in that part of the ocean. The trade was prosecuted by men whose names are still distinguished among us as those of the master-spirits of American commerce, — the Thorndikes, the Perkinses, Lambs, Sturgis, Cushing, and others of Boston, Astor and others of New York. The greater number of the vessels sent from the United States were fine ships or brigs laden with valuable cargoes of West-India productions, British manufactured articles, and French, Italian, and Spanish wines and spirits; and the owners were men of large capital and high reputation in the commercial world, some of whom were able to compete with the British companies, and even to control their movements.

During all this period, though constant accessions were made to the knowledge of the coast by means of commercial adventure, the interior of the continent, from the Mississippi to the ocean, remained unknown. The intercourse of the people of the United States with the native tribes was restricted by several causes. One was the possession of Louisiana by the Spaniards; another, the retention by the British of several important posts south of the Great Lakes, within the acknowledged territory of the Union. At length, by the treaty of 1794 between Great Britain and the United States, those posts were given up to the Americans; and by treaty with France, in 1803, Louisiana, which had come into possession of that power in 1800, was ceded to the United States. From this period, the Government and people of the United States ceased to be indifferent to the immense and important region whose destinies were committed to them; and the ensuing narrative will relate the first attempt made by national authority to occupy and explore the country.

CHAPTER II.

LEWIS AND CLARKE.

IN the year 1786, John Ledyard of Connecticut, who had been with Capt. Cook in his voyage of discovery to the north-west coast of America in 1776–1780, was in Paris, endeavoring to engage a mercantile company in the fur-trade of that coast. He had seen, as he thought, unequalled opportunities for lucrative traffic in the exchange of the furs of that country for the silks and teas of China. But his representations were listened to with incredulity by the cautious merchants of Europe, and he found it impossible to interest any so far as to induce them to fit out an expedition for the object proposed.

Disappointed and needy, he applied for advice and assistance to Mr. Jefferson, at that time the American minister at the court of France. Ledyard had no views of pecuniary gain in the contemplated enterprise: he sought only an opportunity of indulging his love of adventure by exploring regions at that time unknown. Mr. Jefferson, as the guardian of his country's interests and the friend of science, was warmly interested in any scheme which contemplated the opening of the vast interior regions of the American continent to the occupancy of civilized man. Since it was impossible to engage mercantile adventurers to fit out an expedition by sea, Mr. Jefferson proposed to Ledyard that he should go as a traveller, by land, through the Russian territories, as far as the eastern coast of the continent of Asia, and from thence get such conveyance as he could to the neighboring coast of America, and thus reach the spot where his main journey was to begin. Ledyard eagerly embraced the proposal. Permission was obtained from the Empress Catharine of Russia, and the enterprising traveller, in December, 1786, set forth. He traversed Denmark and Sweden; passed round the head of the Gulf of Bothnia, after an unsuccessful attempt to cross it on the ice; and reached St. Petersburg in March, 1787, without money, shoes, or stockings, having gone this immense journey on foot in an arctic winter. At St. Petersburg he obtained notice, money to the amount of twenty guineas, and permission to accompany a convoy of stores to Yakoutsk, in Siberia.

But, for some unexplained reason, he was arrested at that place by order of the empress, and conveyed back to Europe; being cautioned, on his release, not again to set foot within the Russian territories, under penalty of death. This harsh treatment is supposed to have arisen from the jealousy of the Russian fur-traders, who feared that Ledyard's proceedings would rouse up rivals in their trade.

Mr. Jefferson did not, upon this disappointment, abandon the idea of an exploration of the interior of the American continent. At his suggestion, the American Philosophical Society of Philadelphia took measures, in 1792, to send suitable persons to make a similar transit of the continent in the opposite direction; that is, by ascending the Missouri, and descending the Columbia. Nothing was effected, however, at that time, except awakening the attention of Capt. Meriwether Lewis, a young officer in the American army, a neighbor and relative of Gen. Washington. He eagerly sought to be employed to make the contemplated journey.

In 1803, Mr. Jefferson, being then President of the United States, proposed to Congress to send an exploring party to trace the Missouri to its source; to cross the highlands, and follow the best water communication which might offer itself, to the Pacific Ocean. Congress approved the proposal, and voted a sum of money to carry it into execution. Capt. Lewis, who had then been two years with Mr. Jefferson as his private secretary, immediately renewed his solicitations to have the direction of the expedition. Mr. Jefferson had now had opportunity of knowing him intimately, and believed him to be brave, persevering, familiar with the Indian character and customs, habituated to the hunting life, honest, and of sound judgment. He trusted that he would be careful of those committed to his charge, yet steady in the maintenance of discipline. On receiving his appointment, Capt. Lewis repaired to Philadelphia, and placed himself under its distinguished professors, with a view to acquire familiarity with the nomenclature of the natural sciences. He selected, as his companion in the proposed expedition, William Clarke, a brother-officer, known and esteemed by him.

While these things were going on, the treaty with France was concluded, by which the country of Louisiana was ceded to the United States. This event, which took place in 1803, greatly increased the interest felt by the people of the United States in the proposed expedition.

In the spring of 1804, the preparations being completed, the explorers commenced their route. The party consisted of nine young men from Kentucky, fourteen soldiers of the United-States army who volunteered their services, two French watermen, an interpreter, a hunter, and a black servant of Capt. Clarke. In addition to these, a further force of fifteen men attended on the commencement of the expedition to secure safety during the transit through some Indian tribes whose hostility was apprehended. The necessary stores were divided into seven bales and one box, the latter containing a small portion of each article in case of a loss of any one of the bales. The stores consisted of clothing, working tools, ammunition, and other articles of prime necessity. To these were added fourteen bales and one box of Indian presents, composed of richly laced coats and other articles of dress, medals, flags, knives, and tomahawks for the chiefs; ornaments of different kinds, particularly beads, looking-glasses, handkerchiefs, paints, and generally such articles as were deemed best calculated for the taste of the Indians. The company embarked on board of three boats. The first was a keel-boat, fifty-five feet long, carrying one large square sail and twenty-two oars. A deck of ten feet, at each end, formed a forecastle and cabin. This was accompanied by two open boats of six oars. Two horses were to be led along the banks of the river, for bringing home game, or hunting in case of scarcity.

The narrative of the expedition was written by the commanders from day to day, and published after their return. We shall tell the story of their adventures nearly in the language of their own journal, with such abridgments as our plan renders necessary.

May 14, 1804. — All the preparations being completed, they left their encampment this day. The character of the river itself was the most interesting object of examination for the first part of their voyage. Having advanced, in two months, about four hundred and fifty miles, they write as follows: " The ranges of hills on opposite sides of the river are twelve or fifteen miles apart, rich plains and prairies, with the river, occupying the intermediate space, partially covered near the river with cotton-wood or Balm-of-Gilead poplar. The whole lowland between the parallel ranges of hills seems to have been formed of mud of the river, mixed with sand and clay. The sand of the neighboring banks, added to that brought down by the stream, forms sand-bars, projecting into the river. These drive the stream to the opposite bank, the loose texture of which it undermines, and at length deserts its ancient bed for a new passage. It is thus that the banks of the Missouri are constantly falling in, and the river changing its bed.

"On one occasion, the party encamped on a sand-bar in the river. Shortly after midnight, the sleepers were startled by the sergeant on guard crying out that the sand-bar was sinking: and the alarm was timely given; for scarcely had they got off with the boats before the bank under which they had been lying fell in; and, by the time the opposite shore was reached, the ground on which they had been encamped sunk also.

"We had occasion here to observe the process of the undermining of these hills by the Missouri. The first attacks seem to be made on the hills which overhang the river. As soon as the violence of the current destroys the grass at the foot of them, the whole texture appears loosened, and the ground dissolves, and mixes with the water. At one point, a part of the cliff, nearly three-quarters of a mile in length, and about two hundred feet in height, had fallen into the river. As the banks are washed away, the trees fall in, and the channel becomes filled with buried logs."

RIVER SCENERY.

"July 12. — We remained to-day for the purpose of making lunar observations. Capt. Clarke sailed a few miles up the Namaha River, and landed on a spot where he found numerous artificial mounds.

NOTE.

A late traveller, Rev. Samuel Parker, speaks thus of these mounds: " The mounds, which some have called the work of unknown generations of men, were scattered here in all varieties of form and magnitude, thousands in number. Some of them were conical, some elliptical, some square, and some parallelograms. One group attracted my attention particularly. They were twelve in number, of conical form, with their bases joined, and twenty or thirty feet high. They formed two-thirds of a circle, with an area of two hundred feet in diameter. If these were isolated, who would not say they were artificial ? But, when they are only a group among a thousand others, who will presume to say they all are the work of man ? . . .

"It is said by those who advocate the belief that they are the work of ancient nations; that they present plain evidence of this in the fact that they contain human bones, articles of pottery, and the like. That some of them have been used for burying-places, is undoubtedly true ; but may it not be questioned whether they were *made*, or only *selected*, for burying-places ?. No one who has ever seen the thousands and ten thousands scattered through the Valley of the Mississippi will be so credulous as to believe that a hundredth part of them were the work of man."

"From the top of the highest mound, a delightful prospect presented itself,— the lowland of the Missouri covered with an undulating grass nearly five feet high, gradually rising into a second plain, where rich weeds and flowers were interspersed with copses of the Osage plum. Farther back from the river were seen small groves of trees, an abundance of grapes, the wild cherry of the Missouri,— resembling our own, but larger, and growing on a small bush. The plums are of three kinds,— two of a yellow color, and distinguished by one of the species being larger than the other; a third species of red color. All have an excellent flavor, particularly the yellow kind."

PIPE-CLAY ROCK.

"Aug. 21.— We passed the mouth of the Great Sioux River. Our Indian interpreter tells us that on the head waters of this river is the quarry of red rock of which the Indians make their pipes; and the necessity of procuring that article has introduced a law of nations, by which the banks of the stream are sacred; and even tribes at war meet without hostility at these quarries, which possess a right of asylum. Thus we find, even among savages, certain principles deemed sacred, by which the rigors of their merciless system of warfare are mitigated."

CHAPTER III.

THE SIOUX.

THE Indian tribes which our adventurers had thus far encountered had been friendly, or at least inoffensive; but they were feeble bands, and all of them lived in terror of their powerful neighbors, the Sioux. On the 23d of September, the party reached a region inhabited by the Tetons, a tribe of Sioux. The journal gives an account of their intercourse with these new acquaintances as follows: —

"The morning was fine; and we raised a flag-staff, and spread an awning, under which we assembled, with all the party under arms. The chiefs and warriors from the Indian camp, about fifty in number, met us; and Capt. Lewis made a speech to them. After this, we went through the ceremony of acknowledging the chiefs by giving to the grand chief a medal, a flag of the United States, a laced uniform coat, a cocked hat and feather; to the two other chiefs, a medal and some small presents; and to two warriors of consideration, certificates. We then invited the chiefs on board, and showed them the boat, the air-gun, and such curiosities as we thought might amuse them. In this we succeeded too well; for after giving them a quarter of a glass of whiskey, which they seemed to like very much, it was with much difficulty we could get rid of them. They at last accompanied Capt. Clarke back to shore in a boat with five men; but no sooner had the party landed than three of the Indians seized the cable of the boat, and one of the soldiers of the chief put his arms round the mast. The second chief, who affected intoxication, then said that we should not go on; that they had not received presents enough from us. Capt. Clarke told him that we would not be prevented from going on; that we were not squaws, but warriors; that we were sent by our great Father, who could in a moment exterminate them. The chief replied that he, too, had warriors; and was proceeding to lay hands on Capt. Clarke, who immediately drew his sword, and made a signal to the boat to prepare for action. The Indians who surrounded him drew their arrows from their quivers, and were bending their bows, when the swivel in the large boat was pointed towards them, and twelve of our most determined men jumped into the small boat, and joined Capt. Clarke. This movement made an impression on them; for the grand chief ordered the young men away from the boat, and the chiefs withdrew, and held a short council with the warriors. Being unwilling to irritate them, Capt. Clarke then went forward, and offered his hand to the first and second chiefs, who refused to take it. He then turned from them, and got into the boat, but had not gone more than a stone's-throw, when the two chiefs and two of the warriors waded in after him; and he took them on board.

"Sept. 26.— Our conduct yesterday seemed to have inspired the Indians with respect; and, as we were desirous of cultivating their acquaintance, we complied with their wish that we should give them an opportunity of treating us well, and also suffer their squaws and children to see us and our boat, which would be perfectly new to them. Accordingly, after passing a small island and several sand-bars, we came to on the south shore, where a crowd of men, women, and children, were waiting to receive us. Capt. Lewis went on shore, and, observing that their disposition seemed friendly, resolved to remain during the night to a dance which they were preparing for us. The captains, who went on shore one after the other, were met on the landing by ten well-dressed young men, who took them up in a robe highly decorated, and carried them to a large council-house, where they were placed on a dressed buffalo-skin by the side of the grand chief. The hall, or council-room, was in the shape of three-quarters of a circle, covered at the top and sides with skins well dressed, and sewed together. Under this shelter sat about seventy men, forming a circle round the chief, before whom were placed a Spanish flag and the one we had given them yesterday. In the vacant space in the centre, the pipe of peace was raised on two forked sticks about six or eight inches from the ground, and under it the down of the swan was scattered. A large fire, at which they were cooking, stood near, and a pile of about four hundred pounds of buffalo-meat, as a present for us.

"As soon as we were seated, an old man rose, and, after approving what we had done, begged us to take pity upon their unfortunate situation. To this we replied with assurances of protection. After he had ceased, the great chief rose, and delivered an harangue to the same effect. Then, with great solemnity, he took some of the more delicate parts of the dog, which was cooked for the festival, and held it to the flag by way of sacrifice: this done, he held up the pipe of peace, and first pointed it towards the heavens, then to the four quarters of the globe, and then to the earth; made a short speech; lighted the pipe, and presented it to us. We smoked, and he again harangued his people; after which the repast was served up to us. It consisted of the dog, which they had just been cooking; this being a great dish among the Sioux, and used at all festivals. To this was added *pemitigon*, a dish made of buffalo-meat, dried, and then pounded, and mixed raw with fat; and a root like the potato, dressed like the preparation of Indian-corn called hominy. Of all these luxuries, which were placed before us in platters, with horn spoons, we took the pemitigon and the potato, which we found good; but we could as yet partake but sparingly of the dog. We ate and smoked for an hour, when it became dark. Every thing was then cleared away for the dance; a large fire being made in the centre of the house, giving at once light and warmth to the ball-room. The orchestra was composed of about ten men, who played on a sort of tambourine formed of skin stretched across a hoop, and made a jingling noise with a long stick, to which the hoofs of deer and goats were hung. The third instrument was a small skin bag, with pebbles in it. These, with five or six young men for the vocal part, made up the band.

"The women then came forward highly decorated; some with poles in their hands, on which were hung the scalps of their enemies; others with guns, spears, or different trophies, taken in war by their husbands, brothers, or connections. Having arranged themselves in two columns, as soon as the music began they danced towards each other till they met in the centre; when the rattles were shaken, and they all shouted, and returned back to their places. They have no steps, but shuffle along the ground; nor does the music appear to be any thing more than a confusion of noises, distinguished only by hard or gentle blows upon the buffalo-skin. The song is perfectly extemporaneous. In the pauses of the dance, any man of the company comes forward, and recites, in a low, guttural tone, some little story or incident, which is either martial or ludicrous. This is taken up by the orchestra and the dancers, who repeat it in a higher strain, and dance to it. Sometimes they alternate, the orchestra first performing; and, when it ceases, the women raise their voices, and make a music more agreeable, that is, less intolerable, than that of the musicians.

"The harmony of the entertainment had nearly been disturbed by one of the musicians, who, thinking he had not received a due share of the tobacco we had distributed during the evening, put himself into a passion, broke one of the drums, threw two of them into the fire, and left the band. They were taken out of the fire: a buffalo-robe, held in one hand, and beaten with the other, supplied the place of the lost drum or tambourine; and no notice was taken of the offensive conduct of the man. We staid till twelve o'clock at night, when we informed the chiefs that they must be fatigued with all these attempts to amuse us, and retired, accompanied by four chiefs, two of whom spent the night with us on board."

THE SIOUX.

"The tribe which we this day saw are a part of the great Sioux nation, and are known by the name of the *Teton Okandandas:* they are about two hundred men in number, and their chief residence is on both sides of the Missouri, between the Cheyenne and Teton Rivers.

"The men shave the hair off their heads, except a small tuft on the top, which they suffer to grow, and wear in plaits over the shoulders. To this they seem much attached, as the loss of it is the usual sacrifice at the death of near relations. In full dress, the men of consideration wear a hawk's feather or calumet feather, worked with porcupine-quills, and fastened to the top of the head, from which it falls back. The face and body are generally painted with a mixture of grease and coal. Over the shoulders is a loose robe or mantle of buffalo-skin, adorned with porcupine-quills, which are loosely fixed so as to make a jingling noise when in motion, and painted with various uncouth figures unintelligible to us, but to them emblematic of military exploits or any other incident. The hair of the robe is worn next the skin in fair weather; but, when it rains, the hair is put outside. Under this robe they wear in winter a kind of shirt, made either of skin or cloth, covering the arms and body. Round the middle is fixed a girdle of cloth or elk-skin, about an inch in width, and closely tied to the body. To this is attached a piece of cloth or blanket or skin about a foot wide, which passes between the legs, and is tucked under the girdle both before and behind. From the hip to the ankle, the man is covered with leggings of dressed antelope-skins, with seams at the sides two inches in width, and ornamented by little tufts of hair, the product of the scalps they have taken in war, which are scattered down the leg.

"The moccasons are of dressed buffalo-skin, the hair being worn inwards. On great occasions, or whenever they are in full dress, the young men drag after them the entire skin of a polecat, fixed to the heel of the moccason.

"The hair of the women is suffered to grow long, and is parted from the forehead across the head; at the back of which it is either collected into a kind of bag, or hangs down over the shoulders. Their moccasons are like those of the men, as are also the leggings, which do not reach beyond the knee, where they are met by a long, loose mantle of skin, which reaches nearly to the ankles. This is fastened over the shoulders by a string, and has no sleeves; but a few pieces of the skin hang a short distance down the arm. Sometimes a girdle fastens this skin round the waist, and over all is thrown a robe like that worn by the men.

"Their lodges are very neatly constructed. They consist of about one hundred cabins, made of white buffalo-hide, with a larger cabin in the centre for holding councils and dances. They are built round with poles about fifteen or twenty feet high, covered with white skins. These lodges may be taken to pieces, packed up, and carried with the nation, wherever they go, by dogs, which bear great burdens. The women are chiefly employed in dressing buffalo-skins. These people seem well-disposed, but are addicted to stealing any thing which they can take without being observed."

CHAPTER IV.

SUMMARY OF TRAVEL TO WINTER-QUARTERS.

SEPT. 1, 1804.— The daily progress of the expedition from this date is marked by no incidents of more importance than the varying fortunes of travel, as they found the river more or less favorable to navigation, and the game more or less abundant on the banks. Their progress was from twelve to twenty miles a day. In general, their sails served them; but they were sometimes obliged to resort to the use of towlines, which, being attached to a tree or other firm object on the shore, enabled the men to pull the boat along. This seems but a slow method of voyaging; yet they found it by no means the slowest, and were sorry when the nature of the banks, being either too lofty or too low, precluded their use of it. Their narrative is, however, varied by accounts of the scenery and natural productions of the country through which they passed, and by anecdotes of the Indians. While they are making their toilsome advance up the river, let us see what they have to tell us of the strange people and remarkable objects which they found on their way.

PRAIRIE-DOGS.

"We arrived at a spot on the gradual descent of the hill, nearly four acres in extent, and covered with small holes. These are the residences of little animals called prairie-dogs, who sit erect near the mouth of the hole, and make a whistling noise, but, when alarmed, take refuge in their holes. In order to bring them out, we poured into one of the holes five barrels of water, without filling it; but we dislodged and caught the owner. After digging down another of the holes for six feet, we found, on running a pole into it, that we had not yet dug half-way to the bottom. We discovered two frogs in the hole; and near it we killed a rattlesnake, which had swallowed a small prairie-dog. We have been told, though we never witnessed the fact, that a sort of lizard and a snake live habitually with these animals.

"The prairie-dog is well named, as it resembles a dog in most particulars, though it has also some points of similarity to the squirrel. The head resembles the squirrel in every respect, except that the ear is shorter. The tail is like that of the ground-squirrel; the toe-nails are long, the fur is fine, and the long hair is gray."

ANTELOPES.

"Of all the animals we have seen, the antelope possesses the most wonderful fleetness. Shy and timorous, they generally repose only on the ridges, which command a view in all directions. Their sight distinguishes the most distant danger; their power of smell defeats the attempt at concealment; and, when alarmed, their swiftness seems more like the flight of birds than the movement of an animal over the ground. Capt. Lewis, after many unsuccessful attempts, succeeded in approaching, undiscovered, a party of seven, which were on an eminence. The only male of the party frequently encircled the summit of the hill, as if to discover if any danger threatened the party. When Capt. Lewis was at the distance of two hundred yards, they became alarmed, and fled. He immediately ran to the spot they had left. A ravine concealed them from him; but the next moment they appeared on a second ridge, at the distance of three miles. He doubted whether they could be the same; but their number, and the direction in which they fled, satisfied him that it was the same party: yet the distance they had made in the time was such as would hardly have been possible to the swiftest racehorse."

PELICAN ISLAND.

"42. — This name we gave to a long island, from the numbers of pelicans which were feeding on it. One of them being killed, we poured into his bag five gallons of water."

NOTE.

"The antelopes are becoming very numerous. Their speed exceeds that of any animal I have ever seen. Our hounds can do nothing in giving them the chase: so soon are they left far in the rear, that they do not follow them more than ten or twenty rods before they return, looking ashamed of their defeat. Our hunters occasionally take the antelope by coming upon them by stealth. When they are surprised, they start forward a very small space, then turn, and, with high-lifted heads, stare for a few seconds at the object which has alarmed them, and then, with a half-whistling snuff, bound off, seeming to be as much upon wings as upon feet. They resemble the goat, but are far more beautiful. Though they are of different colors, yet they are generally red, and have a large, fine, prominent eye. Their flesh is good for food, and about equals venison." — *Parker's Tour.*

INDIAN VILLAGES AND AGRICULTURE.

"We halted for dinner at a deserted village, which we suppose to have belonged to the Ricaras. It is situated in a low plain on the river, and consists of about eighty lodges, of an octagon form, neatly covered with earth, placed as close to each other as possible, and picketed round. The skin-canoes, mats, buckets, and articles of furniture, found in the lodges, induce us to suppose that it was left in the spring. We found three different kinds of squashes growing in the village.

"Another village, which we reached two days later, was situated on an island, which is three miles long, and covered with fields, in which the Indians raise corn, beans, and potatoes. We found here several Frenchmen living among the Indians, as interpreters or traders. The Indians gave us some corn, beans, and dried squashes; and we gave them a steel mill, with which they were much pleased. We sat conversing with the chiefs some time, during which they treated us to a bread made of corn and beans, also corn and beans boiled, and a large rich bean which they take from the mice of the prairie, who discover and collect it. We gave them some sugar, salt, and a sun-glass."

YORK, THE NEGRO.

"The object which seemed to astonish the Indians most was Capt. Clarke's servant, York, — a sturdy negro. They had never seen a human being of that color, and therefore flocked round him to examine the monster. By way of amusement, he told them that he had once been a wild animal, and been caught and tamed by his master, and, to convince them, showed them feats of strength, which, added to his looks, made him more terrible than we wished him to be. At all the villages he was an object of astonishment. The children would follow him constantly, and, if he chanced to turn towards them, would run with great terror."

STONE-IDOL CREEK.

"We reached the mouth of a creek, to which we gave the name of Stone-Idol Creek; for, on passing up, we discovered, that, a few miles back from the Missouri, there are two stones resembling human figures, and a third like a dog; all which are objects of great veneration among the Ricaras. Their history would adorn the "Metamorphoses" of Ovid. A young man was in love with a girl whose parents refused their consent to the marriage. The youth went out into the fields to mourn his misfortunes: a sympathy of feeling led the girl to the same spot; and the faithful dog would not fail to follow his master. After wandering together, and having nothing but grapes to subsist on, they were at last converted into stone, which, beginning at the feet, gradually invaded the nobler parts, leaving nothing unchanged but a bunch of grapes, which the female holds in her hands to this day. Such is the account given by the Ricara chief, which we had no means of testing, except that we found one part of the story very agreeably confirmed; for on the banks of the creek we found a greater abundance of fine grapes than we had seen elsewhere."

GOATS.

" Great numbers of goats are crossing the river, and directing their course to the westward. We are told that they spend the summer in the plains east of the Missouri, and at this season (October) are returning to the Black Mountains, where they subsist on leaves and shrubbery during the winter, and resume their migrations in the spring. At one place, we saw large flocks of them in the water. They had been gradually driven into the river by the Indians, who now lined the shore so as to prevent their escape, and were firing on them; while boys went into the river, and killed them with sticks. They seemed to have been very successful; for we counted fifty-eight which they had killed. In the evening they made a feast, that lasted till late at night, and caused much noise and merriment.

"The country through which we passed has wider river-bottoms and more timber than those we have been accustomed to see; the hills rising at a distance, and by gradual ascents. We have seen great numbers of elk, deer, goats, and buffaloes, and the usual attendants of these last, — the wolves, which follow their movements, and feed upon those who die by accident, or are too feeble to keep pace with the herd. We also wounded a white bear, and saw some fresh tracks of those animals, which are twice as large as the tracks of a man."

THE PRAIRIE ON FIRE.

"In the evening, the prairie took fire, either by accident or design, and burned with great fury; the whole plain being enveloped in flames. So rapid was its progress, that a man and a woman were burned to death before they could reach a place of safety. Another man, with his wife and child, were much burned, and several other persons narrowly escaped destruction. Among the rest, a boy of the half-breed escaped unhurt in the midst of the flames. His safety was ascribed by the Indians to the Great Spirit, who had saved him on account of his being white. But a much more natural cause was the presence of mind of his mother, who, seeing no hopes of carrying off her son, threw him on the ground, and, covering him with the fresh hide of a buffalo, escaped herself from the flames. As soon as the fire had passed, she returned, and found him untouched; the skin having prevented the flame from reaching the grass where he lay."

A COUNCIL.

" After making eleven miles, we reached an old field, where the Mandans had cultivated grain last summer. We encamped for the night about half a mile below the first village of the Mandans. As soon as we arrived, a crowd of men, women, and children, came down to see us. Capt. Lewis returned with the principal chiefs to the village, while the others remained with us during the evening. The object which seemed to surprise them most was a corn-mill, fixed to the boat, which we had occasion to use; while they looked on, and were delighted at observing the ease with which it reduced the grain to powder.

"Among others who visited us was the son of the grand chief of the Mandans, who had both his little fingers cut off at the second joint. On inquiring into this injury, we found that the custom was to express grief for the death of relations by some corporeal suffering, and that the usual mode was to lose a joint of the little finger, or sometimes of other fingers.

"Oct. 29, 1804. — The morning was fine, and we prepared our presents and speech for the council. At ten o'clock, the chiefs were all assembled under an awning of our sails. That the impression might be the more forcible, the men were all paraded; and the council opened by a discharge from the swivel of the boat. Capt. Lewis then delivered a speech, which, like those we had already made, intermingled advice with assurances of friendship and trade. While he was speaking, the Ahnahaway chief grew very restless, and observed that he could not wait long, as his camp was exposed to the hostilities of the Shoshonees. He was instantly rebuked with great dignity, by one of the chiefs, for this violation of decorum at such a moment, and remained quiet during the rest of the council. This being over, we proceeded to distribute the presents with great ceremony. One chief of each town was acknowledged by the gift of a flag, a medal with the likeness of the President of the United States, a uniform coat, hat, and feather. To the second chiefs we gave a medal representing some domestic animals, and a loom for weaving; to the third chiefs, medals with the impression of a farmer sowing grain. A variety of other products were distributed; but none seemed to give more satisfaction than an iron corn-mill which we gave them.

"In the evening, our men danced among themselves to the music of the violin, to the great amusement of the Indians."

THEY ENCAMP FOR THE WINTER.

"Friday, Nov. 7, 1804. — Capt. Clarke having examined the shores, and found a position where there was plenty of timber, we encamped, and began to fell trees to build our huts. The timber which we employ is cotton-wood (poplar) and elm, with some ash of inferior size. By the 8th, our huts were advanced very well; on the 13th, we unloaded the boat, and stowed away the contents in a storehouse which we had built.

"Nov. 20. — This day we moved into our huts,

which are now completed. We call our place Fort Mandan. It is situated on a point of low ground on the north side of the Missouri, covered with tall and heavy cotton-wood. The works consist of two rows of huts or sheds, forming an angle where they join each other; each row containing four rooms of fourteen feet square and seven feet high, with plank ceiling, and the roof slanting so as to form a loft above the rooms, the highest part of which is eighteen feet from the ground. The backs of the huts formed a wall of that height; and, opposite the angle, the place of the wall was supplied by picketing. In the area were two rooms for stores and provisions. The latitude, by observation, is 47° 22', long. 101°; and the computed distance from the mouth of the Missouri, sixteen hundred miles.

"Nov. 21. — We are now settled in our winter habitation, and shall wait with much impatience the first return of spring to continue our journey."

CHAPTER V.

INDIAN TRIBES.

THE villages near which we are established are the residence of three distinct nations, — the Mandans, the Ahnahaways, and the Minnetarees. The Mandans say, that, many years ago, their tribe was settled in nine villages, the ruins of which we passed about eighty miles below. Finding themselves wasting away before the small-pox and the Sioux, they moved up the river, and planted themselves opposite the Ricaras. Their numbers are very much reduced, and they now constitute but two villages, — one on each side of the river, and at a distance of three miles from each other. Both villages together may raise about three hundred and fifty men."

AHNAHAWAYS.

"Four miles from the lower Mandan village is one inhabited by the Ahnahaways. This nation formerly dwelt on the Missouri, about thirty miles below where they now live. The Assinaboins and Sioux forced them to a spot five miles higher, and thence, by a second. emigration, to their present situation, in order to obtain an asylum near the Minnetarees. Their whole force is about fifty men."

MINNETAREES.

"About half a mile from this village, and in the same open plain with it, is a village of Minnetarees, who are about one hundred and fifty men in number. One and a half miles above this village is a second of the same tribe, who may be considered the proper Minnetaree nation. It is situated in a beautiful plain, and contains four hundred and fifty warriors. The Mandans say that this people came out of the water to the east, and settled near them. The Minnetarees, however, assert that they grew where they now live, and will never emigrate from the spot; the Great Spirit having declared, that, if they move, they will all perish.

"The inhabitants of these villages, all of which are within the compass of six miles, live in harmony with each other. Their languages differ to some extent; but their long residence together has enabled them to understand one another's speech as to objects of daily occurrence, and obvious to the senses.

"All these tribes are at deadly feud with the Sioux, who are much more powerful, and are consequently objects of continual apprehension. The presence of our force kept the peace for the present.

"Almost the whole of that vast tract of country comprised between the Mississippi, the Red River of Lake Winnipeg, the Saskatchawan, and the Missouri, is loosely occupied by a great nation whose primitive name is Dahcotas, but who are called Sioux by the French, Sues by the English. They are divided into numerous tribes, named Yanktons, Tetons, Assinaboins, &c. These tribes are sometimes at war with one another, but still acknowledge relationship, and are recognized by similarity of language and by tradition."

RELIGION.

"The religion of the Mandans consists in the belief of one Great Spirit presiding over their destinies. This Being must be in the nature of a good genius, since it is associated with the healing art; and the Great Spirit is synonymous with Great Medicine, — a name also applied to every thing they do not comprehend. They also believe in a multiplicity of inferior spirits. Each individual selects for himself the particular object of his devotion, which is termed his Medicine, and is either an invisible being, or more commonly some animal, which thenceforward becomes his protector, or his intercessor with the Great Spirit. To propitiate the Medicine, every attention is lavished, and every personal consideration is sacrificed. 'I was lately owner of seventeen horses,' said a Mandan; 'but I have offered them all up to my Medicine, and am now poor.' He had in reality taken them into the plain, and, turning them loose, committed them to the care of his Medicine, and abandoned them.

" Their belief in a future state is connected with a tradition of their origin. The whole nation, they say, once dwelt in one large village underground. A grape-vine extended its roots down to their habitation; and the earth, being broken round its stem, gave them a view of the light. Some of the more adventurous climbed up the vine, and were delighted with the sight of the earth, which they found covered with buffaloes, and rich with every kind of fruit. Returning with the grapes they had gathered, their countrymen were so pleased with the taste, that the whole nation resolved to leave their dull residence for the upper region. Men, women, and children ascended by means of the vine; but, when about half the nation had reached the surface, a corpulent woman, who was clambering up the vine, broke it with her weight, and, falling, closed up the cavity. Those who had reached the surface, thus excluded from their original seats, cherish the hopes of returning there when they die."

INDIAN MANNERS.

The following extract imparts some traits of Indian manners: —

"Nov. 22. — This morning, the sentinel informed us that an Indian was about to kill his wife near the fort. We went to the house of our interpreter, where we found the parties, and, after forbidding any violence, inquired into the cause of his intending to commit such an atrocity. It appeared that, some days ago, a quarrel had taken place between him and his wife, in consequence of which she had taken refuge in the house where the wives of our interpreter lived. By running away, she forfeited her life, which might be lawfully taken by the husband. He was now come for the purpose of completing his revenge. We gave him a few presents, and tried to persuade him to take his wife home. The grand chief, too, happened to arrive at the same moment, and reproached him with his violence; till at length husband and wife went off together, but by no means in a state of much apparent connubial felicity."

THE WEATHER.

" Dec. 12, 1804. — The thermometer at sunrise was thirty-eight degrees below zero; on the 16th, twenty-two below; on the 17th, forty-five below. On the 19th, it moderated a little. Notwithstanding the cold, we observed the Indians at the village engaged, out in the open air, at a game which resembles billiards. The platform, which answered for a table, was formed with timber, smoothed and joined so as to be as level as the floor of one of our houses. Instead of balls, they had circular disks made of clay-stone, and flat like checkers."

THE ARGALI.

" Dec. 22. — A number of squaws brought corn to trade for small articles with the men. Among other things, we procured two horns of the animal called by the hunters the Rocky-Mountain sheep, and by naturalists the argali. The animal is about the size of a small elk or large deer; the horns winding like those of a ram, which they resemble also in texture, though larger and thicker.

"Dec. 23. — The weather was fine and warm. We were visited by crowds of Indians of all description, who came either to trade, or from mere curiosity. Among the rest, Kagohami, the Little Raven, brought his wife and son, loaded with corn; and she entertained us with a favorite Mandan dish, — a mixture of pumpkins, beans, corn, and choke-cherries, all boiled together in a kettle, and forming a composition by no means unpalatable.

"Dec. 25. — Christmas Day. We were awakened before day by a discharge of fire-arms from the party. We had told the Indians not to visit us, as it was one of our great Medicine-days; so that the men remained at home, and amused themselves in various ways, particularly with dancing, in which they take great pleasure. The American flag was hoisted for the first time in the fort; the best provisions we had were brought out; and this, with a little brandy, enabled them to pass the day in great festivity."

THE BLACKSMITH.

"Dec. 27. — We were fortunate enough to have among our men a good blacksmith, whom we set to work to make a variety of articles. His operations seemed to surprise the Indians who came to see us; but nothing could equal their astonishment at the bellows, which they considered a *very great Medicine.*"

THE DYING CHIEF.

"Kagohami came to see us early. His village was afflicted by the death of one of their aged chiefs, who, from his account, must have been more than a hundred years old. Just as he was dying, he requested his grand-children to dress him in his best robe, and carry him up to a hill, and seat him on a stone, with his face down the river, towards their old village, that he might go straight to his brother, who had passed before him to the ancient village underground."

THE MEDICINE-STONE.

" Oheenaw and Shahaka came down to see us, and mentioned that several of their countrymen had gone to consult their *Medicine-stone* as to the prospects of the following year. This Medicine-stone is the great oracle of the Mandans, and whatever it announces is believed with implicit confidence. Every spring; and on some occasions during the summer, a deputation visits the sacred spot, where there is a thick, porous stone twenty feet in circumference, with a smooth surface. Having reached the place, the ceremony of smoking to it is performed by the deputies, who alternately take a whiff themselves, and then present the pipe to the stone. After this, they retire to an adjoining wood for the night, during which it may be safely presumed all the embassy do not sleep; and, in the morning, they read the destinies of the nation in the white marks on the stone, which those who made them are at no loss to decipher. The Minnetarees have a stone of a similar kind, which has the same qualities, and the same influence over the nation."

THE INDIANS' ENDURANCE OF COLD.

"Jan. 10, 1805. — The weather now exhibited the intensity of cold. This morning, at sunrise, the mercury stood at forty degrees below zero. One of the men, separated from the rest in hunting, was out all night. In the morning he returned, and told us that he had made a fire, and kept himself tolerably warm. A young Indian, about thirteen years of age, came in soon after. He had been overtaken by the night, and had slept in the snow, with no covering but a pair of deer-skin moccasons and leggings, and a buffalo-robe. His feet were frozen; but we restored them by putting them in cold water, rendering him every attention in our power. Another Indian, who had been missing, returned about the same time. Although his dress was very thin, and he had slept in the snow, without a fire, he had not suffered any inconvenience. These Indians support the rigors of the season in a way which we had hitherto thought impossible."

SUPPLIES OF FOOD.

"Our supplies are chiefly procured by hunting; but occasional additions are made by the Indians, sometimes in the way of gifts, and sometimes in exchange for the services of the blacksmith, who is a most important member of the party.

"Feb. 18.— Our stock of meat is exhausted, so that we must confine ourselves to vegetable diet till the return of our hunters. For this, however, we are at no loss, since yesterday and to-day our blacksmith got large quantities of corn from the Indians who came to the fort.

"Sunday, March 3.— The men are all employed in preparing the boats. We are visited by a party of Indians with corn. A flock of ducks passed up the river to-day.

"Wednesday, 13.—We had a fine day, and a south-west wind. Many Indians came to see us, who are so anxious for battle-axes, that our smiths have not a moment's leisure, and procure us an abundance of corn."

HUNTING BUFFALOES ON THE ICE.

"March 25, 1805.—A fine day, the wind south-west. The river rose nine inches, and the ice began breaking away. Our canoes are now nearly ready, and we expect to set out as soon as the river is sufficiently clear of ice to permit us to pass.

"March 29.—The ice came down this morning in great quantities. We have had few Indians at the fort for the last three or four days, as they are now busy in catching the floating buffaloes. Every spring, as the river is breaking up, the surrounding plains are set on fire, and the buffaloes tempted to cross the river in search of the fresh grass which immediately succeeds to the burning. On their way, they are often insulated on a large cake or mass of ice which floats down the river. The Indians now select the most favorable points for attack, and, as the buffalo approaches, run with astonishing agility across the trembling ice, sometimes pressing lightly a cake of not more than two feet square. The animal is, of course, unsteady, and his footsteps insecure, on this new element, so that he can make but little resistance; and the hunter who has given him his death-wound paddles his icy boat to the shore, and secures his prey."

CHAPTER VI.

THE MARCH RESUMED.

FROM the 1st of November, 1804, to the 1st of April, 1805, the expedition remained stationary at their fort. Some of their number had been sent back to the States with despatches to the Government, and with specimens of the natural productions of the country. On resuming their march on the 4th of April, the party consisted of thirty-two persons. Besides the commanders, there were three sergeants, — Ordway, Prior, and Gass; twenty-three privates, besides Capt. Clark's black servant York; two interpreters, — George Drewyer and Toussaint Chaboneau. The wife of Chaboneau, an Indian woman, with her young child, accompanied her husband. All this party, with the luggage, was stored in six small canoes and two pirogues. They left the fort with fair weather, and, after making four miles, encamped on the north side of the river, nearly opposite the first Mandan village. We continue their journal.

THE RIVER-SHORE.

"April 8. — The river-banks exhibit indications of volcanic agency. The bluffs which we passed to-day are upwards of one hundred feet high, composed of yellow clay and sand, with horizontal strata of carbonated wood resembling pit-coal, from one to five feet in thickness, scattered through the bluff at different elevations. Great quantities of pumice-stone and lava are seen in many parts of the hills, where they are broken and washed into gullies by the rain. We passed a bluff which is on fire, and throws out quantities of smoke, which has a strong, sulphurous smell. On the sides of the hills is a white substance, which appears in considerable quantities on the surface, and tastes like a mixture of common salt with Glauber salts. Many of the springs which come from the foot of the hills are so impregnated with this substance, that the water has an unpleasant taste, and a purgative effect."

THE PRAIRIE-MICE.

"April, 1805. — We saw, but could not procure, an animal that burrows in the ground, similar to the burrowing-squirrel, except that it is only one-third of its size. This may be the animal whose works we have often seen in the plains and prairies. They consist of a little hillock of ten or twelve pounds of loose earth, which would seem to have been reversed from a flower-pot; and no aperture is seen in the ground from which it could have been brought. On removing gently the earth, you discover that the soil has been broken in a circle of about an inch and a half in diameter, where the ground is looser, though still no opening is perceptible. When we stopped for dinner, the Indian woman went out, and, penetrating with a sharp stick the holes of the mice, brought a quantity of wild artichokes, which the mice collect, and hoard in large quantities. The root is white, of an ovate form, from one to three inches long, and generally of the size of a man's finger; and two, four, and sometimes six roots are attached to a single stalk. Its flavor, as well as the stalk that issues from it, resemble those of the Jerusalem artichoke, except that the latter is much larger."

THE YELLOW-STONE RIVER.

"Certain signs, known to the hunters, induced them to believe that we were at no great distance from the Yellow-stone River. In order to prevent delay, Capt.

Lewis determined to go on by land in search of that river, and make the necessary observations, so as to enable us to proceed immediately after the boats should join him.

"On leaving the party, he pursued his route along the foot of the hills; ascending which, the wide plains watered by the Missouri and the Yellow-stone spread themselves before his eye, occasionally varied with the wood of the banks, enlivened by the windings of the two rivers, and animated by vast herds of buffaloes, deer, elk, and antelope."

NATURAL HISTORY.

"May, 1805.— We reached the mouth of a river flowing from the north, which, from the unusual number of porcupines near it, we called Porcupine River. These animals are so careless and clumsy, that we can approach very near without disturbing them as they are feeding on the young willows. The porcupine is common in all parts of the territory, and for its quills is held in high estimation by the Indians. It is interesting to see with how much ingenuity, and in how many various forms, the Indians manufacture these quills into ornamental work, such as moccasons, belts, and various other articles."

WOLVES.

"The wolves are very numerous, and of two species. First, the small wolf, or burrowing dog of the prairies, which is found in almost all the open plains. It is of an intermediate size, between the fox and dog, very delicately formed, fleet and active. The ears are large, erect, and pointed; the head long and pointed, like that of a fox; the tail long and bushy; the hair and fur of a pale reddish-brown, and much coarser than that of the fox. These animals usually associate in bands of ten or twelve, and are rarely, if ever, seen alone; not being able singly to attack a deer or antelope. They live, and rear their young, in burrows, which they fix near some pass much frequented by game, and sally out in a body against any animal which they think they can overpower, but, on the slightest alarm, retreat to their burrows, making a noise exactly like that of a small dog.

"The second species is lower, shorter in the legs, and thicker, than the Atlantic wolf. They do not burrow, nor do they bark, but howl; and they frequent the woods and plains, and skulk along the herds of buffaloes, in order to attack the weary or wounded."

ELK.

"Among the animals of the deer kind, the elk is the largest and most majestic. It combines beauty with magnitude and strength; and its large, towering horns give it an imposing appearance. Its senses are so keen in apprehension, that it is difficult to be approached; and its speed in flight is so great, that it mocks the chase. Its flesh resembles beef, but is less highly flavored, and is much sought for by the Indians and hunters. Its skin is esteemed, and much used in articles of clothing and for moccasons."

BEAVERS.

"We saw many beavers to-day. The beaver seems to contribute very much to the widening of the river and the formation of islands. They begin by damming up the channels of about twenty yards width between the islands. This obliges the river to seek another outlet; and, as soon as this is effected, the channel stopped by the beaver becomes filled with mud and sand. The industrious animal is thus driven to another channel, which soon shares the same fate; till the river spreads on all sides, and cuts the projecting points of land into islands.

"The beaver dams differ in shape, according to the nature of the place in which they are built. If the water in the river or creek have but little motion, the dam is almost straight; but, when the current is more rapid, it is always made with a considerable curve, convex toward the stream. The materials made use of are drift-wood, green willows, birch, and poplars, if they can be got; also mud and stones, intermixed in such a manner as must evidently contribute to the strength of the dam. In places which have been long frequented by beavers undisturbed, their dams, by frequent repairing, become a solid bank, capable of resisting a great force both of water and ice; and as the willow, poplar, and birch generally take root, and shoot up, they, by degrees, form a kind of regular planted hedge, in some places so tall that birds build their nests among the branches. The beaver-houses are constructed of the same materials as their dams, and are always proportioned in size to the number of inhabitants, which seldom exceeds four old and six or eight young ones. The houses are of a much ruder construction than their dams: for, notwithstanding the sagacity of these animals, it has never been observed that they aim at any other convenience in their house than to have a dry place to lie on; and there they usually eat their victuals, such as they take out of the water. Their food consists of roots of plants, like the pond-lily, which grows at the bottom of the lakes and rivers. They also eat the bark of trees, particularly those of the poplar, birch, and willow.

"The instinct of the beavers leading them to live in associations, they are in an unnatural position, when, in any locality, their numbers are so much reduced as to prevent their following this instinct. The beaver near the settlement is sad and solitary: his works have been swept away, his association broken up, and he is reduced to the necessity of burrowing in the river-bank, instead of building a house for himself. Such beavers are called 'terriers.' One traveller says that these solitaries are also called 'old bachelors.'"

THE WHITE, BROWN, OR GRISLY BEAR.

"April 29. — All these names are given to the same species, which probably changes in color with the season, or with the time of life. Of the strength and ferocity of this animal, the Indians give dreadful accounts. They never attack him but in parties of six or eight persons, and, even then, are often defeated with the loss of some of the party.

"May 18. — One of our men who had been suffered to go ashore came running to the boats with cries and every symptom of terror. As soon as he could command his breath, he told us, that, about a mile below, he had shot a white bear, which immediately turned and ran towards him, but, being wounded, had not been able to overtake him. Capt. Lewis, with seven men, went in search of the bear, and, having found his track, followed him by the blood for a mile, came up with him, and shot him with two balls through the skull. He was a monstrous animal, and a most formidable enemy. Our man had shot him through the centre of the lungs: yet the bear had pursued him furiously for half a mile; then returned more than twice that distance, and, with his talons, dug himself a bed in the earth, two feet deep and five feet long, and was perfectly alive when they found him, which was at least two hours after he received the wound. The fleece and skin of the bear were a heavy burden for two men; and the oil amounted to eight gallons.

"The wonderful power of life of these animals, added to their great strength, renders them very formidable. Their very track in the mud or sand, which we have sometimes found eleven inches long and seven and a quarter wide, exclusive of the talons, is alarming; and we had rather encounter two Indians than a single brown bear. There is no chance of killing them by a single shot, unless the ball is sent through the brain; and this is very difficult to be done, on account of two large muscles which cover the side of the forehead, and the sharp projection of the frontal bone, which is very thick."

NOTE.

Their strength is astonishingly great. Lieut. Stein of the dragoons, a man of undoubted veracity, told me he saw some buffaloes passing near some bushes where a grisly bear lay concealed: the bear, with one stroke, tore three ribs from a buffalo, and left it dead. — *Parker.*

Although endowed with such strength, and powers of destruction, the grisly bear is not disposed to begin the attack. Mr. Drummond, a later traveller, states, that, in his excursions over the Rocky Mountains, he had frequent opportunity of observing the manners of these animals; and it often happened, that in turning the point of a rock, or sharp angle of a valley, he came suddenly upon one or more of them. On such occasions they reared on their hind-legs, and made a loud noise like a person breathing quick, but much harsher. He kept his ground, without attempting to molest them; and they on their part, after attentively regarding him for some time, generally wheeled round, and galloped off: though, from their known disposition, there is little doubt but he would have been torn in

THE BLACK BEAR.

"The black bear, common in the United States, is scarcely more than half the size of the grisly bear. Its favorite food is berries of various kinds; but, when these are not to be procured, it lives upon roots, insects, fish, eggs, and such birds and quadrupeds as it can surprise. It passes the winter in a torpid state, selecting a spot for its den under a fallen tree, and, having scratched away a portion of the soil, retires to the place at the commencement of a snow-storm, when the snow soon furnishes it with a close, warm covering. Its breath makes a small opening in the den, and the quantity of hoar-frost which gathers round the hole serves to betray its retreat to the hunter. In more southern districts, where the timber is of larger size, bears often shelter themselves in hollow trees."

BUFFALOES.

"The buffalo is about as large as our domestic cattle; and their long, shaggy, woolly hair, which covers

---

pieces, had he lost his presence of mind and attempted to fly. When he discovered them at a distance, he often frightened them away by beating on a large tin box in which he carried his specimens of plants.

their head, neck, and shoulders, gives them a formidable appearance, and, at a distance, something like that of the lion. In many respects, they resemble our horned cattle; are cloven-footed, chew the cud, and select the same kind of food. Their flesh is in appearance and taste much like beef, but of superior flavor. Their heads are formed like the ox, perhaps a little more round and broad; and, when they run, they carry them rather low. Their horns, ears, and eyes, as seen through their shaggy hair, appear small, and, cleared from their covering, are not large. Their legs and feet are small and trim; the fore-legs covered with the long hair of the shoulders, as low down as the knee. Though their figure is clumsy in appearance, they run swiftly, and for a long time without much slackening their speed; and, up steep hills or mountains, they more than equal the best horses. They unite in herds, and, when feeding, scatter over a large space; but, when fleeing from danger, they collect into dense columns: and, having once laid their course, they are not easily diverted from it, whatever may oppose. So far are they from being a fierce or revengeful animal, that they are very shy and timid; and in no case did we see them offer to make an attack but in self-defence, and then they always sought the first opportunity to escape. When they run, they lean alternately from side to side. They are fond of rolling upon the ground like horses, which is not practised by our domestic cattle. This is so much their diversion, that large places are found without grass, and considerably excavated by them."

NOTE.

Rev. Mr. Parker thus describes a buffalo-hunt: —

"To-day we unexpectedly saw before us a large herd of buffaloes. All halted to make preparation for the chase. The young men, and all the good hunters, prepared themselves, selected the swiftest horses, examined the few guns they had, and also took a supply of arrows with their bows. They advanced towards the herd of buffaloes with great caution, lest they should frighten them before they should make a near approach, and also to reserve the power of their horses for the chase, when it should be necessary to bring it into full requisition. When the buffaloes took the alarm, and fled, the rush was made, each Indian selecting for himself the one to which he happened to come nearest. All were in swift motion, scouring the valley. A cloud of dust began to rise; firing of guns, and shooting of arrows, followed in close succession. Soon, here and there, buffaloes were seen prostrated; and the women, who followed close in the rear, began the work of securing the acquisition, and the men were away again in pursuit of the flying herd. Those in the chase, when as near as two rods, shoot and wheel, expecting the wounded animal to turn upon them. The horses seemed to understand the way to avoid danger. As soon as the wounded

INDIAN METHOD OF HUNTING THE BUFFALO.

"May 30, 1805. — We passed a precipice about one hundred and twenty feet high, under which lay scattered the fragments of at least a hundred carcasses of buffaloes. These buffaloes had been chased down the precipice in a way very common on the Missouri, and by which vast herds are destroyed in a moment. The mode of hunting is to select one of the most active and fleet young men, who is disguised by a buffalo-skin round his body; the skin of the head, with the ears and horns, fastened on his own head in such a way as to deceive the buffaloes. Thus dressed, he fixes himself at a convenient distance between a herd of buffaloes and any of the river precipices, which sometimes extend for some miles. His companions, in the mean time, get in the rear and side of the herd, and, at a given signal, show themselves, and advance towards the buffaloes. They instantly take the alarm; and, finding the hunters beside them, they run toward the disguised Indian, or decoy, who leads them on, at full speed, toward

animal flies again, the chase is renewed; and such is the alternate wheeling and chasing, until the buffalo sinks beneath his wounds."

the river; when, suddenly securing himself in some crevice of the cliff which he had previously fixed on, the herd is left on the brink of the precipice. It is then in vain for the foremost to retreat, or even to stop. They are pressed on by the hindmost rank, who, seeing no danger but from the hunters, goad on those before them, till the whole are precipitated over the cliff, and the shore is covered with their dead bodies. Sometimes, in this perilous adventure, the Indian decoy is either trodden under foot, or, missing his footing in the cliff, is urged down the precipice by the falling herd."

WHICH IS THE TRUE RIVER?

"June 3, 1805. — We came to for the night, for the purpose of examining in the morning a large river which enters opposite to us. It now became an interesting question, which of those two streams is what the Indians call Ahmateahza, or the Missouri, which, they tell us, has its head waters very near to the Columbia. On our right decision much of the fate of the expedition depends; since, if, after ascending to the Rocky Mountains or beyond them, we should find that the river we have been tracing does not come near the Columbia, and be obliged to turn back, we shall have lost the travelling season, and seriously disheartened our men. We determined, therefore, to examine well before deciding on our course, and, for this purpose, despatched two canoes with three men up each of the streams, with orders to ascertain the width, depth, and rapidity of the currents, so as to judge of their comparative bodies of water. Parties were also sent out by land to penetrate the country, and discover from the rising grounds, if possible, the distant bearings of the two rivers. While they were gone, the two commanders ascended together the high grounds in the fork of the two rivers, whence they had an extensive prospect of the surrounding country. On every side, it was spread into one vast plain covered with verdure, in which innumerable herds of buffaloes were roaming, attended by their enemies the wolves. Some flocks of elk also were seen; and the solitary antelopes were scattered, with their young, over the plain. The direction of the rivers could not be long distinguished, as they were soon lost in the extent of the plain.

" On our return, we continued our examination. The width of the north branch is two hundred yards; that of the south is three hundred and seventy-two. The north, though narrower, is deeper than the south: its waters also are of the same whitish-brown color, thickness, and turbidness as the Missouri. They run in the same boiling and roaring manner which has uniformly characterized the Missouri; and its bed is composed of some gravel, but principally mud. The south fork is broader, and its waters are perfectly transparent. The current is rapid, but the surface smooth and unruffled; and its bed is composed of round and flat smooth stones, like those of rivers issuing from a mountainous country.

"In the evening, the exploring parties returned, after ascending the rivers in canoes for some distance, then continuing on foot, just leaving themselves time to return by night. Their accounts were far from deciding the important question of our future route; and we therefore determined each of us to ascend one of the rivers during a day and a half's march, or farther, if necessary for our satisfaction.

"Tuesday, June 4, 1805. — This morning, Capt. Lewis and Capt. Clarke set out, each with a small party, by land, to explore the two rivers. Capt. Lewis traced the course of the north fork for fifty-nine miles, and found, that, for all that distance, its direction was northward; and, as the latitude we were now in was

47° 24′, it was highly improbable, that, by going farther north, we should find between this and the Sascatchawan any stream which can, as the Indians assure us the Missouri does, possess a navigable current for some distance within the Rocky Mountains.

" These considerations, with others drawn from the observations of Capt. Clarke upon the south branch, satisfied the chiefs that the South River was the true Missouri; but the men generally were of a contrary opinion, and much of their belief depended upon Crusatte, an experienced waterman on the Missouri, who gave it as his opinion that the north fork was the main river. In order that nothing might be omitted which could prevent our falling into error, it was agreed that one of us should ascend the southern branch by land until he reached either the falls or the mountains. In the mean time, in order to lighten our burdens as much as possible, we determined to deposit here all the heavy baggage which we could possibly spare, as well as some provisions, salt, powder, and tools. The weather being fair, we dried all our baggage and merchandise, and made our deposit, or *cache.* Our cache is made in this manner: In the high plain on the side of the river, we choose a dry situation, and, drawing a small circle of about twenty inches diameter, remove the sod as carefully as possible. The hole is then sunk perpendicularly a foot deep, or more if the ground be not firm. It is now worked gradually wider as it deepens, till at length it becomes six or seven feet deep, shaped nearly like a kettle, or the lower part of a large still, with the bottom somewhat sunk at the centre. As the earth is dug, it is carefully laid on a skin or cloth, in which it is carried away, and thrown into the river, so as to leave no trace of it. A floor to the cache is then made of dry sticks, on which is thrown hay, or a hide perfectly dry. The goods, being well aired and dried, are laid on this floor, and prevented from touching the sides by other dried sticks, as the baggage is stowed away. When the hole is nearly full, a skin is laid over the goods; and, on this, earth is thrown, and beaten down, until, with the addition of the sod, the whole is on a level with the ground, and there remains no appearance of an excavation. Careful measurements are taken to secure the ready recovery of the cache on the return; and the deposit is left in perfect confidence of finding every thing safe and sound after the lapse of months, or even years."

THE FALLS OF THE MISSOURI.

"June 12. — This morning, Capt. Lewis set out with four men on an exploration, to ascend the southern branch, agreeably to our plan. He left the bank of the river in order to avoid the deep ravines, which generally extend from the shore to a distance of two or three miles in the plain. On the second day, having travelled about sixty miles from the point of departure, on a sudden their ears were saluted with the agreeable sound of falling water; and, as they advanced, a spray which seemed driven by the wind rose above the plain like a column of smoke, and vanished in an instant. Towards this point, Capt. Lewis directed his steps; and the noise, increasing as he approached, soon became too powerful to be ascribed to any thing but the Great Falls of the Missouri. Having travelled seven miles after first hearing the sound, he reached the falls. The hills, as he approached the river, were difficult of transit, and two hundred feet high. Down these he hurried, and, seating himself on a rock, enjoyed the spectacle of this stupendous object, which, ever since the creation, had been lavishing its magnificence upon the desert, unseen by civilized man.

"The river, immediately at its cascade, is three hundred yards wide, and is pressed in by a perpendicular cliff, which rises to about one hundred feet, and extends up the stream for a mile. On the other side, the bluff is also perpendicular for three hundred yards above the falls. For ninety or a hundred yards from the left cliff, the water falls in one smooth, even sheet, over a precipice eighty feet in height. The remaining part of the river rushes with an accelerated current, but, being received as it falls by irregular rocks below, forms a brilliant spectacle of perfectly white foam, two hundred yards in length, and eighty in height. The spray is dissipated into a thousand shapes, on all of which the sun impresses the brightest colors of the rainbow. The principal cascade is succeeded by others of less grandeur, but of exceeding beauty and great variety, for about twenty miles in extent." *

A PORTAGE.

"June 21. — Having reached the falls, we found ourselves obliged to get past them by transporting our boats overland by what is called a *portage*. The

---

* Dimensions of Niagara Falls, — American, 960 feet wide, 162 feet high; English, 700 feet wide, 150 feet high.

distance was eighteen miles. It was necessary to construct a truck or carriage to transport the boats; and the making of the wheels and the necessary framework took ten days. The axle-trees, made of an old mast, broke repeatedly, and the cottonwood tongues gave way; so that the men were forced to carry as much baggage as they could on their backs. The prickly pear annoyed them much by sticking through their moccasons. It required several trips to transport all the canoes and baggage; and, though the men put double soles to their moccasons, the prickly pear, and the sharp points of earth formed by the trampling of the buffaloes during the late rains, wounded their feet; and, as the men were laden as heavily as their strength would permit, the crossing was very painful. They were obliged to halt and rest frequently; and, at almost every stopping-place, they would throw themselves down, and fall asleep in an instant. Yet no one complained, and they went on with cheerfulness.

"Having decided to leave here one of the pirogues, we set to work to fit up a boat of skins, upon a frame of iron which had been prepared at the armory at Harper's Ferry. It was thirty-six feet long, four feet and a half wide at top, and twenty-six inches wide at bottom. It was with difficulty we found the necessary timber to complete it, even tolerably straight sticks, four and a half feet long. The sides were formed of willow-bark, and, over this, elk and buffalo skins."

A NARROW ESCAPE.

" June 29. — Capt. Clarke, having lost some notes and remarks which he had made on first ascending the river, determined to go up along its banks in order to supply the deficiency. He had reached the falls, accompanied by his negro-servant York, and by Chaboneau, the half-breed Indian interpreter, and his wife with her young child. On his arrival there, he observed a dark cloud in the west, which threatened rain; and looked around for some shelter. About a quarter of a mile above the falls he found a deep ravine, where there were some shelving rocks, under which they took refuge. They were perfectly sheltered from the rain, and therefore laid down their guns, compass, and other articles which they carried with them. The shower was at first moderate; it then increased to a heavy rain, the effects of which they did not feel. Soon after, a torrent of rain and hail descended. The rain seemed to fall in a solid mass, and, instantly collecting in the ravine, came rolling down in a dreadful torrent, carrying the mud and rocks, and every thing that opposed it. Capt. Clarke fortunately saw it a moment before it reached them, and springing up, with his gun in his left hand, with his right he clambered up the steep bluff, pushing on the Indian woman with her child in her arms. Her husband, too, had seized her hand, and was pulling her up the hill, but was so terrified at the danger, that, but for Capt. Clarke, he would have been lost, with his wife and child. So instantaneous was the rise of the water, that, before Capt. Clarke had secured his gun and begun to ascend the bank, the water was up to his waist; and he could scarce get up faster than it rose, till it reached the height of fifteen feet, with a furious current, which, had they waited a moment longer, would have swept them into the river, just above the falls, down which they must inevitably have been carried. As it was, Capt. Clarke lost his compass, Chaboneau his gun, shot-pouch, and tomahawk; and the Indian woman had just time to grasp her child before the net in which it lay was carried down the current."

PROGRESS RESUMED.

"July 4. — The boat was now completed, except what was in fact the most difficult part, — the making her seams secure. Having been unsuccessful in all our attempts to procure tar, we have formed a composition of pounded charcoal with beeswax and buffalo-tallow to supply its place. If this resource fail us, it will be very unfortunate, as, in every other respect, the boat answers our purpose completely. Although not quite dry, she can be carried with ease by five men: she is very strong, and will carry a load of eight thousand pounds, with her complement of men.

"July 9. — The boat having now become sufficiently dry, we gave it a coat of the composition, then a second, and launched it into the water. She swam perfectly well. The seats were then fixed, and the oars fitted. But after a few hours' exposure to the wind, which blew with violence, we discovered that nearly all the composition had separated from the skins, so that she leaked very much. To repair this misfortune without pitch was impossible; and, as none of that article was to be procured, we were obliged to abandon her, after having had so much labor in the construction.

"It now becomes necessary to provide other means for transporting the baggage which we had intended to stow in her. For this purpose, we shall want two canoes; but for many miles we have not seen a single tree fit to be used for that purpose. The hunters, however, report that there is a low ground about eight miles above us by land, and more than twice that distance by water, in which we may probably find trees large enough. Capt. Clarke has therefore determined to set out by land for that place, with ten of the best workmen, who will be occupied in building the canoes, till the rest of the party, after taking the boat to pieces and making the necessary deposits, shall transport the baggage, and join them with the other six canoes.

"Capt. Clarke accordingly proceeded on eight miles by land; the distance by water being twenty-three miles. Here he found two cottonwood-trees, and proceeded to convert them into boats. The rest of the party took the iron boat to pieces, and deposited it in a *cache*, or hole, with some other articles of less importance.

"July 11.— Sergeant Ordway, with four canoes and eight men, set sail in the morning to the place where Capt. Clarke had fixed his camp. The canoes were unloaded and sent back, and the remainder of the baggage in a second trip was despatched to the upper camp.

"July 15. — We rose early, embarked all our baggage on board the canoes, which, though eight in number, were heavily laden, and at ten o'clock set out on our journey.

"July 16. — We had now arrived at the point where the Missouri emerges from the Rocky Mountains. The current of the river becomes stronger as we advance, and the spurs of the mountain approach towards the river, which is deep, and not more than seventy yards wide. The low grounds are now but a few yards in width; yet they furnish room for an Indian road, which winds under the hills on the north side of the river. The general range of these hills is from south-east to north-west; and the cliffs themselves are about eight hundred feet above the water, formed almost entirely of a hard black rock, on which are scattered a few dwarf pine and cedar trees.

"As the canoes were heavily laden, all the men not employed in working them walked on shore. The navigation is now very laborious. The river is deep, but with little current; the low grounds are very narrow; the cliffs are steep, and hang over the river so much, that, in places, we could not pass them, but were obliged to cross and recross from one side of the river to the other in order to make our way."

CHAPTER VII.

JOURNEY CONTINUED.

JULY 4. — Since our arrival at the falls, we have repeatedly heard a strange noise coming from the mountains, in a direction a little to the north of west. It is heard at different periods of the day and night, sometimes when the air is perfectly still and without a cloud; and consists of one stroke only, or of five or six discharges in quick succession. It is loud, and resembles precisely the sound of a six-pound piece of ordnance, at the distance of three miles. The Minnetarees frequently mentioned this noise, like thunder, which they said the mountains made; but we had paid no attention to them, believing it to be some superstition, or else a falsehood. The watermen also of the party say that the Pawnees and Ricaras give the same account of a noise heard in the Black Mountains, to the westward of them. The solution of the mystery, given by the philosophy of the watermen, is, that it is occasioned by the bursting of the rich mines of silver confined within the bosom of the mountain.*

"An elk and a beaver are all that were killed to-day: the buffaloes seem to have withdrawn from our neighborhood. We contrived, however, to spread a comfortable table in honor of the day; and in the evening gave the men a drink of spirits, which was the last of our stock."

VEGETATION.

"July 15. — We find the prickly-pear — one of the greatest beauties, as well as one of the greatest inconveniences, of the plains — now in full bloom. The sunflower too, a plant common to every part of the Missouri, is here very abundant, and in bloom. The Indians of the Missouri, and more especially those who do not cultivate maize, make great use of this plant for bread, and in thickening their soup. They first parch, and then pound it between two stones

---

* There are many stories, from other sources, confirmatory of these noises in mountainous districts. One solution, suggested by Humboldt, — who does not, however, record the fact as of his own observation, — is, that "this curious phenomenon announces a disengagement of hydrogen, produced by a bed of coal in a state of combustion." This solution is applicable only to mountains which contain coal, unless chemical changes in other minerals might be supposed capable of producing a similar effect.

until it is reduced to a fine meal. Sometimes they add a portion of water, and drink it thus diluted; at other times they add a sufficient proportion of marrow-fat to reduce it to the consistency of common dough, and eat it in that manner. This last composition we preferred to the rest, and thought it at that time very palatable.

"There are also great quantities of red, purple, yellow, and black currants. The currants are very pleasant to the taste, and much preferable to those of our gardens. The fruit is not so. acid, and has a more agreeable flavor."

THE BIG-HORNED OR MOUNTAIN RAM.

"July 18. — This morning we saw a large herd of the big-horned animals, who were bounding among the rocks in the opposite cliff with great agility. These inaccessible spots secure them from all their enemies; and the only danger they encounter is in wandering among these precipices, where we should suppose it scarcely possible for any animal to stand. A single false step would precipitate them at least five hundred feet into the river.

"The game continues abundant. We killed to-day the largest male elk we have yet seen. On placing it in its natural, erect position, we found that it measured five feet three inches from the point of the hoof to the top of the shoulder.

"The antelopes are yet lean. This fleet and quick-sighted animal is generally the victim of its curiosity. When they first see the hunters, they run with great velocity. If the hunter lies down on the ground, and lifts up his arm, his hat, or his foot, the antelope returns on a light trot to look at the object, and sometimes goes and returns two or three times, till at last he approaches within reach of the rifle. So, too, they sometimes leave their flock to go and look at the wolves, who crouch down, and, if the antelope be frightened at first, repeat the same manœuvre, and sometimes relieve each other, till they decoy the antelope from his party near enough to seize it."

THE GATES OF THE ROCKY MOUNTAINS.

"July 20. — During the day, in the confined valley through which we are passing, the heat is almost insupportable; yet, whenever we obtain a glimpse of the lofty tops of the mountains, we are tantalized with a view of the snow. A mile and a half farther on, the rocks approach the river on both sides, forming a most sublime and extraordinary spectacle. For six miles, these rocks rise perpendicularly from the water's edge to the height of nearly twelve hundred feet. They are composed of a black granite near the base; but judging from its lighter color above, and from fragments that have fallen from it, we suppose the upper part to be flint, of a yellowish-brown and cream color. Nothing can be imagined more tremendous than the frowning darkness of these rocks, which project over the river, and menace us with destruction. The river, one hundred and fifty yards in width, seems to have forced its channel down this solid mass: but so reluctantly has it given way, that, during the whole distance, the water is very deep even at the edges; and, for the first three miles, there is not a spot, except one of a few yards in extent, on which a man could stand between the water and the towering perpendicular of the mountain. The convulsion of the passage must have been terrible; since, at its outlet, there are vast columns of rock torn from the mountain, which are strewed on both sides of the river, the trophies, as it were, of victory. We were obliged to go on some time after dark, not being able to find a spot large enough to encamp on. This extraordinary range of rocks we called the Gates of the Rocky Mountains."

NATURAL PRODUCTIONS.

"July 29. — This morning the hunters brought in some fat deer of the long-tailed red kind, which are the only kind we have found at this place. There are numbers of the sandhill-cranes feeding in the meadows. We caught a young one, which, though it had nearly attained its full growth, could not fly. It is very fierce, and strikes a severe blow with its beak. The kingfisher has become quite common this side of the falls; but we have seen none of the summer duck since leaving that place. Small birds are also abundant in the plains. Here, too, are great quantities of grasshoppers, or crickets; and, among other animals, large ants, with a reddish-brown body and legs, and a black head, which build little cones of gravel ten or twelve inches high, without a mixture of sticks, and with but little earth. In the river we see a great abundance of fish, but cannot tempt them to bite by any thing on our hooks."

THE FORKS OF THE MISSOURI.

"July 28, 1805. — From the height of a limestone cliff, Capt. Lewis observed the three forks of the Missouri, of which this river is one. The middle and south-west forks unite at half a mile above the entrance of the south-east fork. The country watered by these rivers, as far as the eye could command, was a beautiful combination of meadow and elevated plain, covered with a rich grass, and possessing more timber than is usual on the Missouri. A range of high mountains, partially covered with snow, is seen at a considerable distance, running from south to west.

"To the south-east fork the name of Gallatin was assigned, in honor of the Secretary of the Treasury. On examining the other two streams, it was difficult to decide which was the larger or real Missouri: they are each ninety yards wide, and similar in character and appearance. We were therefore induced to discontinue the name of Missouri, and to give to the south-west branch the name of Jefferson, in honor of the President of the United States and the projector of the enterprise; and called the middle branch Madison, after James Madison, Secretary of State.

"July 30. — We reloaded our canoes, and began to ascend Jefferson River. The river soon became very crooked; the current, too, is rapid, impeded with shoals, which consist of coarse gravel. The islands are numerous. On the 7th of August, we had, with much fatigue, ascended the river sixty miles, when we reached the junction of a stream from the northwest, which we named Wisdom River. We continued, however, to ascend the south-east branch, which we were satisfied was the true continuation of the Jefferson."

THE SHOSHONEES, OR SNAKE INDIANS.

"July 28. — We are now very anxious to see the Snake Indians. After advancing for several hundred miles into this wild and mountainous country, we may soon expect that the game will abandon us. With no information of the route, we may be unable to find a passage across the mountains when we reach the head of the river, at least such an one as will lead us to the Columbia. And, even were we so fortunate as to find a branch of that river, the timber which we have hitherto seen in these mountains does not promise us any wood fit to make canoes; so that our chief dependence is on meeting some tribe from whom we may procure horses.

"Sacajawea, our Indian woman, informs us that we are encamped on the precise spot where her countrymen, the Snake Indians, had their huts five years ago, when the Minnetarees came upon them, killed most of the party, and carried her away prisoner.

She does not, however, show any distress at these recollections, nor any joy at the prospect of being restored to her country; for she seems to possess the folly, or the philosophy, of not suffering her feelings to extend beyond the anxiety of having plenty to eat, and trinkets to wear.

"Aug. 9. — Persuaded of the absolute necessity of procuring horses to cross the mountains, it was determined that one of us should proceed in the morning to the head of the river, and penetrate the mountains till he found the Shoshonees, or some other nation, who could assist us in transporting our baggage. Immediately after breakfast, Capt. Lewis took Drewyer, Shields, and McNeal; and, slinging their knapsacks, they set out, with a resolution to meet some nation of Indians before they returned, however long it might be.

"Aug. 11. — It was not till the third day after commencing their search that they met with any success. Capt. Lewis perceived with the greatest delight, at the distance of two miles, a man on horseback coming towards them. On examining him with the glass, Capt. Lewis saw that he was of a different nation from any we had hitherto met. He was armed with a bow and a quiver of arrows, and mounted on an elegant horse without a saddle; while a small string, attached to the under-jaw, answered as a bridle. Convinced that he was a Shoshonee, and knowing how much our success depended upon the friendly offices of that nation, Capt. Lewis was anxious to approach without alarming him. He therefore advanced towards the Indian at his usual pace. When they were within a mile of each other, the Indian suddenly stopped. Capt. Lewis immediately followed his example; took his blanket from his knapsack, and, holding it with both hands at the two corners, threw it above his head, and unfolded it as he brought it to the ground, as if in the act of spreading it. This signal, which originates in the practice of spreading a robe or a skin as a seat for guests to whom they wish to show kindness, is the universal sign of friendship among the Indians. As usual, Capt. Lewis repeated this signal three times. Still the Indian kept his position, and looked with an air of suspicion on Drewyer and Shields, who were now advancing on each side. Capt. Lewis was afraid to make any signal for them to halt, lest he should increase the suspicions of the Indian, who began to be uneasy; and they were too distant to hear his voice. He therefore took from his pack some beads, a looking-glass, and a few trinkets, which he had brought for the purpose; and, leaving his gun, advanced unarmed towards the Indian, who remained in the same position till Capt. Lewis came within two hundred yards of him, when he turned his horse, and began to move off slowly. Capt. Lewis then called out to him, as loud as he could, 'Tabba bone,' — which, in the Shoshonee language, means *White man;* but, looking over his shoulder, the Indian kept his eyes on Drewyer and Shields, who were still advancing, till Capt. Lewis made a signal to them to halt. This, Drewyer obeyed; but Shields did not observe it, and still went forward. The Indian, seeing Drewyer halt, turned his horse about, as if to wait for Capt. Lewis, who had now reached within one hundred and fifty paces, repeating the words, 'Tabba bone,' and holding up the trinkets in his hand; at the same time stripping up his sleeve to show that he was white. The Indian suffered him to advance within one hundred paces, then suddenly turned his horse, and, giving him the whip, leaped across the creek, and disappeared in an instant among the willows. They followed his track four miles, but could not get sight of him again, nor find any encampment to which he belonged.

"Meanwhile the party in the canoes advanced slowly up the river till they came to a large island, to which they gave the name of Three-thousand-mile Island, on account of its being at that distance from the mouth of the Missouri."

CHAPTER VIII.

THE SOURCES OF THE MISSOURI AND COLUMBIA.

AUG. 12, 1805. — Capt. Lewis decided to advance along the foot of the mountains, hoping to find a road leading across them. At the distance of four miles from his camp, he found a large, plain, Indian road, which entered the valley from the north-east. Following this road towards the south-west, the valley, for the first five miles, continued in the same direction; then the main stream turned abruptly to the west, through a narrow bottom between the mountains. We traced the stream, which gradually became smaller, till, two miles farther up, it had so diminished, that one of the men, in a fit of enthusiasm, with one foot on each side of the rivulet, thanked God that he had lived to bestride the Missouri. Four miles from thence, we came to the spot where, from the foot of a mountain, issues the remotest water of the mighty river

"We had now traced the Missouri to its source, which had never before been seen by civilized man; and as we quenched our thirst at the pure and icy fountain, and stretched ourselves by the brink of the little rivulet which yielded its distant and modest tribute to the parent ocean, we felt rewarded for all our labors.

"We left reluctantly this interesting spot, and, pursuing the Indian road, arrived at the top of a ridge, from whence we saw high mountains, partially covered with snow, still to the west of us. The ridge on which we stood formed, apparently, the dividing-line between the waters of the Pacific and Atlantic Oceans. We followed a descent much steeper than that on the eastern side, and, at the distance of three-quarters of a mile, reached a handsome, bold creek of cold, clear water, running to the westward. We stopped for a moment, to taste, for the first time, the waters of the Columbia; and then followed the road across hills and valleys, till we found a spring, and a sufficient quantity of dry willow-brush for fuel; and there halted for the night."

THEY MEET WITH INDIANS.

"Aug. 13.— Very early in the morning, Capt. Lewis resumed the Indian road, which led him in a western direction, through an open, broken country. At five miles' distance, he reached a creek about ten yards wide, and, on rising the hill beyond it, had a view of a handsome little valley about a mile in width, through which they judged, from the appearance of the timber, that a stream probably flowed. On a sudden, they discovered two women, a man, and some dogs, on an eminence about a mile before them. The strangers viewed them apparently with much attention; and then two of them sat down, as if to await Capt. Lewis's arrival. He went on till he had reached within about half a mile; then ordered his party to stop, put down his knapsack and rifle, and, unfurling the flag, advanced alone towards the Indians.

"The women soon retreated behind the hill; but the man remained till Capt. Lewis came within a hundred yards of him, when he, too, went off, though Capt. Lewis called out 'Tabba bone' ('White man'), loud enough to be heard distinctly. The dogs, however, were less shy, and came close to him. He therefore thought of tying a handkerchief with some beads round their necks, and then to let them loose, to convince the fugitives of his friendly intentions; but the dogs would not suffer him to take hold of them, and soon left him.

"He now made a signal to the men, who joined him; and then all followed the track of the Indians, which led along a continuation of the same road they had been travelling. It was dusty, and seemed to have been much used lately both by foot-passengers and horsemen.

"They had not gone along it more than a mile, when, on a sudden, they saw three female Indians, from whom they had been concealed by the deep ravines which intersected the road, till they were now within thirty paces of them. One of them, a young woman, immediately took to flight: the other two, an old woman and little girl, seeing we were too near for them to escape, sat on the ground, and, holding down their heads, seemed as if reconciled to the death which they supposed awaited them. Capt. Lewis instantly put down his rifle, and, advancing towards them, took the woman by the hand, raised her up, and repeated the words, 'Tabba bone,' at the same time stripping up his sleeve to show that he was a white man; for his hands and face had become by exposure quite as dark as their own.

"She appeared immediately relieved from her alarm; and, Drewyer and Shields now coming up, Capt. Lewis gave her some beads, a few awls, pewter mirrors, and a little paint, and told Drewyer to request the woman to recall her companion, who had escaped to some distance, and, by alarming the Indians, might cause them to attack him, without any time for explanation. She did as she was desired, and the young woman returned readily. Capt. Lewis gave her an equal portion of trinkets, and painted the tawny cheeks of all three of them with vermilion, which, besides its ornamental effect, has the advantage of being held among the Indians as emblematic of peace.

"After they had become composed, he informed them by signs of his wish to go to their camp in order to see their chiefs and warriors. They readily complied, and conducted the party along the same road down the river. In this way they marched two miles, when they met a troop of nearly sixty warriors, mounted on excellent horses, riding at full speed towards them. As they advanced, Capt. Lewis put down his gun, and went with the flag about fifty paces in advance. The chief, who, with two men, was riding in front of the main body, spoke to the women, who now explained that the party was composed of white men, and showed exultingly the presents they had received. The three men immediately leaped from their horses, came up to Capt. Lewis, and embraced him with great cordiality,— putting their left arm over his right shoulder, and clasping his back,— applying at the same time their left cheek to his, and frequently vociferating, 'Ah-hi-e!'—'*I am glad! I am glad!*'

"The whole body of warriors now came forward, and our men received the caresses, and no small share of the grease and paint, of their new friends. After this fraternal embrace, Capt. Lewis lighted a pipe, and offered it to the Indians, who had now seated themselves in a circle around our party. But, before they would receive this mark of friendship, they pulled off their moccasons; a custom which, we afterwards learned, indicates their sincerity when they smoke with a stranger.

"After smoking a few pipes, some trifling presents were distributed among them, with which they seemed very much pleased, particularly with the blue beads and the vermilion.

"Capt. Lewis then informed the chief that the object of his visit was friendly, and should be explained as soon as he reached their camp; but that in the mean time, as the sun was oppressive, and no water near, he wished to go there as soon as possible. They now put on their moccasons; and their chief, whose name was Cameawait, made a short speech to the warriors. Capt. Lewis then gave him the flag, which he informed him was the emblem of peace, and that now and for the future it was to be the pledge of union between us and them. The chief then moved on, our party followed, and the rest of the warriors brought up the rear.

"At the distance of four miles from where they had first met the Indians, they reached the camp, which was in a handsome, level meadow on the bank of the river. Here they were introduced into a leathern lodge which was assigned for their reception. After being seated on green boughs and antelope-skins, one of the warriors pulled up the grass in the centre of the lodge, so as to form a vacant circle of two feet in diameter, in which he kindled a fire. The chief then produced his pipe and tobacco; the warriors all pulled off their moccasons, and our party were requested to take off their own. This being done, the chief lighted his pipe at the fire, and then, retreating from it, began a speech several minutes long; at the end of which he pointed the stem of his pipe towards the four cardinal points of the heavens, beginning with the east, and concluding with the north. After this ceremony, he presented the stem in the same way to Capt. Lewis, who, supposing it an invitation to smoke, put out his hand to receive the pipe; but the chief drew it back, and continued to repeat the same offer three times; after which he pointed the stem to the heavens, then took three whiffs himself, and presented it again to Capt. Lewis. Finding that this last offer was in good earnest, he smoked a little, and returned it. The pipe was then held to each of the white men, and, after they had taken a few whiffs, was given to the warriors.

"The bowl of the pipe was made of a dense, transparent, green stone, very highly polished, about two and a half inches long, and of an oval figure; the bowl being in the same direction with the stem. The tobacco is of the same kind with that used by the Minnetarees and Mandans of the Missouri. The Shoshonees do not cultivate this plant, but obtain it from the bands who live farther south.

"The ceremony of smoking being concluded, Capt. Lewis explained to the chief the purposes of his visit; and, as by this time all the women and children of the camp had gathered around the lodge to indulge in a view of the first white men they had ever seen, he distributed among them the remainder of the small articles he had brought with him.

"It was now late in the afternoon, and our party had tasted no food since the night before. On apprising the chief of this fact, he said that he had nothing but berries to eat, and presented some cakes made of service-berries and choke-cherries which had been dried in the sun. Of these, Capt. Lewis and his companions made as good a meal as they were able.

"The chief informed him that the stream which flowed by them discharged itself, at the distance of half a day's march, into another of twice its size; but added that there was no timber there suitable for building canoes, and that the river was rocky and rapid. The prospect of going on by land was more pleasant; for there were great numbers of horses feeding round the camp, which would serve to transport our stores over the mountains.

"An Indian invited Capt. Lewis into his lodge,

and gave him a small morsel of boiled antelope, and a piece of fresh salmon, roasted. This was the first salmon he had seen, and perfectly satisfied him that he was now on the waters of the Pacific.

"On returning to the lodge, he resumed his conversation with the chief; after which he was entertained with a dance by the Indians. The music and dancing — which were in no respect different from those of the Missouri Indians — continued nearly all night; but Capt. Lewis retired to rest about twelve o'clock, when the fatigues of the day enabled him to sleep, though he was awaked several times by the yells of the dancers."

CHAPTER IX.

THE PARTY IN THE BOATS.

AUGUST, 1805.—While these things were occurring to Capt. Lewis, the party in the boats were slowly and laboriously ascending the river. It was very crooked, the bends short and abrupt, and obstructed by so many shoals, over which the canoes had to be dragged, that the men were in the water three-fourths of the day. They saw numbers of otters, some beavers, antelopes, ducks, geese, and cranes; but they killed nothing except a single deer. They caught, however, some very fine trout. The weather was cloudy and cool; and at eight o'clock a shower of rain fell.

Next day, as the morning was cold, and the men stiff and sore from the fatigues of yesterday, they did not set out till seven o'clock. The river was shallow, and, as it approached the mountains, formed one continued rapid, over which they were obliged to drag the boats with great labor and difficulty. By these means, they succeeded in making fourteen miles; but this distance did not exceed more than six and a half in a straight line.

Several successive days were passed in this manner (the daily progress seldom exceeding a dozen miles), while the party anxiously expected to be rejoined by Capt. Lewis and his men, with intelligence of some relief by the aid of friendly Indians. In the mean time, Capt. Lewis was as anxiously expecting their arrival, to confirm the good impressions he had made on the Indians, as well as to remove some lurking doubts they still felt as to his intentions.

CAPT. LEWIS AMONG THE SHOSHONEES.

Aug. 14. — In order to give time for the boats to reach the forks of Jefferson River, Capt. Lewis determined to remain where he was, and obtain all the information he could with regard to the country. Having nothing to eat but a little flour and parched meal, with the berries of the Indians, he sent out Drewyer and Shields, who borrowed horses of the natives, to hunt. At the same time, the young warriors set out for the same purpose.

There are but few elk or black-tailed deer in this region; and, as the common red deer secrete themselves in the bushes when alarmed, they are soon safe from the arrows of the Indian hunters, which are but feeble weapons against any animal which the huntsmen cannot previously run down. The chief game of the Shoshonees, therefore, is the antelope, which, when pursued, runs to the open plains, where the horses have full room for the chase. But such is this animal's extraordinary fleetness and wind, that a single horse has no chance of outrunning it, or tiring it down; and the hunters are therefore obliged to resort to stratagem. About twenty Indians, mounted on fine horses, and armed with bows and arrows, left the camp. In a short time, they descried a herd of ten antelopes. They immediately separated into little squads of two or three, and formed a scattered circle round the herd for five or six miles, keeping at a wary distance, so as not to alarm them till they were perfectly enclosed. Having gained their positions, a small party rode towards the herd; the huntsman preserving his seat with wonderful tenacity, and the horse his footing, as he ran at full speed over the hills, and down the ravines, and along the edges of precipices. They were soon outstripped by the antelopes, which, on gaining the other limit of the circle, were driven back, and pursued by fresh hunters. They turned, and flew, rather than ran, in another direction; but there, too, they found new enemies. In this way they were alternately driven backwards and forwards, till at length, notwithstanding the skill of the hunters, they all escaped; and the party, after running two hours, returned without having caught any thing, and their horses foaming with sweat. This chase, the greater part of which was seen from the camp, formed a beautiful scene; but to the hunters it is exceedingly laborious, and so unproductive, even when they are able to worry the animal down and shoot him, that forty or fifty hunters will sometimes be engaged for half a day without obtaining more than two or three antelopes. Soon after they returned, our two huntsmen came in with no better success. Capt. Lewis therefore made a little paste with the flour, and the addition of some berries formed a tolerable repast.

Having now secured the good-will of Cameahwait, Capt. Lewis informed him of his wish, — that he would speak to the warriors, and endeavor to engage them to accompany him to the forks of Jefferson River, where, by this time, another chief, with a large party of white men, were waiting his return. He added, that it would be necessary to take about thirty horses to transport the merchandise; that they should be well rewarded for their trouble; and that, when all the party should have reached the Shoshonee camp, they would remain some time among them, and trade for horses, as well as concert plans for furnishing them in future with regular supplies of merchandise. Cameahwait readily consented to do as requested; and, after collecting the tribe together, he made a long harangue, and in about an hour and a half returned, and told Capt. Lewis that they would be ready to accompany him next morning.

Capt. Lewis rose early, and, having eaten nothing yesterday except his scanty meal of flour and berries, felt the pain of extreme hunger. On inquiry, he found that his whole stock of provisions consisted of two pounds of flour. This he ordered to be divided into two equal parts, and one-half of it boiled with the berries into a sort of pudding; and, after presenting a large share to the chief, he and his three men breakfasted on the remainder. Cameahwait was delighted with this new dish. He took a little of the flour in his hand, tasted it, and examined it very carefully, asking if it was made of roots.

Capt. Lewis explained how it was produced, and the chief said it was the best thing he had eaten for a long time.

Breakfast being finished, Capt. Lewis endeavored to hasten the departure of the Indians, who seemed reluctant to move, although the chief addressed them twice for the purpose of urging them. On inquiring the reason, Capt. Lewis learned that the Indians were suspicious that they were to be led into an ambuscade, and betrayed to their enemies. He exerted himself to dispel this suspicion, and succeeded so far as to induce eight of the warriors, with Cameahwait, to accompany him. It was about twelve o'clock when his small party left the camp, attended by Cameahwait and the eight warriors. At sunset they reached the river, and encamped about four miles above the narrow pass between the hills, which they had noticed in their progress some days before. Drewyer had been sent forward to hunt; but he returned in the evening unsuccessful; and their only supply, therefore, was the remaining pound of flour, stirred in a little boiling water, and divided between the four white men and two of the Indians.

Next morning, as neither our party nor the Indians had any thing to eat, Capt. Lewis sent two of his hunters out to procure some provision. At the same time, he requested Cameahwait to prevent his young men from going out, lest, by their noise, they might alarm the game. This measure immediately revived their suspicions, and some of them followed our two men to watch them. After the hunters had been gone about an hour, Capt. Lewis mounted, with one of the Indians behind him, and the whole party set out. Just then, they saw one of the spies coming back at full speed across the plain. The chief stopped, and seemed uneasy: the whole band were moved with fresh suspicions; and Capt. Lewis himself was anxious, lest, by some unfortunate accident, some hostile tribe might have wandered that way. The young Indian had hardly breath to say a few words as he came up, when the whole troop dashed forward as fast as their horses could carry them; and Capt. Lewis, astonished at this movement, was borne along for nearly a mile, before he learned, with great satisfaction, that it was all caused by the spy's having come to announce that one of the white men had killed a deer.

When they reached the place where Drewyer, in cutting up the deer, had thrown out the intestines, the Indians dismounted in confusion, and ran, tumbling over each other, like famished dogs: each tore away whatever part he could, and instantly began to devour it. Some had the liver, some the kidneys: in short, no part on which we are accustomed to look with disgust escaped them. It was, indeed, impossible to see these wretches ravenously feeding on the refuse of animals, and the blood streaming from their mouths, without deploring how nearly the condition of savages approaches that of the brute creation. Yet, though suffering with hunger, they did not attempt to take (as they might have done) by force the whole deer, but contented themselves with what had been thrown away by the hunter. Capt. Lewis had the deer skinned, and, after reserving a quarter of it, gave the rest of the animal to the chief, to be divided among the Indians, who immediately devoured the whole without cooking.

THEY MEET THE BOAT PARTY.

As they were now approaching the place where they had been told they should see the white men, Capt. Lewis, to guard against any disappointment, explained the possibility of our men not having reached the forks, in consequence of the difficulty of the navigation; so that, if they should not find us at that spot, they might be assured of our being not far below. After stopping two hours to let the horses graze, they remounted, and rode on rapidly, making one of the Indians carry the flag, so that the party in the boats might recognize them as they approached. To their great mortification, on coming within sight of the forks, no canoes were to be seen.

Uneasy, lest at this moment he should be abandoned, and all his hopes of obtaining aid from the Indians be destroyed, Capt. Lewis gave the chief his gun, telling him, if the enemies of his nation were in the bushes, he might defend himself with it; and that the chief might shoot him as soon as they discovered themselves betrayed. The other three men at the same time gave their guns to the Indians, who now seemed more easy, but still suspicious. Luckily, he had a hold on them by other ties than their generosity. He had promised liberal exchanges for their horses; but, what was still more attractive, he had told them that one of their country-women, who had been taken by the Minnetarees, accompanied the party below: and one of the men had spread the report of our having with us a man perfectly black, whose hair was short and curled. This last account had excited a great degree of curiosity; and they seemed more desirous of seeing this monster than of obtaining the most favorable barter for their horses.

In the mean time, the boat party under Capt. Clarke, struggling against rapids and shallows, had made their way to a point only four miles by land, though ten by water, from where Capt. Lewis and the Indians were. Capt. Clarke had seen from an eminence the forks of the river, and sent the hunters up. They must have left it only a short time before Capt. Lewis's arrival.

Aug. 17. — Capt. Lewis rose early, and despatched Drewyer and the Indian down the river in quest of the boats. They had been gone about two hours, and the Indians were all anxiously waiting for some news, when an Indian who had straggled a short distance down the river returned, with a report that he had seen the white men, who were not far below, and were coming on. The Indians were all delighted; and the chief, in the warmth of his affection, renewed his embrace to Capt. Lewis, who, though quite as much gratified, would willingly have spared that manifestation of it. The report proved true. On commencing the day's progress, Capt. Clarke, with Chaboneau and his wife, walked by the river-side; but they had not gone more than a mile, when Capt. Clarke saw Sacajawea, the Indian woman, who was some distance in advance, begin to dance, and show every mark of extravagant joy, pointing to several Indians, whom he now saw advancing on horseback. As they approached, Capt. Clarke discovered Drewyer among them, from whom he learned the situation of Capt. Lewis and his party. While the boats were performing the circuit, Capt. Clarke went towards the forks with the Indians, who, as they went along, sang aloud with the greatest appearance of delight.

They soon drew near the camp; and, as they approached it, a woman made her way through the crowd towards Sacajawea, when, recognizing each other, they embraced with the most tender affection. The meeting of these two young women had in it something peculiarly touching. They had been companions in childhood, and, in the war with the Minnetarees, had both been taken prisoners in the same battle. They had shared the same captivity, till one had escaped, leaving her friend with scarce a hope of ever seeing her again.

While Sacajawea was renewing among the women the friendships of former days, Capt. Clarke went on, and was received by Capt. Lewis and the chief, who, after the first embraces and salutations, conducted him to a sort of circular tent constructed of willow-branches. Here he was seated on a white robe; and the chief tied in his hair six small shells resembling pearls,— an ornament highly valued by these people. After smoking, a conference was held, Sacajawea acting as interpreter. Capt. Lewis told them he had been sent to discover the best route by which merchandise could be conveyed to them, and, since no trade would be begun before our return, it was naturally desirable that we should proceed with as little delay as possible; that we were under the necessity of requesting them to furnish us with horses to transport our baggage across the mountains, and a guide to show us the route; but that they should be amply remunerated for their horses, as well as for any other service they should render us. In the mean time, our first wish was that they should immediately collect as many horses as were necessary to transport our baggage to their village, where, at our leisure, we would trade with them for as many horses as they could spare.

The speech made a favorable impression. The chief thanked us for our friendly intentions, and declared their willingness to render us every service. He promised to return to the village next day, and to bring all his own horses, and to encourage his people to bring theirs. We then distributed our presents. To Cameahwait we gave a medal of the small size, with the likeness of President Jefferson, and on the reverse a figure of hands clasped, with a pipe and tomahawk. To this were added a uniform-coat, a shirt, a pair of scarlet leggings, a lump of tobacco, and some small articles. Each of the other chiefs received similar presents, excepting the dress-coat. These honorary gifts were followed by presents of paint, moccasons, awls, knives, beads, and looking-glasses. They had abundant sources of surprise in all they saw. The appearance of the men, their arms, their clothing, the canoes, the strange looks of the negro, and the sagacity of our dog, all in turn shared their admiration, which was raised to astonishment by a shot from the air-gun. This was immediately pronounced a *Great Medicine*, by which they mean something produced by the Great Spirit himself in some incomprehensible way.

CHAPTER X.

THE DESCENT OF THE COLUMBIA.

AUGUST, 1805.— Our Indian information as to the navigation of the Columbia was of a very discouraging character. It was therefore agreed that Capt. Clarke should set off in the morning with eleven men, furnished, besides their arms, with tools for making canoes; that he should take Chaboneau and his wife to the camp of the Shoshonees, where he was to leave them to hasten the collection of horses; that he was then to lead his men down to the Columbia; and if he found it navigable, and the timber in sufficient quantity, should begin to build canoes. As soon as he should have decided on the question of proceeding, whether down the river or across the mountains, he was to send back one of the men, with information of his decision, to Capt. Lewis, who would tarry meanwhile at the Shoshonee village.

Aug. 20.— Capt. Clarke set out at six o'clock.

Passing through a continuation of hilly, broken country, he met several parties of Indians. An old man among them was pointed out, who was said to know more of the nature of the country north than any other person; and Capt. Clarke engaged him as a guide.

The first point to ascertain was the truth of the Indian information as to the difficulty of descending the river. For this purpose, Capt. Clarke and his men set out at three o'clock in the afternoon, accompanied by his Indian guide. At the distance of four miles he crossed the river, and, eight miles from the camp, halted for the night. As Capt. Lewis was the first white man who had visited its waters, Capt. Clarke gave the stream the name of Lewis's River.

Aug. 23.—Capt. Clarke set out very early; but as his route lay along the steep side of a mountain, over irregular and broken masses of rocks, which wounded the horses' feet, he was obliged to proceed slowly. At the distance of four miles, he reached the river; but the rocks here became so steep, and projected so far into the stream, that there was no mode of passing except through the water. This he did for some distance, though the current was very rapid, and so deep, that they were forced to swim their horses. After following the edge of the stream for about a mile, he reached a small meadow, below which the whole current of the river beat against the shore on which he was, and which was formed of a solid rock, perfectly inaccessible to horses. He therefore resolved to leave the horses and the greater part of the men at this place, and continue his examination of the river on foot, in order to determine if there were any possibility of descending it in canoes.

With his guide and three men he proceeded, clambering over immense rocks, and along the sides of precipices which bordered the stream. The river presented a succession of shoals, neither of which could be passed with loaded canoes; and the baggage must therefore be transported for considerable distances over the steep mountains, where it would be impossible to employ horses. Even the empty boats must be let down the rapids by means of cords, and not even in this way without great risk both to the canoes and the men.

Disappointed in finding a route by way of the river, Capt. Clarke now questioned his guide more particularly respecting an Indian road which came in from the north. The guide, who seemed intelligent, drew a map on the sand, and represented this road as leading to a great river where resided a nation called Tushepaws, who, having no salmon on their river, came by this road to the fish-wears on Lewis's River. After a great deal of conversation, or rather signs, Capt. Clarke felt persuaded that his guide knew of a road from the Shoshonee village they had left, to the great river toward the north, without coming so low down as this, on a road impracticable for horses. He therefore hastened to return thither, sending forward a man on horseback with a note to Capt. Lewis, apprising him of the result of his inquiries.

From the 25th to the 29th of August, Capt. Clarke and his men were occupied in their return to the Shoshonee village, where Capt. Lewis and party were awaiting them. During their march, the want of provisions was such, that if it had not been for the liberality of the Indians, who gave them a share of their own scanty supplies, they must have perished. The main dependence for food was upon salmon and berries. It was seldom they could get enough of these for a full meal; and abstinence and the strange diet caused some sickness. Capt. Lewis, on the contrary, had found the game sufficiently abundant to supply their own party, and to spare some to the Indians; so that, when their friends rejoined them, they had it in their power to immediately relieve their wants.

THE SHOSHONEES.

The Shoshonees are a small tribe of the nation called Snake Indians, — a vague denomination, which embraces at once the inhabitants of the southern parts of the Rocky Mountains, and of the plains on each side. The Shoshonees, with whom we now are, amount to about a hundred warriors, and three times that number of women and children. Within their own recollection, they formerly lived in the plains; but they have been driven into the mountains by the roving Indians of the Saskatchawan country, and are now obliged to visit only occasionally and by stealth the country of their ancestors. From the middle of May to the beginning of September, they reside on the waters of the Columbia. During this time, they subsist chiefly on salmon; and, as that fish disappears on the approach of autumn, they are obliged to seek subsistence elsewhere. They then cross the ridge to the waters of the Missouri, down which they proceed cautiously till they are joined by other bands of their own nation, or of the Flatheads, with whom they associate against the common enemy. Being now strong in numbers, they venture to hunt buffaloes in the plains eastward of the mountains, near which they spend the winter, till the return of the salmon invites them to the Columbia.

In this loose and wandering existence, they suffer the extremes of want: for two-thirds of the year they are forced to live in the mountains, passing whole weeks without meat, and with nothing to eat but a few fish and roots.

Yet the Shoshonees are not only cheerful, but gay; and their character is more interesting than that of any other Indians we have seen. They are frank and communicative; fair in their dealings; and we have had no reason to suspect that the display of our new and valuable wealth has tempted them into a single act of theft. While they have shared with us the little they possess, they have always abstained from begging any thing of us.

Their wealth is in horses. Of these they have at least seven hundred, among which are about forty colts, and half that number of mules. The original stock was procured from the Spaniards; but now they raise their own, which are generally of good size, vigorous, and patient of fatigue as well as of hunger. Every warrior has one or two tied to a stake near his hut day and night, so as to be always prepared for action. The mules are obtained in the course of trade from the Spaniards of California. They are highly valued. The worst are considered as worth the price of two horses.

The Shoshonee warrior always fights on horseback. He possesses a few bad guns, which are reserved for war; but his common arms are the bow and arrow, a shield, a lance, and a weapon called *pogamogon*, which consists of a handle of wood, with a stone weighing about two pounds, and held in a cover of leather, attached to the handle by a leather thong. At the other end is a loop, which is passed round the wrist, so as to secure the hold of the instrument, with which they strike a very severe blow.

The bow is made of cedar or pine, covered on the outer side with sinews and glue. Sometimes it is made of the horn of an elk, covered on the back like those of wood. The arrows are more slender than those of other Indians we have seen. They are kept, with the implements for striking fire, in a narrow quiver formed of different kinds of skin. It is just long enough to protect the arrows from the weather, and is fastened upon the back of the wearer by means of a strap passing over the right shoulder, and under the left arm. The shield is a circular piece of buffalo-skin, about two feet four inches in diameter, ornamented with feathers, with a fringe round it of dressed leather, and adorned with paintings of strange figures.

Besides these, they have a kind of armor, something like a coat of mail, which is formed by a great many folds of antelope-skins, united by a mixture of glue and sand. With this they cover their own bodies and those of their horses, and find it impervious to the arrow.

The caparison of their horses is a halter and saddle. The halter is made of strands of buffalo-hair platted together; or is merely a thong of raw hide, made pliant by pounding and rubbing. The halter is very long, and is never taken from the neck of the horse when in constant use. One end of it is first tied round the neck in a knot, and then brought down to the under-jaw, round which it is formed into a simple noose, passing through the mouth. It is then drawn up on the right side, and held by the rider in his left hand, while the rest trails after him to some distance. With these cords dangling alongside of them, the horse is put to his full speed, without fear of falling; and, when he is turned to graze, the noose is merely taken from his mouth.

The saddle is formed, like the pack-saddles used by

the French and Spaniards, of two flat, thin boards, which fit the sides of the horse, and are kept together by two cross-pieces, one before and the other behind, which rise to a considerable height, making the saddle deep and narrow. Under this, a piece of buffalo-skin, with the hair on, is placed, so as to prevent the rubbing of the board; and, when the rider mounts, he throws a piece of skin or robe over the saddle, which has no permanent cover. When stirrups are used, they consist of wood covered with leather; but stirrups and saddles are conveniences reserved for women and old men. The young warriors rarely use any thing except a small, leather pad stuffed with hair, and secured by a girth made of a leathern thong. In this way, they ride with great expertness; and they have particular dexterity in catching the horse when he is running at large. They make a noose in the rope, and although the horse may be at some distance, or even running, rarely fail to fix it on his neck; and such is the docility of the animal, that, however unruly he may seem, he surrenders as soon as he feels the rope on him.

The horse becomes an object of attachment. A favorite is frequently painted, and his ears cut into various shapes. The mane and tail, which are never drawn nor trimmed, are decorated with feathers of birds; and sometimes a warrior suspends at the breast of his horse the finest ornaments he possesses.

Thus armed and mounted, the Shoshonee is a formidable enemy, even with the feeble weapons which he is still obliged to use. When they attack at full speed, they bend forward, and cover their bodies with the shield, while with the right hand they shoot under the horse's neck.

INDIAN HORSES AND RIDERS.

They are so well supplied with horses, that every man, woman, and child is mounted; and all they have is packed upon horses. Small children, not more than three years old, are mounted alone, and generally upon colts. They are tied upon the saddle to keep them from falling, especially when they go to sleep, which they often do when they become fatigued. Then they lie down upon the horse's shoulders; and, when they awake, they lay hold of their whip, which is fastened to the wrist of their right hand, and apply it smartly to their horses: and it is astonishing to see how these little creatures will guide and run them. Children that are still younger are put into an incasement made with a board at the back, and a wicker-work around the other parts, covered with cloth inside and without, or, more generally, with dressed skins; and they are carried upon the mother's back, or suspended from a high knob upon the fore part of their saddles.

CHAPTER XI.

CLARKE'S RIVER.

AUG. 31.—Capt. Lewis, during the absence of his brother-officer, had succeeded in procuring from the Indians, by barter, twenty-nine horses,—not quite one for each man. Capt. Clarke having now rejoined us, and the weather being fine, we loaded our horses, and prepared to start. We took our leave of the Shoshonees, and accompanied by the old guide, his four sons, and another Indian, began the descent of the river, which Capt. Clarke had named Lewis's River. After riding twelve miles, we encamped on the bank; and, as the hunters had brought in three deer early in the morning, we did not feel in want of provisions.

On the 31st of August, we made eighteen miles. Here we left the track of Capt. Clarke, and began to explore the new route recommended by the Indian guide, and which was our last hope of getting out of the mountains.

. During all day, we rode over hills, from which are many drains and small streams, and, at the distance of eighteen miles, came to a large creek, called Fish Creek, emptying into the main river, which is about six miles from us.

Sept. 2. — This morning, all the Indians left us, except the old guide, who now conducted us up Fish Creek. We arrived shortly after at the forks of the creek. The road we were following now turned in a contrary direction to our course, and we were left without any track; but, as no time was to be lost, we began to cut our road up the west branch of the creek. This we effected with much difficulty. The thickets of trees and brush through which we were obliged to cut our way required great labor. Our course was over the steep and rocky sides of the hills, where the horses could not move without danger of slipping down, while their feet were bruised by the rocks, and stumps of trees. Accustomed as these animals were to this kind of life, they suffered severely. Several of them fell to some distance down the sides of the hills, some turned over with the baggage, one was crippled, and two gave out exhausted with fatigue. After crossing the creek several times, we had made five miles with great labor, and encamped in a small, stony, low ground. It was not, however, till after dark that the whole party was collected; and then, as it rained, and we killed nothing, we passed an uncomfortable night. We had been too busily occupied with the horses to make any hunting excursion; and, though we saw many beaver-dams in the creek, we saw none of the animals.

Next day, our experiences were much the same, with the addition of a fall of snow at evening. The day following, we reached the head of a stream which directed its course more to the westward, and followed it till we discovered a large encampment of Indians. When we reached them, and alighted from our horses, we were received with great cordiality. A council was immediately assembled, white robes were thrown over our shoulders, and the pipe of peace introduced. After this ceremony, as it was too late to go any farther, we encamped, and continued smoking and conversing with the chiefs till a late hour.

Next morning, we assembled the chiefs and warriors, and informed them who we were, and the purpose for which we visited their country. All this was, however, conveyed to them in so many different languages, that it was not comprehended without difficulty. We therefore proceeded to the more intelligible language of presents, and made four chiefs by giving a medal and a small quantity of tobacco to each. We received in turn, from the principal chiefs, a present, consisting of the skins of an otter and two antelopes; and were treated by the women to some dried roots and berries. We then began to traffic for horses, and succeeded in exchanging seven, and purchasing eleven.

These Indians are a band of the Tushepaws, a numerous people of four hundred and fifty tents, residing on the head waters of the Missouri and Columbia Rivers, and some of them lower down the latter river. They seemed kind and friendly, and willingly shared with us berries and roots, which formed their only stock of provisions. Their only wealth is their horses, which are very fine, and so numerous that this band had with them at least five hundred.

We proceeded next day, and, taking a north-west direction, crossed, within a distance of a mile and a half, a small river from the right. This river is the main stream; and, when it reaches the end of the valley, it is joined by two other streams. To the river thus formed we gave the name of Clarke's River, he being the first white man who ever visited its waters.

We followed the course of the river, which is from twenty-five to thirty yards wide, shallow, and stony, with the low grounds on its borders narrow; and encamped on its right bank, after making ten miles. Our stock of flour was now exhausted, and we had but little corn; and, as our hunters had killed nothing except two pheasants, our supper consisted chiefly of berries.

The next day, and the next, we followed the river, which widened to fifty yards, with a valley four or five miles broad. At ten miles from our camp was a creek, which emptied itself on the west side of the river. It was a fine bold creek of clear water, about twenty yards wide; and we called it Traveller's Rest: for, as our guide told us we should here leave the river, we determined to make some stay for the purpose of collecting food, as the country through which we were to pass has no game for a great distance.

Toward evening, one of the hunters returned with three Indians whom he had met. We found that they were Tushepaw Flatheads in pursuit of strayed horses. We gave them some boiled venison and a few presents, such as a fish hook, a steel to strike fire, and a little powder; but they seemed better pleased with a piece of ribbon which we tied in the hair of each of them. Their people, they said, were numerous, and resided on the great river in the plain below the mountains. From that place, they added, the river was navigable to the ocean. The distance from this place is five "sleeps," or days' journeys.

On resuming our route, we proceeded up the right side of the creek (thus leaving Clarke's River), over a country, which, at first plain and good, became afterwards as difficult as any we had yet traversed.

We had now reached the sources of Traveller's-rest Creek, and followed the road, which became less rugged. At our encampment this night, the game having entirely failed us, we killed a colt, on which we made a hearty supper. We reached the river, which is here eighty yards wide, with a swift current and a rocky channel. Its Indian name is Kooskooskee.

KOOSKOOSKEE RIVER.

Sept. 16. — This morning, snow fell, and continued all day; so that by evening it was six or eight inches deep. It covered the track so completely, that we were obliged constantly to halt and examine, lest we should lose the route. The road is, like that of yesterday, along steep hillsides, obstructed with fallen timber, and a growth of eight different species of pine, so thickly strewed, that the snow falls from them upon us as we pass, keeping us continually wet to the skin. We encamped in a piece of low ground, thickly timbered, but scarcely large enough to permit us to lie level. We had made thirteen miles. We were wet, cold, and hungry; yet we could not procure any game, and were obliged to kill another horse for our supper. This want of provisions, the extreme fatigue to which we were subjected, and the dreary prospect before us, began to dispirit the men. They are growing weak, and losing their flesh very fast.

After three days more of the same kind of experience, on Friday, 20th September, an agreeable change occurred. Capt. Clarke, who had gone forward in hopes of finding game, came suddenly upon a beautiful open plain partially stocked with pine. Shortly after, he discovered three Indian boys, who, observing the party, ran off, and hid themselves in the grass. Capt. Clarke immediately alighted, and, giving his horse and gun to one of the men, went after the boys. He soon relieved their apprehensions, and sent them forward to the village, about a mile off, with presents of small pieces of ribbon. Soon after the boys had reached home, a man came out to meet the party, with great caution; but he conducted them to a large tent in the village, and all the inhabitants gathered round to view with a mixture of fear and pleasure the wonderful strangers. The conductor now informed Capt. Clarke, by signs, that the spacious tent was the residence of the great chief, who had set out three days ago, with all the warriors, to attack some of their enemies towards the south-west; that, in the mean time, there were only a few men left to guard the women and children. They now set before them a small piece of buffalo-meat, some dried salmon, berries, and several kinds of roots. Among these last was one which is round, much like an onion in appearance, and sweet to the taste. It is called *quamash,* and is eaten either in its natural state, or boiled into a kind of soup, or made into a cake, which is called *pasheco.* After our long abstinence, this was a sumptuous repast. We returned the kindness of the people with a few small presents, and then went on, in company with one of the chiefs, to a second village in the same plain, at a distance of two miles. Here the party was treated with great kindness, and passed the night.

The two villages consist of about thirty double tents; and the people call themselves Chopunnish, or Pierced-nose. The chief drew a chart of the river on the sand, and explained that a greater chief than himself, who governed this village, and was called the Twisted-hair, was now fishing at the distance of half a day's ride down the river. His chart made the Kooskooskee to fork a little below his camp, below which the river passed the mountains. Here was a great fall of water, near which lived white people, from whom they procured the white beads and brass ornaments worn by the women.

Capt. Clarke engaged an Indian to guide him to the Twisted-hair's camp. For twelve miles, they proceeded through the plain before they reached the river-hills, which are very high and steep. The whole valley from these hills to the Rocky Mountains is a beautiful level country, with a rich soil covered with grass. There is, however, but little timber, and the ground is badly watered. The plain is so much sheltered by the surrounding hills, that the weather is quite warm (Sept. 21), while the cold of the mountains was extreme.

From the top of the river-hills we descended for three miles till we reached the water-side, between eleven and twelve o'clock at night. Here we found a small camp of five women and three children; the chief himself being encamped, with two others, on a small island in the river. The guide called to him, and he came over. Capt. Clarke gave him a medal, and they smoked together till one o'clock.

Next day, Capt. Clarke passed over to the island with the Twisted-hair, who seemed to be cheerful and sincere. The hunters brought in three deer; after which Capt. Clarke left his party, and, accompanied by the Twisted-hair and his son, rode back to the village, where he found Capt. Lewis and his party just arrived.

The plains were now crowded with Indians, who came to see the white men and the strange things they brought with them; but, as our guide was a perfect stranger to their language, we could converse by signs only. Our inquiries were chiefly directed to the situation of the country. The Twisted-hair drew a chart of the river on a white elk-skin. According to this, the Kooskooskee forks a few miles from this place: two days' journey towards the south is another and larger fork, on which the Shoshonee Indians fish; five days' journey farther is a large river from the north-west, into which Clarke's River empties itself. From the junction with that river to the falls is five days' journey farther. On all the forks, as well as on the main river, great numbers of Indians reside; and at the falls are establishments of whites. This was the story of the Twisted-hair.

Provision here was abundant. We purchased a quantity of fish, berries, and roots; and in the afternoon went on to the second village. We continued our purchases, and obtained as much provision as our horses could carry in their present weak condition. Great crowds of the natives are round us all night; but we have not yet missed any thing, except a knife and a few other small articles.

Sept. 24. — The weather is fair. All round the village the women are busily employed in gathering and dressing the pasheco-root, large quantities of which are heaped up in piles all over the plain.

We feel severely the consequence of eating heartily after our late privations. Capt. Lewis and two of his men were taken very ill last evening, and to-day he can hardly sit on his horse. Others could not mount without help; and some were forced to lie down by the side of the road for some time.

Our situation rendered it necessary to husband our remaining strength; and it was determined to proceed down the river in canoes. Capt. Clarke therefore set out with Twisted-hair and two young men in quest of timber for canoes.

Sept. 27, 28, and 29. — Sickness continued. Few of the men were able to work; yet preparations were made for making five canoes. A number of Indians collect about us in the course of the day to gaze at the strange appearance of every thing belonging to us.

Oct. 4. — The men were now much better, and Capt. Lewis so far recovered as to walk about a little. The canoes being nearly finished, it became necessary to dispose of the horses. They were therefore collected to the number of thirty-eight, and, being branded and marked, were delivered to three Indians, — the two brothers and the son of a chief; the chief having promised to accompany us down the river. To each of these men we gave a knife and some small articles; and they agreed to take good care of the horses till our return.

We had all our saddles buried in a *cache* near the river, about half a mile below, and deposited at the same time a canister of powder and a bag of balls.

THE VOYAGE DOWN THE KOOSKOOSKEE RIVER.

Oct. 7.—This morning, all the canoes were put in the water, and loaded, the oars fitted, and every preparation made for setting out. When we were all ready, the chief who had promised to accompany us was not to be found: we therefore proceeded without him. The Kooskooskee is a clear, rapid stream, with a number of shoals and difficult places. This day and the next, we made a distance of fifty miles. We passed several encampments of Indians on the islands and near the rapids, which situations are chosen as the most convenient for taking salmon. At one of these camps we found the chief, who, after promising to descend the river with us, had left us. He, however, willingly came on board, after we had gone through the ceremony of smoking.

Oct. 10.—A fine morning. We loaded the canoes, and set off at seven o'clock. After passing twenty miles, we landed below the junction of a large fork of the river, from the south. Our arrival soon attracted the attention of the Indians, who flocked from all directions to see us. Being again reduced to fish and roots, we made an experiment to vary our food by purchasing a few dogs; and, after having been accustomed to horse-flesh, felt no disrelish to this new dish. The Chopunnish have great numbers of dogs, but never use them for food; and our feeding on the flesh of that animal brought us into ridicule as dog-eaters.

This southern branch is, in fact, the main stream of Lewis's River, on whose upper waters we encamped when among the Shoshonees. At its mouth, Lewis's River is about two hundred and fifty yards wide, and its water is of a greenish-blue color. The Kooskooskee, whose waters are clear as crystal, is one hundred and fifty yards in width; and, after the union, the joint-stream extends to the width of three hundred yards.

The Chopunnish, or Pierced-nose Indians, who reside on the Kooskooskee and Lewis's Rivers, are in person stout, portly, well-looking men. The women are small, with good features, and generally handsome, though the complexion of both sexes is darker than that of the Tushepaws. In dress, they resemble that nation, being fond of displaying their ornaments. The buffalo or elk-skin robe, decorated with beads, sea-shells (chiefly mother-of-pearl), attached to an otter-skin collar, is the dress of the men. The same ornaments are hung in the hair, which falls in front in two cues: they add feathers, paints of different colors (principally white, green, and blue), which they find in their own country. In winter, they wear a shirt of dressed skins; long, painted leggings, and moccasons; and a plait of twisted grass round the neck.

The dress of the women is more simple, consisting of a long shirt of the mountain-sheep skin, reaching down to the ankles, without a girdle. To this are tied little pieces of brass and shells, and other small articles; but the head is not at all ornamented.

The Chopunnish have few amusements; for their life is painful and laborious, and all their exertions are necessary to earn a precarious subsistence. During the summer and autumn, they are busily occupied in fishing for salmon, and collecting their winter store of roots. In winter, they hunt the deer on snowshoes over the plains; and, towards spring, cross the mountains to the Missouri in pursuit of the buffalo.

The soil of these prairies is a light-yellow clay. It is barren, and produces little more than a bearded grass about three inches high, and the prickly-pear, of which we found three species. The first is the broad-leaved kind, common to this river with the Missouri; the second has a leaf of a globular form, and is also frequent on the upper part of the Missouri; the third is peculiar to this country. It consists of small, thick leaves of a circular form, which grow from the margin of each other. These leaves are armed with a great number of thorns, which are strong, and appear to be barbed. As the leaf itself is very slightly attached to the stem, as soon as one thorn touches the moccason, it adheres, and brings with it the leaf, which is accompanied with a re-enforcement of thorns. This species was a greater annoyance on our march than either of the others.

CHAPTER XII.

FROM THE JUNCTION OF THE KOOSKOOSKEE WITH LEWIS'S RIVER TO THE COLUMBIA.

FROM the mouth of the Kooskooskee to that of the Lewis is about a hundred miles; which distance they descended in seven days. The navigation was greatly impeded by rapids, which they passed with more or less danger and difficulty; being greatly indebted to the assistance of the Indians, as they thankfully acknowledge. Sometimes they were obliged to unload their boats, and to carry them round by land. All these rapids are fishing-places, greatly resorted to in the season.

On the 17th of October (1805), having reached the junction of Lewis's River with the Columbia, they found by observation that they were in latitude 46° 15′, and longitude 119°. They measured the two rivers by angles, and found, that, at the junction, the Columbia is 960 yards wide; and Lewis's River,

575: but, below their junction, the joint river is from one to three miles in width, including the islands. From the point of junction, the country is a continued plain, rising gradually from the water. There is through this plain no tree, and scarcely any shrub, except a few willow-bushes; and, even of smaller plants, there is not much besides the prickly-pear, which is abundant.

In the course of the day, Capt. Clarke, in a small canoe, with two men, ascended the Columbia. At the distance of five miles, he came to a small but not dangerous rapid. On the bank of the river opposite to this is a fishing-place, consisting of three neat houses. Here were great quantities of salmon drying on scaffolds; and, from the mouth of the river upwards, he saw immense numbers of dead salmon strewed along the shore, or floating on the water.

The Indians, who had collected on the banks to view him, now joined him in eighteen canoes, and accompanied him up the river. A mile above the rapids, he observed three houses of mats, and landed to visit them. On entering one of the houses, he found it crowded with men, women, and children, who immediately provided a mat for him to sit on; and one of the party undertook to prepare something to eat. He began by bringing in a piece of pine-wood that had drifted down the river, which he split into small pieces with a wedge made of the elk's horn, by means of a mallet of stone curiously carved. The pieces were then laid on the fire, and several round stones placed upon them. One of the squaws now brought a bucket of water, in which was a large salmon about half dried; and, as the stones became heated, they were put into the bucket till the salmon was sufficiently boiled. It was then taken out, put on a platter of rushes neatly made, and laid before Capt. Clarke. Another was boiled for each of his men. Capt. Clarke found the fish excellent.

At another island, four miles distant, the inhabitants were occupied in splitting and drying salmon. The multitudes of this fish are almost inconceivable. The water is so clear, that they can readily be seen at the depth of fifteen or twenty feet; but at this season they float in such quantities down the stream, and are drifted ashore, that the Indians have nothing to do but collect, split, and dry them. The Indians assured him by signs that they often used dry fish as fuel for the common occasions of cooking. The evening coming on, he returned to camp.

Capt. Clarke, in the course of his excursion, shot

several grouse and ducks; also a prairie-cock, — a bird of the pheasant kind, about the size of a small turkey. It measured, from the beak to the end of the toe, two feet six inches; from the extremity of the wings, three feet six inches; and the feathers of the tail were thirteen inches long. This bird we have seen nowhere except upon this river. Its chief food is the grasshopper, and the seeds of wild plants peculiar to this river and the Upper Missouri.

ADVENTURE OF CAPT. CLARKE.

Oct. 19. — Having resumed their descent of the Columbia, they came to a very dangerous rapid. In order to lighten the boats, Capt. Clarke landed, and walked to the foot of the rapid. Arriving there before either of the boats, except a canoe, he sat down on a rock to wait for them; and, seeing a crane fly across the river, shot it, and it fell near him. Several Indians had been, before this, passing on the opposite side; and some of them, alarmed at his appearance or the report of the gun, fled to their houses. Capt. Clarke was afraid that these people might not have heard that white men were coming: therefore, in order to allay their uneasiness before the whole party should arrive, he got into the canoe with three men, and rowed over towards the houses, and, while crossing, shot a duck, which fell into the water. As he approached, no person was to be seen, except three men; and they also fled as he came near the shore. He landed before five houses close to each other; but no person appeared: and the doors, which were of mat, were closed. He went towards one of them with a pipe in his hand, and, pushing aside the mat, entered the lodge, where he found thirty-two persons, men and women, with a few children, all in the greatest consternation; some hanging down their heads; others crying, and wringing their hands. He went up to them all, and shook hands with them in the most friendly manner. Their apprehensions gradually subsided, but revived on his taking out a burning-glass (there being no roof to the lodge), and lighting his pipe. Having at length restored some confidence by the gift of some small presents, he visited some other houses, where he found the inhabitants similarly affected. Confidence was not completely attained until the boats arrived, and then the two chiefs who accompanied the party explained the friendly intentions of the expedition. The sight of Chaboneau's wife also dissipated any remaining doubts, as it is not the practice among the Indians to allow women to accompany a war-party.

To account for their fears, they told the two chiefs that they had seen the white men fall from the sky. Having heard the report of Capt. Clarke's rifle, and seen the birds fall, and not having seen him till after the shot, they fancied that he had himself dropped from the clouds.

This belief was strengthened, when, on entering the lodge, he brought down fire from heaven by means of his burning-glass. We soon convinced them that we were only mortals; and, after one of our chiefs had explained our history and objects, we all smoked together in great harmony.

Our encampment that night was on the river-bank opposite an island, on which were twenty-four houses of Indians, all of whom were engaged in drying fish. We had scarcely landed when about a hundred of them came over to visit us, bringing with them a present of some wood, which was very acceptable. We received them in as kind a manner as we could, smoked with them, and gave the principal chief a string of wampum; but the highest satisfaction they enjoyed was in the music of our two violins, with which they seemed much delighted. They remained all night at our fires.

AN INDIAN BURYING-PLACE.

We walked to the head of the island for the purpose of examining a vault, or burying-place, which we had remarked in coming along. The place in which the dead are deposited is a building about sixty feet long and twelve feet wide, formed by placing in the ground poles, or forks, six feet high, across which a long pole is extended the whole length of the structure. Against this ridge-pole are placed broad boards, and pieces of wood, in a slanting direction, so as to form a shed. The structure stands east and west, open at both ends. On entering the western end, we observed a number of bodies wrapped carefully in leather robes, and arranged in rows on boards, which were then covered with a mat. This part of the building was destined for those who had recently died. A little farther on, limbs, half decayed, were scattered about; and in the centre of the building was a large pile of them heaped promiscuously. At the eastern extremity was a mat, on which twenty-one skulls were arranged in a circular form: the mode of interment being first to wrap the body in robes; and, as it decays, the bones are thrown into the heap, and the skulls placed together in order.

From the different boards and pieces of wood which form the vault were suspended on the inside fishing-nets, baskets, wooden bowls, robes, skins, trenchers, and trinkets of various kinds, intended as offerings of affection to deceased relatives. On the outside of the vault were the skeletons of several horses, and great quantities of bones in the neighborhood, which induced us to believe that these animals were sacrificed at the funeral-rites of their masters.

In other parts of the route, the travellers found a different species of cemetery. The dead were placed in canoes, and these canoes were raised above the ground by a scaffolding of poles. The motive was supposed to be to protect them from wild beasts.

FALLS OF THE COLUMBIA.

About a hundred and fifty miles below the junction of Lewis's River, we reached the Great Falls. At the commencement of the pitch, which includes the falls, we landed, and walked down to examine them, and ascertain on which side we could make a portage most easily. From the lower end of the island, where the rapids begin, to the perpendicular fall, is about two miles. Here the river contracts, when the water is low, to a very narrow space; and, with only a short distance of swift water, it makes its plunge twenty feet perpendicularly; after which it rushes on, among volcanic rocks, through a channel four miles in length, and then spreads out into a gentle, broad current.

We will interrupt the narrative here to introduce from later travellers some pictures of the remarkable region to which our explorers had now arrived. It was not to be expected that Capts. Lewis and Clarke should have taxed themselves, in their anxious and troubled march, to describe natural wonders, however striking.

Lieut. Frémont thus describes this remarkable spot : —

THE DALLES. — "In a few miles we descended to the river, which we reached at one of its highly interesting features, known as the Dalles of the Columbia. The whole volume of the river at this place passes between the walls of a chasm, which has the appearance of having been rent through the basaltic strata which form the valley-rock of the region. At the narrowest place, we found the breadth, by measurement, fifty-eight yards, and the average height of the walls above the water twenty-five feet, forming a trough between the rocks; whence the name, probably applied by a Canadian voyageur."

The same scene is described by Theodore Winthrop in his " Canoe and Saddle : " —

" The Dalles of the Columbia, upon which I was now looking,

must be studied by the American Dante, whenever he comes, for imagery to construct his Purgatory, if not his Inferno. At Walla-walla, two great rivers, Clarke's and Lewis's, drainers of the continent north and south, unite to form the Columbia. It flows furiously for a hundred and twenty miles westward. When it reaches the dreary region where the outlying ridges of the Cascade chain commence, it finds a great, low surface, paved with enormous polished sheets of basaltic rock. These plates, in French, *dalles*, give the spot its name. The great river, a mile wide not far above, finds but a narrow rift in this pavement for its passage. The rift gradually draws its sides closer, and, at the spot now called the Dalles, subdivides into three mere slits in the sharp-edged rock. At the highest water, there are other minor channels; but generally this continental flood is cribbed and compressed within its three chasms suddenly opening in the level floor, each chasm hardly wider than a leap a hunted fiend might take."

It is not easy to picture to one's self, from these descriptions, the peculiar scenery of the Dalles. Frémont understands the name as signifying a *trough;* while Winthrop interprets it as *plates*, or *slabs*, of rock. The following description by Lieut. (now Gen.) Henry L. Abbot, in his " Report of Explorations for a Railroad Route," &c., will show that the term, in each of its meanings, is applicable to different parts of the channel: —

" At the Dalles of the Columbia, the river rushes through a

chasm only about two hundred feet wide, with vertical, basaltic sides, rising from twenty to thirty feet above the water. Steep hills closely border the chasm, leaving in some places scarcely room on the terrace to pass on horseback. The water rushes through this basaltic trough with such violence, that it is always dangerous, and in some stages of the water impossible, for a boat to pass down. The contraction of the river-bed extends for about three miles. Near the lower end of it, the channel divides into several sluices, and then gradually becomes broader, until, where it makes a great bend to the south, it is over a quarter of a mile in width."

After this interruption, the journal is resumed:—

"We soon discovered that the nearest route was on the right side, and therefore dropped down to the head of the rapid, unloaded the canoes, and took all the baggage over by land to the foot of the rapid. The distance is twelve hundred yards, part of it over loose sands, disagreeable to pass. The labor of crossing was lightened by the Indians, who carried some of the heavy articles for us on their horses. Having ascertained the best mode of bringing down the canoes, the operation was conducted by Capt. Clarke, by hauling the canoes over a point of land four hundred and fifty-seven yards to the water. One mile farther down, we reached a pitch of the river, which, being divided by two large rocks, descends with great rapidity over a fall eight feet in height. As the boats could not be navigated down this steep descent, we were obliged to land, and let them down as gently as possible by strong ropes of elk-skin, which we had prepared for the purpose. They all passed in safety, except one, which, being loosed by the breaking of the ropes, was driven down, but was recovered by the Indians below."

Our travellers had now reached what have since been called the Cascade Mountains; and we must interrupt their narrative to give some notices of this remarkable scenery from later explorers. We quote from Abbot's Report: —

"There is great similarity in the general topographical features of the whole Pacific slope. The Sierra Nevada in California, and the Cascade range in Oregon, form a continuous wall of mountains nearly parallel to the coast, and from one hundred to two hundred miles distant from it. The main crest of this range is rarely elevated less than six thousand feet above the level of the sea, and many of its peaks tower into the region of eternal snow."

Lieut. Abbot thus describes a view of these peaks and of the Columbia River: —

"At an elevation of five thousand feet above the sea, we stood upon the summit of the pass. For days we had been struggling blindly through dense forests ; but now the surrounding country lay spread out before us for more than a hundred miles. The five grand snow-peaks, Mount St. Helens, Mount Ranier, Mount Adams, Mount Hood, and Mount Jefferson, rose majestically above a rolling sea of dark fir-covered ridges, some of which the approaching winter had already begun to mark with white. On every side, as far as the eye could reach, terrific convulsions of Nature had recorded their fury; and not even a thread of blue smoke from the camp-fire of a wandering savage disturbed the solitude of the scene."

THE COLUMBIA RIVER. — "The Columbia River forces its way through the Cascade range by a pass, which, for wild and sublime natural scenery, equals the celebrated passage of the Hudson through the Highlands. For a distance of about fifty miles, mountains covered with clinging spruces, firs, and pines, where not too precipitous to afford even these a foothold, rise abruptly from the water's edge to heights varying from one thousand to three thousand feet. Vertical precipices of columnar basalt are occasionally seen, rising from fifty to a hundred feet above the river level. In other places, the long mountain-walls of the river are divided by lateral cañons (pronounced *canyons*), containing small tributaries, and occasionally little open spots of good land, liable to be overflowed at high water."

CAÑONS. — The plains east of the Cascade Mountains, through the whole extent of Oregon and California, are covered with a volcanic deposit composed of trap, basalt, and other rocks of the same class. This deposit is cleft by chasms often more than a thousand feet deep, at the bottom of which there usually flows a stream of clear, cold water. This is sometimes the only water to be procured for the distance of many miles; and the traveller may be perishing with thirst while he sees far below him a sparkling stream, from which he is separated by precipices of enormous height and perpendicular descent. To chasms of this nature the name of *cañons* has been applied, borrowed from the Spaniards of Mexico. We quote Lieut. Abbot's description of the cañon of Des Chutes River, a tributary of the Columbia : —

"Sept. 30. — As it was highly desirable to determine accurately the position and character of the cañon of Des Chutes River, I started this morning with one man to follow down the creek to its mouth, leaving the rest of the party in camp. Having yesterday experienced the inconveniences of travelling in the bottom of a cañon, I concluded to try to-day the northern bluff. It was a dry, barren plain, gravelly, and sometimes sandy, with a few bunches of grass scattered here and there. Tracks of antelopes or deer were numerous. After crossing one small ravine, and riding about five miles from camp, we found ourselves on the edge of the vast cañon of the river, which, far below us, was rushing through a narrow trough of basalt, resembling the Dalles of the Columbia. We estimated the depth of the cañon at a thousand feet. On each side, the precipices were very steep, and marked in many places by horizontal lines of vertical, basaltic columns, fifty or sixty feet in height. The man who was with me rolled a large rock, shaped like a grindstone, and weighing about two hundred pounds, from the summit. It thundered down for at least a quarter of a mile, — now over a vertical precipice, now over a steep mass of detritus, until at length it plunged into the river with a hollow roar, which echoed and re-echoed through the gorge for miles. By ascending a slight hill, I obtained a fine view of the surrounding country. The generally level character of the great basaltic table-land around us was very manifest from this point. Bounded on the west by the Cascade Mountains, the plain extends far towards the south, — a sterile, treeless waste."

THE CASCADES. — "About forty miles below the Dalles, all navigation is suspended by a series of rapids called the Cascades. The wild grandeur of this place surpasses description. The river rushes furiously over a narrow bed filled with bowlders, and bordered by mountains which echo back the roar of the waters. The descent at the principal rapids is thirty-four feet; and the total fall at the Cascades, sixty-one feet. Salmon pass up the river in great numbers; and the Cascades, at certain seasons of the year, are a favorite fishing resort with the Indians, who build slight stagings over the water's edge, and spear the fish, or catch them in rude dip-nets, as they slowly force their way up against the current."

We now return to our travellers.

INDIAN MODE OF PACKING SALMON.

Near our camp are five large huts of Indians engaged in drying fish, and preparing it for market.

The manner of doing this is by first opening the fish, and exposing it to the sun on scaffolds. When it is sufficiently dried, it is pounded between two stones till it is pulverized, and is then placed in a basket, about two feet long and one in diameter, neatly made of grass and rushes, and lined with the skin of the salmon, stretched and dried for the purpose. Here they are pressed down as hard as possible, and the top covered with skins of fish, which are secured by cords through the holes of the basket. These baskets are then placed in some dry situation, the corded part upwards; seven being usually placed as close as they can be together, and five on the top of them. The whole is then wrapped up in mats, and made fast by cords. Twelve of these baskets, each of which contains from ninety to a hundred pounds, form a stack, which is now left exposed till it is sent to market. The fish thus preserved are kept sound and sweet for several years; and great quantities of it, they inform us, are sent to the Indians who live lower down the river, whence it finds its way to the whites who visit the mouth of the Columbia. We observe, both near the lodges and on the rocks in the river, great numbers of stacks of these pounded fish.

Beside the salmon, there are great quantities of

salmon-trout, and another smaller species of trout, which they save in another way. A hole of any size being dug, the sides and bottom are lined with straw, over which skins are laid. On these the fish, after being well dried, is laid, covered with other skins, and the hole closed with a layer of earth, twelve or fifteen inches deep. These supplies are for their winter food.

The stock of fish, dried and pounded, was so abundant, that Capt. Clarke counted one hundred and seven stacks of them, making more than ten thousand pounds.

THE INDIAN BOATMEN.

The canoes used by these people are built of white cedar or pine, very light, wide in the middle, and tapering towards the ends; the bow being raised, and ornamented with carvings of the heads of animals. As the canoe is the vehicle of transportation, the Indians have acquired great dexterity in the management of it, and guide it safely over the roughest waves.

We had an opportunity to-day of seeing the boldness of the Indians. One of our men shot a goose, which fell into the river, and was floating rapidly towards the great shoot, when an Indian, observing it, plunged in after it. The whole mass of the waters of the Columbia, just preparing to descend its narrow channel, carried the bird down with great rapidity. The Indian followed it fearlessly to within a hundred and fifty feet of the rocks, where, had he arrived, he would inevitably have been dashed to pieces; but, seizing his prey, he turned round, and swam ashore with great composure. We very willingly relinquished our right to the bird in favor of the Indian, who had thus secured it at the hazard of his life. He immediately set to work, and picked off about half the feathers, and then, without opening it, ran a stick through it, and carried it off to roast.

INDIAN HOUSES.

While the canoes were coming on, impeded by the difficulties of the navigation, Capt. Clarke, with two men, walked down the river-shore, and came to a village belonging to a tribe called Echeloots. The village consisted of twenty-one houses, scattered promiscuously over an elevated position. The houses were nearly equal in size, and of similar construction. A large hole, twenty feet wide and thirty in length, is dug to the depth of six feet. The sides are lined with split pieces of timber in an erect position, rising a short distance above the surface of the ground. These timbers are secured in their position by a pole, stretched along the side of the building, near the eaves, supported by a post at each corner. The timbers at the gable-ends rise higher, the middle pieces being the tallest. Supported by these, there is a ridge-pole running the whole length of the house, forming the top of the roof. From this ridge-pole to the eaves of the house are placed a number of small poles, or rafters, secured at each end by fibres of the cedar. On these poles is laid a covering of white cedar or arbor-vitæ, kept on by strands of cedar-fibres. A small distance along the whole length of the ridge-pole is left uncovered for the admission of light, and to permit the smoke to escape. The entrance is by a small door at the gable-end, thirty inches high, and fourteen broad. Before this hole is hung a mat; and on pushing it aside, and crawling through, the descent is by a wooden ladder, made in the form of those used among us.

One-half of the inside is used as a place of deposit for their dried fish, and baskets of berries: the other half, nearest the door, remains for the accommodation of the family. On each side are arranged, near the walls, beds of mats, placed on platforms or bedsteads, raised about two feet from the ground. In the middle of the vacant space is the fire, or sometimes two or three fires, when, as is usually the case, the house contains several families.

The inhabitants received us with great kindness, and invited us to their houses. On entering one of them, we saw figures of men, birds, and different animals, cut and painted on the boards which form the sides of the room, the figures uncouth, and the workmanship rough; but doubtless they were as much esteemed by the Indians as our finest domestic adornments are by us. The chief had several articles, such as scarlet and blue cloth, a sword, a jacket, and hat, which must have been procured from the whites. On one side of the room were two wide split boards, placed together so as to make space for a rude figure of a man, cut and painted on them. On pointing to this, and asking what it meant, he said something, of which all we understood was " good," and then stepped to the image, and brought out his bow and quiver, which, with some other warlike implements, were kept behind it. The chief then directed his wife to hand him his *Medicine-bag*, from which he brought out fourteen fore-fingers, which he told us had once belonged to the same number of his enemies. They were shown with great exultation; and after an harangue, which we were left to presume was in praise of his exploits, the fingers were carefully replaced among the valuable contents of the red Medicine-bag. This bag is an object of religious regard, and it is a species of sacrilege for any one but its owner to touch it.

In all the houses are images of men, of different shapes, and placed as ornaments in the parts of the house where they are most likely to be seen.

A SUBMERGED FOREST.

Oct. 30. — The river is now about three-quarters of a mile wide, with a current so gentle, that it does not exceed a mile and a half an hour; but its course is obstructed by large rocks, which seem to have fallen from the mountains. What is, however, most singular, is, that there are stumps of pine-trees scattered to some distance in the river, which has the appearance of having been dammed below, and forced to encroach on the shore.

NOTE.

Rev. S. Parker says, "We noticed a remarkable phenomenon, — trees standing in their natural position in the river, where the water is twenty feet deep. In many places, they

THE RIVER WIDENS. — THEY MEET THE TIDE.

Nov. 2, 1805. — Longitude about 122°. At this point the first tide-water commences, and the river widens to nearly a mile in extent. The low grounds, too, become wider; and they, as well as the mountains on each side, are covered with pine, spruce, cotton-wood, a species of ash, and some alder. After being so long accustomed to the dreary nakedness of the country above, the change is as grateful to the eye as it is useful in supplying us with fuel.

The ponds in the low grounds on each side of the river are resorted to by vast quantities of fowls, such as swans, geese, brants, cranes, storks, white gulls, cormorants, and plover. The river is wide, and con-

---

were so numerous, that we had to pick our way with our canoe as through a forest. The water is so clear, that I had an opportunity of examining their position down to their spreading roots, and found them in the same condition as when standing in their native forest. It is evident that there has been an uncommon subsidence of a tract of land, more than twenty miles in length, and more than a mile in width. That the trees are not wholly decayed down to low-water mark, proves that the subsidence is comparatively of recent date; and their undisturbed natural position proves that it took place in a tranquil manner, not by any tremendous convulsion of Nature."

tains a great number of sea-otters. In the evening, the hunters brought in game for a sumptuous supper, which we shared with the Indians, great numbers of whom spent the night with us. During the night, the tide rose eighteen inches near our camp.

A LARGE VILLAGE. — COLUMBIA VALLEY.

Nov. 4. — Next day, we landed on the left bank of the river, at a village of twenty-five houses. All of these were thatched with straw, and built of bark, except one, which was about fifty feet long, built of boards, in the form of those higher up the river; from which it differed, however, in being completely above ground, and covered with broad split boards. This village contains about two hundred men of the Skilloot nation, who seem well provided with canoes, of which there were fifty-two (some of them very large) drawn up in front of the village.

On landing, we found an Indian from up the river, who had been with us some days ago, and now invited us into a house, of which he appeared to own a part. Here he treated us with a root, round in shape, about the size of a small Irish potato, which they call *wappatoo*. It is the common arrowhead, or sagittifolia, so much esteemed by the Chinese, and, when roasted in the embers till it becomes soft, has an agreeable taste, and is a very good substitute for bread.

Here the ridge of low mountains running north-west and south-east crosses the river, and forms the western boundary of the plain through which we have just passed.* This great plain, or valley, is about sixty miles wide in a straight line; while on the right and left it extends to a great distance. It is a fertile and delightful country, shaded by thick groves of tall timber, watered by small ponds, and lying on both sides of the river. The soil is rich, and capable of any species of culture; but, in the present condition of the Indians, its chief production is the wappatoo-root, which grows spontaneously and exclusively in this region. Sheltered as it is on both sides, the temperature is much milder than that of the surrounding country. Through its whole extent, it is inhabited by numerous tribes of Indians, who either reside in it permanently, or visit its waters in quest of fish and wappatoo-roots. We gave it the name of the Columbia Valley.

---

* Since called the Coast range.

COFFIN ROCK.

Among some interesting islands of basalt, there is one called Coffin Rock, situated in the middle of the river, rising ten or fifteen feet above high-freshet water. It is almost entirely covered with canoes, in which the dead are deposited, which gives it its name. In the section of country from Wappatoo Island to the Pacific Ocean, the Indians, instead of committing their dead to the earth, deposit them in canoes; and these are placed in such situations as are most secure from beasts of prey, upon such precipices as this island, upon branches of trees, or upon scaffolds made for the purpose. The bodies of the dead are covered with mats, and split planks are placed over them. The head of the canoe is a little raised, and at the foot there is a hole made for water to escape.

THEY REACH THE OCEAN.

Next day we passed the mouth of a large river, a hundred and fifty yards wide, called by the Indians Cowalitz. A beautiful, extensive plain now presented itself; but, at the distance of a few miles, the hills again closed in upon the river, so that we could not for several miles find a place sufficiently level to fix our camp upon for the night.

Thursday, Nov. 7.—The morning was rainy, and the fog so thick, that we could not see across the river. We proceeded down the river, with an Indian for our pilot, till, after making about twenty miles, the fog cleared off, and we enjoyed the delightful prospect of the OCEAN, the object of all our labors, the reward of all our endurance. This cheering view exhilarated the spirits of all the party, who listened with delight to the distant roar of the breakers.

For ten days after our arrival at the coast, we were harassed by almost incessant rain. On the 12th, a violent gale of wind arose, accompanied with thunder, lightning, and hail. The waves were driven with fury against the rocks and trees, which had till then afforded us a partial defence. Cold and wet; our clothes and bedding rotten as well as wet; the canoes, our only means of escape from the place, at the mercy of the waves,—we were, however, fortunate enough to enjoy good health.

Saturday, Nov. 16.—The morning was clear and beautiful. We put out our baggage to dry, and sent several of the party to hunt. The camp was in full view of the ocean. The wind was strong from the south-west, and the waves very high; yet the Indians were passing up and down the bay in canoes, and several of them encamped near us. The hunters brought in two deer, a crane, some geese and ducks, and several brant. The tide rises at this place eight feet six inches, and rolls over the beach in great waves.

AN EXCURSION DOWN THE BAY.

Capt. Clarke started on Monday, 18th November, on an excursion by land down the bay, accompanied by eleven men. The country is low, open, and marshy, partially covered with high pine and a thick undergrowth. At the distance of about fifteen miles they reached the cape, which forms the northern boundary of the river's mouth, called Cape Disappointment, so named by Capt. Meares, after a fruitless search for the river. It is an elevated circular knob, rising with a steep ascent a hundred and fifty feet or more above the water, covered with thick timber on the inner side, but open and grassy in the exposure next the sea. The opposite point of the bay is a very low ground, about ten miles distant, called, by Capt. Gray, Point Adams.

The water for a great distance off the mouth of the

river appears very shallow; and within the mouth, nearest to Point Adams, there is a large sand-bar, almost covered at high tide. We could not ascertain the direction of the deepest channel; for the waves break with tremendous force across the bay.

Mr. Parker speaks more fully of this peculiarity of the river: —

"A difficulty of such a nature as is not easily overcome exists in regard to the navigation of this river; which is, the sand-bar at its entrance. It is about five miles, across the bar, from Cape Disappointment out to sea. In no part of that distance is the water upon the bar over eight fathoms deep, and in one place only five, and the channel only about half a mile in width. So wide and open is the ocean, that there is always a heavy swell: and, when the wind is above a gentle breeze, there are breakers quite across the bar; so that there is no passing it, except when the wind and tide are both favorable. Outside the bar, there is no anchorage; and there have been instances, in the winter season, of ships lying off and on thirty days, waiting for an opportunity to pass: and a good pilot is always needed. High, and in most parts perpendicular, basaltic rocks line the shores."

The following is Theodore Winthrop's description of the Columbia, taken from his "Canoe and Saddle:" —

"A wall of terrible breakers marks the mouth of the Columbia, — Achilles of rivers.

"Other mighty streams may swim feebly away seaward, may

sink into foul marshes, may trickle through the ditches of an oozy delta, may scatter among sand-bars the currents that once moved majestic and united; but to this heroic flood was destined a short life and a glorious one, — a life all one strong, victorious struggle, from the mountains to the sea. It has no infancy: two great branches collect its waters up and down the continent. They join, and the Columbia is born — to full manhood. It rushes forward jubilant through its magnificent chasm, and leaps to its death in the Pacific."

CHAPTER XIII.

WINTER-QUARTERS.

NOVEMBER, 1805.—Having now examined the coast, it becomes necessary to decide on the spot for our winter-quarters. We must rely chiefly for subsistence upon our arms, and be guided in the choice of our residence by the supply of game which any particular spot may offer. The Indians say that the country on the opposite side of the river is better supplied with elk,—an animal much larger, and more easily killed, than the deer, with flesh more nutritive, and a skin better fitted for clothing. The neighborhood of the sea is, moreover, recommended by the facility of supplying ourselves with salt, and the hope of meeting some of the trading-vessels, which are expected about three months hence, from which we may procure a fresh supply of trinkets for our journey homewards. These considerations induced us to determine on visiting the opposite side of the bay;

and, if there was an appearance of plenty of game, to establish ourselves there for the winter.

Monday, 25th November, we set out; but, as the wind was too high to suffer us to cross the river, we kept near the shore, watching for a favorable change. On leaving our camp, seven Clatsops in a canoe accompanied us, but, after going a few miles, left us, and steered straight across through immense, high waves, leaving us in admiration at the dexterity with which they threw aside each wave as it threatened to come over their canoe.

Next day, with a more favorable wind, we began to cross the river. We passed between some low, marshy islands, and reached the south side of the Columbia, and landed at a village of nine large houses. Soon after we landed, three Indians came down from the village with wappatoo-roots, which we purchased with fish-hooks.

We proceeded along the shore till we came to a remarkable knob of land projecting about a mile and a half into the bay, about four miles round, while the neck of land which unites it to the main is not more than fifty yards across. We went round this projection, which we named Point William; but the waves then became so high, that we could not venture any farther, and therefore landed on a beautiful shore of pebbles of various colors, and encamped near an old Indian hut on the isthmus.

DISCOMFORTS.

Nov. 27. — It rained hard all next day, and the next, attended with a high wind from the south-west. It was impossible to proceed on so rough a sea. We therefore sent several men to hunt, and the rest of us remained during the day in a situation the most cheerless and uncomfortable. On this little neck of land, we are exposed, with a miserable covering which does not deserve the name of a shelter, to the violence of the winds. All our bedding and stores are completely wet, our clothes rotting with constant exposure, and no food except the dried fish brought from the falls, to which we are again reduced. The hunters all returned hungry, and drenched with rain; having seen neither deer nor elk, and the swans and brants too shy to be approached. At noon, the wind shifted to the north-west, and blew with such fury, that many trees were blown down near us. The gale lasted with short intervals during the whole night; but towards morning the wind lulled, though the rain continued, and the waves were still high.

30th. — The hunters met with no better success this day and the next, and the weather continued rainy. But on Monday, 2d December, one of the hunters killed an elk at the distance of six miles from the camp, and a canoe was sent to bring it. This was the first elk we had killed on the west side of the Rocky Mountains; and, condemned as we have been to the dried fish, it forms a most acceptable food.

The rain continued, with brief interruptions, during the whole month of December. There were occasional falls of snow, but no frost or ice.

WINTER-QUARTERS.

Capt. Lewis returned from an excursion down the bay, having left two of his men to guard six elks and five deer which the party had shot. He had examined the coast, and found a river a short distance below, on which we might encamp for the winter, with a sufficiency of elk for our subsistence within reach. This information was very satisfactory, and we decided on going thither as soon as we could move from the point; but it rained all night and the following day.

Saturday, 7th December, 1805, was fair. We therefore loaded our canoes, and proceeded: but the tide was against us, and the waves very high; so that we were obliged to proceed slowly and cautiously. We at length turned a point, and found ourselves in a deep bay. Here we landed for breakfast, and were joined by a party sent out three days ago to look for the six elk. After breakfast, we coasted round the bay, which is about four miles across, and receives two rivers. We called it Meriwether's Bay, from the Christian name of Capt. Lewis, who was, no doubt, the first white man who surveyed it. On reaching the south side of the bay, we ascended one of the rivers for three miles to the first point of highland, on its western bank, and formed our camp in a thick grove of lofty pines about two hundred yards from the water, and thirty feet above the level of the high tides.

THE CLATSOPS AT HOME.

Capt. Clarke started on an expedition to the seashore, to fix upon a place for the salt-works. He took six men with him; but three of them left in pursuit of a herd of elk. He met three Indians loaded with fresh salmon, which they had taken, and were returning to their village, whither they invited him to accompany them. He agreed; and they brought out a canoe hid along the bank of a creek. Capt. Clarke and his party got on board, and in a short time were landed at the village, consisting of twelve houses, inhabited by twelve families of Clatsops. These houses were on the south exposure of a hill, and sunk about four feet deep into the ground; the walls, roof, and gable-ends being formed of split-pine boards; the descent through a small door down a ladder. There were two fires in the middle of the room, and the beds disposed round the walls, two or three feet from the floor, so as to leave room under them for their bags, baskets, and household articles. The floor was covered with mats.

Capt. Clarke was received with much attention. As soon as he entered, clean mats were spread, and fish, berries, and roots set before him on small, neat platters of rushes. After he had eaten, the men of the other houses came and smoked with him. They appeared much neater in their persons than Indians generally are.

Towards evening, it began to rain and blow violently; and Capt. Clarke therefore determined to remain during the night. When they thought his appetite had returned, an old woman presented him, in a bowl made of light-colored horn, a kind of sirup, pleasant to the taste, made from a species of berry common in this country, about the size of a cherry, called by the Indians *shelwel*. Of these berries a bread is also prepared, which, being boiled with roots, forms a soup, which was served in neat wooden trenchers. This, with some cockles, was his repast.

The men of the village now collected, and began to gamble. The most common game was one in which one of the company was banker, and played against all the rest. He had a piece of bone about the size of a large bean; and, having agreed with any one as to the value of the stake, he would pass the bone with great dexterity from one hand to the other, singing at the same time to divert the attention of his adversary. Then, holding up his closed hands, his antagonist was challenged to say in which of them the bone was, and lost or won as he pointed to the right or wrong hand.

To this game of hazard they abandon themselves with great ardor. Sometimes every thing they possess is sacrificed to it; and this evening several of the Indians lost all the beads which they had with them.

This lasted for three hours; when, Capt. Clarke appearing disposed to sleep, the man who had been most attentive, and whose name was Cuskalah, spread two new mats by the fire; and, ordering his wife to retire to her own bed, the rest of the company dispersed at the same time. Capt. Clarke then lay down, and slept as well as the fleas would permit him.

Next morning was cloudy, with some rain. He walked on the sea-shore, and observed the Indians walking up and down, and examining the shore. He was at a loss to understand their object till one of them explained that they were in search of fish, which are thrown on shore by the tide; adding, in English, "Sturgeon is good." There is every reason to suppose that these Clatsops depend for their subsistence during the winter chiefly on the fish thus casually thrown on the coast.

After amusing himself for some time on the beach, Capt. Clarke returned toward the village. One of the Indians asked him to shoot a duck which he pointed out. He did so; and, having accidentally shot off its head, the bird was brought to the village, and all the Indians came round in astonishment. They examined the duck, the musket, and the very small bullet (a hundred to the pound); and then exclaimed in their language, "Good musket: don't understand this kind of musket."

They now placed before him their best roots, fish, and sirup; after which he bought some berry-bread and a few roots in exchange for fish-hooks, and then set out to return by the same route by which he came. He was accompanied by Cuskalah and his brother part of the way, and proceeded to the camp through a heavy rain. The party had been occupied during his absence in cutting down trees and in hunting.

Next day, two of our hunters returned with the pleasing intelligence of their having killed eighteen elk about six miles off. Our huts begin to rise; for, though it rains all day, we continue our labors, and are glad to find that the beautiful balsam-pine splits into excellent boards more than two feet in width.

Dec. 15. — Capt. Clarke, with sixteen men, set out in three canoes to get the elk which were killed. After landing as near the spot as possible, the men were despatched in small parties to bring in the game; each man returning with a quarter of an animal. It was accomplished with much labor and suffering; for the rain fell incessantly.

THE FORT COMPLETED.

We now had the meat-house covered, and all our game carefully hung up in small pieces. Two days after, we covered in four huts. Five men were sent out to hunt, and five others despatched to the seaside, each with a large kettle, in order to begin the manufacture of salt. The rest of the men were employed in making pickets and gates for our fort.

Dec. 31. — As if it were impossible to have twenty-four hours of pleasant weather, the sky last evening clouded up, and the rain began, and continued through the day. In the morning, there came down two canoes, — one from the Wahkiacum village; the other contained three men and a squaw of the Skilloot nation. They brought wappatoo and shanatac roots, dried fish, mats made of flags and rushes, dressed elk-skins, and tobacco, for which, particularly the skins, they asked an extravagant price. We purchased some wappatoo and a little tobacco, very much like that we had seen among the Shoshonees, put up in small, neat bags made of rushes. These we obtained in exchange for a few articles, among which fish-hooks are the most esteemed. One of the Skilloots brought a gun which wanted some repair;

and, when we had put it in order, we received from him a present of about a peck of wappatoo. We then gave him a piece of sheep-skin and blue cloth to cover the lock, and he very thankfully offered a further present of roots. There is an obvious superiority of these Skilloots over the Wahkiacums, who are intrusive, thievish, and impertinent. Our new regulations, however, and the appearance of the sentinel, have improved the behavior of all our Indian visitors. They left the fort before sunset, even without being ordered.

CHAPTER XIV.

A NEW YEAR.

WE were awaked at an early hour by the discharge of a volley of small-arms to salute the new year. This is the only way of doing honor to the day which our situation admits; for our only dainties are boiled elk and wappatoo, enlivened by draughts of water.

Next day, we were visited by the chief, Comowool, and six Clatsops. Besides roots and berries, they brought for sale three dogs. Having been so long accustomed to live on the flesh of dogs, the most of us have acquired a fondness for it; and any objection to it is overcome by reflecting, that, while we subsisted on that food, we were fatter, stronger, and in better health, than at any period since leaving the buffalo country, east of the mountains.

The Indians also brought with them some whale's blubber, which they obtained, they told us, from their neighbors who live on the sea-coast, near one of whose villages a whale has recently been thrown and stranded. It was white, and not unlike the fat of pork, though of a more porous and spongy texture; and, on being cooked, was found to be tender and palatable, in flavor resembling the flesh of the beaver.

Two of the five men who were despatched to make salt returned. They had formed an establishment about fifteen miles south-west of our fort, near some scattered houses of the Clatsops, where they erected a comfortable camp, and had killed a stock of provisions. They brought with them a gallon of the salt of their manufacture, which was white, fine, and very good. It proves to be a most agreeable addition to our food; and, as they can make three or four quarts a day, we have a prospect of a plentiful supply.

THE WHALE.

The appearance of the whale seemed to be a matter of importance to all the neighboring Indians; and in hopes that we might be able to procure some of it for ourselves, or at least purchase some from the Indians, a small parcel of merchandise was prepared, and a party of men got in readiness to set out in the morning. As soon as this resolution was known, Chaboneau and his wife requested that they might be permitted to accompany us. The poor woman urged very earnestly that she had travelled a great way with us to see the great water, yet she had never been down to the coast; and, now that this monstrous fish also was to be seen, it seemed hard that she should not be permitted to see either the ocean or the whale. So reasonable a request could not be denied: they were therefore suffered to accompany Capt. Clarke, who next day, after an early breakfast, set out with twelve men in two canoes.

He proceeded down the river on which we are encamped into Meriwether Bay; from whence he passed up a creek three miles to some high, open land, where he found a road. He there left the canoes, and followed the path over deep marshes to a pond about a mile long. Here they saw a herd of elk; and the men were divided into small parties, and hunted them till after dark. Three of the elk were wounded; but night prevented our taking more than one, which was brought to the camp, and cooked with some sticks of pine which had drifted down the creeks. The weather was beautiful, the sky clear, and the moon shone brightly, — a circumstance the more agreeable, as this is the first fair evening we have enjoyed for two months.

Thursday, Jan. 2. — There was a frost this morning. We rose early, and taking eight pounds of flesh, which was all that remained of the elk, proceeded up the south fork of the creek. At the distance of two miles we found a pine-tree, which had been felled by one of our salt-makers, on which we crossed the deepest part of the creek, and waded through the rest. We then went over an open, ridgy prairie, three-quarters of a mile to the sea-beach; after following which for three miles, we came to the mouth of a beautiful river, with a bold, rapid current, eighty-five yards wide, and three feet deep in its shallowest crossings. On its north-east side are the remains of an old village of Clatsops, inhabited by only a single family, who appeared miserably poor and dirty. We gave the man two fish-hooks to ferry the party over the river, which, from the tribe on its banks, we called Clatsop River. The creek which we had passed on a tree approaches this river within about a hundred yards, and, by means of a portage, supplies a communication with the villages near Point Adams.

After going on for two miles, we found the salt-makers encamped near four houses of Clatsops and Killimucks, who, though poor and dirty, seemed kind and well-disposed. We persuaded a young Indian, by the present of a file and a promise of some other articles, to guide us to the spot where the whale lay. He led us for two and a half miles over the round, slippery stones at the foot of a high hill projecting into the sea, and then, suddenly stopping, and uttering the word "peshack," or bad, explained by signs that we could no longer follow the coast, but must cross the mountain. This threatened to be a most laborious undertaking; for the side was nearly perpendicular, and the top lost in clouds. He, however, followed an Indian path, which wound along, and favored the ascent as much as possible; but it was so steep, that, at one place, we were forced to draw ourselves up for about a hundred feet by means of bushes and roots.

CLARKE'S POINT OF VIEW.

At length, after two hours' labor, we reached the top of the mountain, where we looked down with astonishment on the height of ten or twelve hundred feet which we had ascended. We were here met by fourteen Indians loaded with oil and blubber, the spoils of the whale, which they were carrying in very heavy burdens over this rough mountain. On leaving them, we proceeded over a bad road till night, when we encamped on a small run. We were all much fatigued: but the weather was pleasant; and, for the first time since our arrival here, an entire day has passed without rain.

In the morning we set out early, and proceeded to the top of the mountain, the highest point of which is an open spot facing the ocean. It is situated about thirty miles south-east of Cape Disappointment, and projects nearly two and a half miles into the sea. Here one of the most delightful views imaginable presents itself. Immediately in front is the ocean, which breaks with fury on the coast, from the rocks of Cape Disappointment as far as the eye can discern to the north-west, and against the highlands and irregular piles of rock which diversify the shore to the south-east. To this boisterous scene, the Columbia, with its tributary waters, widening into bays as it approaches the ocean, and studded on both sides with the Chinnook and Clatsop villages, forms a charming contrast; while immediately beneath our feet are stretched rich prairies, enlivened by three beautiful streams, which conduct the eye to small lakes at the foot of the hills. We stopped to enjoy the romantic view from this place, which we distinguished by the name of Clarke's Point of View, and then followed our guide down the mountain.

THE WHALE.

The descent was steep and dangerous. In many places, the hillsides, which are formed principally of yellow clay, have been loosened by the late rains, and are slipping into the sea in large masses of fifty and a hundred acres. In other parts, the path crosses the rugged, perpendicular, basaltic rocks which overhang the sea, into which a false step would have precipitated us.

The mountains are covered with a very thick growth of timber, chiefly pine and fir; some trees of which, perfectly sound and solid, rise to the height of two hundred and ten feet, and are from eight to twelve in diameter. Intermixed is the white cedar, or arbor-vitæ, and some trees of black alder, two or three feet thick, and sixty or seventy in height. At length we reached the sea-level, and continued for two miles along the sand-beach, and soon after reached the place where the waves had thrown the whale on shore. The animal had been placed between two villages of Killimucks; and such had been their industry, that there now remained nothing but the skeleton, which we found to be a hundred and five feet in length. Capt. Clarke named the place Ecola, or Whale Creek.

The natives were busied in boiling the blubber in a large square trough of wood by means of heated stones, preserving the oil thus extracted in bladders and the entrails of the whale. The refuse pieces of the blubber, which still contained a portion of oil, were hung up in large flitches, and, when wanted for use, were warmed on a wooden spit before the fire, and eaten, either alone, or with roots of the rush and shanatac. The Indians, though they had great quantities, parted with it very reluctantly, at such high prices, that our whole stock of merchandise was exhausted in the purchase of about three hundred pounds of blubber and a few gallons of oil.

Next morning was fine, the wind from the northeast; and, having divided our stock of the blubber, we began at sunrise to retrace our steps in order to reach our encampment, which we called Fort Clatsop, thirty-five miles distant, with as little delay as possible. We met several parties of Indians on their way to trade for blubber and oil with the Killimucks: we also overtook a party returning from the village, and could not but regard with astonishment the heavy loads which the women carry over these fatiguing and dangerous paths. As one of the women was descending a steep part of the mountain, her load slipped from her back; and she stood holding it by a strap with one hand, and with the other supporting herself by a bush. Capt. Clarke, being near her, undertook to replace the load, and found it almost as much as he could lift, and above one hundred pounds in weight. Loaded as they were, they kept pace with us till we reached the salt-makers' camp, where we passed the night, while they continued their route.

Next day, we proceeded across Clatsop River to the place where we had left our canoes, and, as the tide was coming in, immediately embarked for the fort, at which place we arrived about ten o'clock at night.

DREWYER, THE HUNTER.

Jan. 12, 1806. — Two hunters had been despatched in the morning; and one of them, Drewyer, had, before evening, killed seven elks. We should scarcely be able to subsist, were it not for the exertions of this excellent hunter. The game is scarce; and none is now to be seen except elk, which, to almost all the men, are very difficult to be procured. But Drewyer, who is the offspring of a Canadian Frenchman and an

Indian woman, has passed his life in the woods, and unites in a wonderful degree the dexterous aim of the frontier huntsman with the sagacity of the Indian in pursuing the faintest tracks through the forest. All our men have indeed become so expert with the rifle, that, when there is game of any kind, we are almost certain of procuring it.

Monday, Jan. 13. — Capt. Lewis took all the men who could be spared, and brought in the seven elk, which they found untouched by the wolves. The last of the candles which we brought with us being exhausted, we now began to make others of elk-tallow. We also employed ourselves in jerking the meat of the elk. We have three of the canoes drawn up out of the reach of the water, and the other secured by a strong cord, so as to be ready for use if wanted.

Jan. 16. — To-day we finished curing our meat; and having now a plentiful supply of elk and salt, and our houses dry and comfortable, we wait patiently for the moment of resuming our journey.

CHAPTER XV.

WINTER LIFE.

JAN. 18, 1806. — We are all occupied in dressing skins, and preparing clothes for our journey homewards. This morning, we sent out two parties of hunters in different directions. We were visited by three Clatsops, who came merely for the purpose of smoking and conversing with us.

Jan. 21. — Two of the hunters came back with three elks, which form a timely addition to our stock of provision. The Indian visitors left us at twelve o'clock.

The Clatsops and other nations have visited us with great freedom. Having acquired much of their language, we are enabled, with the assistance of gestures, to hold conversations with great ease. We find them inquisitive and loquacious; by no means deficient in acuteness. They are generally cheerful, but seldom gay. Every thing they see excites their attention and inquiries.

Their treatment of women and old men depends very much on the usefulness of these classes. Thus, among the Clatsops and Chinnooks, who live upon fish and roots, which the women are equally expert with the men in procuring, the women have a rank and influence far greater than they have among the hunting tribes. On many subjects their judgments and opinions are respected; and, in matters of trade, their advice is generally asked and followed. So with the old men: when one is unable to pursue the chase, his counsels may compensate for his want of activity; but in the next state of infirmity, when he can no longer travel from camp to camp as the tribe roams about for subsistence, he is found to be a burden. In this condition they are abandoned among the Sioux and other hunting-tribes of the Missouri. As the tribe are setting out for some new excursion where the old man is unable to follow, his children or nearest relations place before him a piece of meat and some water; and telling him that he has lived long enough, that it is now time for him to go home to his relations, who can take better care of him than his friends on earth, they leave him without remorse to perish, when his little supply is exhausted.

Though this is doubtless true as a general rule, yet, in the villages of the Minnetarees and Ricaras, we saw no want of kindness to old men: on the contrary, probably because in villages the more abundant means of subsistence renders such cruelty unnecessary, the old people appeared to be treated with attention; and some of their feasts, particularly the buffalo-dances, were intended chiefly as an occasion of contribution for the old and infirm.

FLATHEAD INDIANS.

The custom of flattening the head by artificial pressure during infancy prevails among all the nations we have seen west of the Rocky Mountains. To the east of that barrier the fashion is so perfectly unused, that they designate the western Indians, of whatever tribe, by the common name of Flatheads. The practice is universal among the Killamucks, Clatsops, Chinnooks, and Cathlamahs, — the four nations with whom we have had most intercourse. Soon after the birth of her child, the mother places it in the compressing-frame, where it is kept for ten or twelve months. The operation is so gradual, that it is not attended with pain. The heads of the children, when they are released from the bandage, are not more than two inches thick about the upper edge of the forehead: nor, with all its efforts, can nature ever restore their shape; the heads of grown persons being often in a straight line from the tip of the nose to the top of the forehead.

TEMPERANCE. — GAMBLING.

Their houses usually contain several families, consisting of parents, sons and daughters, daughters-in-law and grand-children, among whom the provisions are in common, and harmony seldom interrupted. As these families gradually expand into tribes, or nations, the paternal authority is represented by the chief of each association. The chieftainship is not hereditary: the chief's ability to render service to his neighbors, and the popularity which follows it, is the foundation of his authority, which does not extend beyond the measure of his personal influence.

The harmony of their private life is protected by their ignorance of spirituous liquors. Although the tribes near the coast have had so much intercourse with the whites, they do not appear to possess any knowledge of those dangerous luxuries; at least, they have never inquired of us for them. Indeed, we have not observed any liquor of an intoxicating quality used among any Indians west of the Rocky Mountains; the universal beverage being pure water. They, however, almost intoxicate themselves by smoking tobacco, of which they are excessively fond. But the common vice of all these people is an attachment to games of chance, which they pursue with a ruinous avidity. The game of the pebble has already been described. Another game is something like the play of ninepins. Two pins are placed on the floor, about the distance of a foot from each other, and a small hole made in the earth behind them. The players then go about ten feet from the hole, into which they try to roll a small piece resembling the men used at checkers. If they succeed in putting it into the hole, they win the stake. If the piece rolls between the pins, but does not go into the hole, nothing is won or lost; but the wager is lost if the checker rolls outside the pins. Entire days are wasted at these games, which are often continued through the night round the blaze of their fires, till the last article of clothing or the last blue bead is lost and won.

TREES.

The whole neighborhood of the coast is supplied with great quantities of excellent timber. The predominant growth is the fir, of which we have seen several species. The first species grows to an immense size, and is very commonly twenty-seven feet in circumference, six feet above the earth's surface. They rise to the height of two hundred and thirty feet, and one hundred and twenty of that height without a limb. We have often found them thirty-six feet in circumference. One of our party measured one, and found it to be forty-two feet in circumference at a point beyond the reach of an ordinary man. This tree was perfectly sound; and, at a moderate calculation, its height may be estimated at three hundred feet.

The second is a much more common species, and constitutes at least one-half of the timber in this neighborhood. It resembles the spruce, rising from one hundred and sixty to one hundred and eighty feet; and is from four to six feet in diameter, straight, round, and regularly tapering.

The stem of the black alder arrives at a great size. It is sometimes found growing to the height of sixty or seventy feet, and is from two to four in diameter.

There is a tree, common on the Columbia River, much resembling the ash, and another resembling the white maple, though much smaller.

The undergrowth consists of honeysuckle, alder, whortleberry, a plant like the mountain-holly, green brier, and fern.

ANIMALS.

The beaver of this country is large and fat: the flesh is very palatable, and, at our table, was a real luxury. On the 7th of January, our hunter found a beaver in his trap, of which he made a bait for taking others. This bait will entice the beaver to the trap as far as he can smell it; and this may be fairly stated. to be at the distance of a mile, as their sense of smelling is very acute.

The sea-otter resides only on the sea-coast or in the neighborhood of the salt water. When fully grown, he attains to the size of a large mastiff dog. The ears, which are not an inch in length, are thick, pointed, fleshy, and covered with short hair; the tail is ten inches long, thick at the point of insertion, and partially covered with a deep fur on the upper side; the legs are very short, covered with fur, and the feet with short hair. The body of this animal is long, and of the same thickness throughout. From the extremity of the tail to the nose, they measure five feet. The color is a uniform dark brown, and when in good condition, and in season, perfectly black. This animal is unrivalled for the beauty, richness, and softness of his fur. The inner part of the fur, when opened, is lighter than the surface in its natural position. There are some black and shining hairs intermixed with the fur, which are rather longer, and add much to its beauty.

HORSES AND DOGS.

The horse is confined chiefly to the nations inhabiting the great plains of the Columbia, extending from latitude forty to fifty north, and occupying the tract of country lying between the Rocky Mountains and a range of mountains which crosses the Columbia River about the great falls. In this region they are very numerous.

They appear to be of an excellent race, lofty, well formed, active, and enduring. Many of them appear like fine English coursers. Some of them are pied, with large spots of white irregularly scattered, and intermixed with a dark-brown bay. The greater part, however, are of a uniform color, marked with stars, and white feet. The natives suffer them to run at large in the plains, the grass of which affords them their only winter subsistence; their masters taking no trouble to lay in a winter's store for them. They will, nevertheless, unless much exercised, fatten on the dry grass afforded by the plains during the winter. The plains are rarely moistened by rain, and the grass is consequently short and thin.

Whether the horse was originally a native of this country or not, the soil and climate appear to be perfectly well adapted to his nature. Horses are said to be found wild in many parts of this country.

The dog is small, about the size of an ordinary cur. He is usually party-colored; black, white, brown, and brindle being the colors most predominant. The head is long, the nose pointed the eyes small, the ears erect and pointed like those of the wolf. The hair is short and smooth, excepting on the tail, where it is long and straight, like that of the ordinary curdog. The natives never eat the flesh of this animal, and he appears to be in no other way serviceable to them but in hunting the elk. To us, on the contrary, it has now become a favorite food; for it is found to be a strong, healthy diet, preferable to lean deer or elk, and much superior to horse-flesh in any state.

BURROWING SQUIRREL.

There are several species of squirrels not different from those found in the Atlantic States. There is also a species of squirrel, evidently distinct, which we denominate the burrowing squirrel. He measures one foot five inches in length, of which the tail comprises two and a half inches only. The neck and legs are short; the ears are likewise short, obtusely pointed, and lie close to the head. The eyes are of a moderate size, the pupil black, and the iris of a dark, sooty brown. The teeth, and indeed the whole contour, resemble those of the squirrel.

These animals associate in large companies, occupying with their burrows sometimes two hundred acres of land. The burrows are separate, and each contains ten or twelve of these inhabitants. There is a little mound in front of the hole, formed of the earth thrown out of the burrow; and frequently there are three or four distinct holes, forming one burrow, with their entrances around the base of a mound. These mounds, about two feet in height and four in diameter, are occupied as watch-towers by the inhabitants of these little communities. The squirrels are irregularly distributed about the tract they thus occupy, — ten, twenty, or thirty yards apart. When any person approaches, they make a shrill whistling sound, somewhat resembling "tweet, tweet, tweet;" the signal for their party to take the alarm, and to retire into their intrenchments. They feed on the grass of their village, the limits of which they never venture to exceed. As soon as the frost commences, they shut themselves up in their caverns, and continue until the spring opens.

BIRDS.

THE GROUSE, OR PRAIRIE-HEN. — This is peculiarly the inhabitant of the great plains of the Columbia, but does not differ from those of the upper portion of the Missouri. In the winter season, this bird is booted to the first joint of the toes. The toes are curiously bordered on their lower edges with narrow, hard scales, which are placed very close to each other, and extend horizontally about one-eighth of an inch on each side of the toes, adding much to the broadness of the feet, — a security which Nature has furnished them for passing over the snow with more ease, — and, what is very remarkable, in the summer season these scales drop from the feet. The color of this bird is a mixture of dark brown, reddish, and yellowish brown, with white confusedly mixed. The reddish-brown prevails most on the upper parts of the body, wings, and tail; and the white, under the belly and the lower parts of the breast and tail. They associate in large flocks in autumn and winter; and, even in summer, are seen in companies of five or six. They feed on grass, insects, leaves of various shrubs in the plains, and the seeds of several species of plants which grow in richer soils. In winter, their food consists of the buds of the willow and cottonwood, and native berries.

The cock of the plains is found on the plains of the Columbia in great abundance. The beak is large, short, covered, and convex; the upper exceeding the lower chap. The nostrils are large, and the back black. The color is a uniform mixture of a dark-brown, resembling the dove, and a reddish or yellowish brown, with some small black specks. The habits of this bird resemble those of the grouse, excepting that his food is the leaf and buds of the pulpy-leaved thorn. The flesh is dark, and only tolerable in point of flavor.

HORNED FROG.

The horned lizard, or horned frog, called, for what reason we never could learn, the prairie buffalo, is a native of these plains as well as of those of the Missouri. The color is generally brown, intermixed with yellowish spots. The animal is covered with minute scales, interspersed with small horny points, or prickles, on the upper surface of the body. The belly and throat resemble those of the frog, and are of a light yellowish-brown. The edge of the belly is likewise beset with small horny projections. The eye is small and dark. Above and behind the eyes there are several bony projections, which resemble horns sprouting from the head.

These animals are found in greatest numbers in the sandy, open plains, and appear most abundant after a shower of rain. They are sometimes found basking in the sunshine, but generally conceal themselves in little holes of the earth. This may account for their appearance in such numbers after rain, as their holes may thus be rendered untenantable.

CHAPTER XVI.

THE RETURN.

MARCH, 1806. — Many reasons had inclined us to remain at Fort Clatsop till the 1st of April. Besides the want of fuel in the Columbian plains, and the impracticability of crossing the mountains before the beginning of June, we were anxious to see some of the foreign traders, from whom, by our ample letters of credit, we might recruit our exhausted stores of merchandise. About the middle of March, however, we became seriously alarmed for the want of food. The elk, our chief dependence, had at length deserted its usual haunts in our neighborhood, and retreated to the mountains. We were too poor to purchase food from the Indians; so that we were sometimes reduced, notwithstanding all the exertions of our hunters, to a single day's provision in advance. The men too, whom the constant rains and confinement had rendered unhealthy, might, we hoped, be benefited by leaving the coast, and resuming the exercise of travelling. We therefore determined to leave Fort Clatsop, ascend the river slowly, consume the month of March in the woody country, where we hoped to find subsistence, and in this way reach the plains about the 1st of April, before which time it will be impossible to cross them.

During the winter, we have been very industrious in dressing skins; so that we now have a sufficient quantity of clothing, besides between three and four hundred pairs of moccasons. But the whole stock of goods on which we are to depend for the purchase of horses or of food, during the long journey of four thousand miles, is so much diminished, that it might all be tied in two handkerchiefs. We therefore feel that our chief dependence must be on our guns, which, fortunately, are all in good order, as we took the precaution of bringing a number of extra locks, and one of our men proved to be an excellent gunsmith. The powder had been secured in leaden canisters; and, though on many occasions they had been under water, it remained perfectly dry: and we now found ourselves in possession of one hundred and forty pounds of powder, and twice that weight of lead, — a stock quite sufficient for the route homewards.

We were now ready to leave Fort Clatsop; but the rain prevented us for several days from calking the canoes, and we were forced to wait for calm weather before we could attempt to pass Point William, which projects about a mile and a half into the sea, forming, as it were, the dividing-line between the river and the ocean; for the water below is salt, while that above is fresh.

On March 23, at one o'clock in the afternoon, we took a final leave of Fort Clatsop. We doubled Point William without any injury, and at six o'clock reached the mouth of a small creek, where we found our hunters. They had been fortunate enough to kill two elks, which were brought in, and served for breakfast next morning.

Next day, we were overtaken by two Wakiacums, who brought two dogs, for which they wanted us to give them some tobacco; but, as we had very little of that article left, they were obliged to go away disappointed. We received at the same time an agreeable supply of three eagles and a large goose, brought in by the hunters.

We passed the entrance of Cowalitz River, seventy miles from our winter camp. This stream enters the Columbia from the north; is one hundred and fifty yards wide; deep and navigable, as the Indians assert, for a considerable distance; and probably waters the country west and north of the Cascade Mountains, which cross the Columbia between the great falls and rapids. During the day, we passed a number of fishing-camps on both sides of the river, and were constantly attended by small parties of Skilloots, who behaved in the most orderly manner, and from whom we purchased as much fish and roots as we wanted, on moderate terms. The night continued as the day had been,— cold, wet, and disagreeable; which is the general character of the weather in this region at this season.

March 29.— At an early hour, we resumed our route, and halted for breakfast at the upper end of an island where is properly the commencement of the great Columbian Valley. We landed at a village of fourteen large wooden houses. The people received us kindly, and spread before us wappatoo and anchovies; but, as soon as we had finished enjoying this hospitality (if it deserves that name), they began to ask us for presents. They were, however, perfectly satisfied with the small articles which we distributed according to custom, and equally pleased with our purchasing some wappatoo, twelve dogs, and two sea-otter skins. We also gave the chief a small medal, which he soon transferred to his wife.

April 1. — We met a number of canoes filled with families descending the river. These people told us that they lived at the Great Rapids, but that a scarcity of provisions there had induced them to come down in hopes of finding subsistence in this fertile valley. All those who lived at the rapids, as well as the nations above them, they said, were in much distress for want of food, having consumed their winter store of dried fish, and not expecting the return of the salmon before the next full moon, which will be on the 2d of May.

This intelligence was disagreeable and embarrassing. From the falls to the Chopunnish nation, the plains afford no deer, elk, or antelope, on which we can rely for subsistence. The horses are very poor at this season; and the dogs must be in the same condition, if their food, the fish, have failed. On the other hand, it is obviously inexpedient to wait for the return of the salmon, since, in that case, we may not reach the Missouri before the ice will prevent our navigating it. We therefore decided to remain here only till we collect meat enough to last us till we reach the Chopunnish nation, with whom we left our horses on our downward journey, trusting that we shall find the animals safe, and have them faithfully returned to us; for, without them, the passage of the mountains will be almost impracticable.

April 2, 1806. — Several canoes arrived to visit us; and among the party were two young men who belonged to a nation, which, they said, resides at the falls of a large river which empties itself into the south side of the Columbia, a few miles below us; and they drew a map of the country with a coal on a mat. In order to verify this information, Capt. Clarke persuaded one of the young men, by the present of a burning-glass, to accompany him to the river, in search of which he immediately set out with a canoe and seven of our men.

In the evening, Capt. Clarke returned from his excursion. After descending about twenty miles, he entered the mouth of a large river, which was concealed, by three small islands opposite its entrance, from those who pass up or down the Columbia. This river, which the Indians call Multnomah, from a nation of the same name residing near it on Wappatoo Island, enters the Columbia one hundred and forty miles above the mouth of the latter river. The current of the Multnomah, which is also called Willamett, is as gentle as that of the Columbia; and it appears to possess water enough for the largest ship, since, on sounding with a line of five fathoms, they could find no bottom.

Capt. Clarke ascended the river to the village of his guide. He found here a building two hundred and twenty-six feet in front, entirely above ground, and all under one roof; otherwise it would seem more like a range of buildings, as it is divided into seven distinct apartments, each thirty feet square. The roof is formed of rafters, with round poles laid on them longitudinally. The whole is covered with a double row of the bark of the white cedar, secured by splinters of dried fir, inserted through it at regular distances. In this manner, the roof is made light, strong, and durable.

In the house were several old people of both sexes, who were treated with much respect, and still seemed healthy, though most of them were perfectly blind.

On inquiring the cause of the decline of their village, which was shown pretty clearly by the remains of several deserted buildings, an old man, father of the guide, and a person of some distinction, brought forward a woman very much marked with the small-pox, and said, that, when a girl, she was near dying with the disorder which had left those marks, and that the inhabitants of the houses now in ruins had fallen victims to the same disease.

WAPPATOO ISLAND AND ROOT.

Wappatoo Island is a large extent of country lying between the Multnomah River and an arm of the Columbia. The island is about twenty miles long, and varies in breadth from five to ten miles. The land is high, and extremely fertile, and on most parts is supplied with a heavy growth of cottonwood, ash, and willow. But the chief wealth of this island consists of the numerous ponds in the interior, abounding with the common arrow-head (*Sagittaria sagittifolia*), to the root of which is attached a bulb growing beneath it, in the mud. This bulb, to which the Indians give the name of *wappatoo*, is the great article of food, and almost the staple article of commerce, on the Columbia. It is never out of season; so that, at all times of the year, the valley is frequented by the neighboring Indians who come to gather it. It is collected chiefly by the women, who employ for the purpose canoes from ten to fourteen feet in length, about two feet wide, and nine inches deep, tapering from the middle, where they are about twenty inches wide. They are sufficient to contain a single person and several bushels of roots; yet so light, that a woman can carry one with ease. She takes one of these canoes into a pond where the water is as high as the breast, and, by means of her toes, separates from the root this bulb, which, on being freed from the mud, rises immediately to the surface of the water, and is thrown into the canoe. In this manner, these patient females remain in the water for several hours, even in the depth of winter. This plant is found through the whole extent of the valley in which we now are, but does not grow on the Columbia farther eastward.

SCENERY OF THE RIVER AND SHORES.

Above the junction of the Multnomah River, we passed along under high, steep, and rocky sides of the mountains, which here close in on each side of the river, forming stupendous precipices, covered with the fir and white cedar. Down these heights frequently descend the most beautiful cascades,— one of which, a large stream, throws itself over a perpendicular rock, three hundred feet above the water; while other smaller streams precipitate themselves from a still greater elevation, and, separating into a mist, again collect, and form a second cascade before they reach the bottom of the rocks.

The hills on both sides of the river are about two hundred and fifty feet high, generally abrupt and craggy, and in many places presenting a perpendicular face of black, hard, basaltic rock. From the top of these hills, the country extends itself, in level plains, to a very great distance.

To one remarkable elevation we gave the name of Beacon Rock. It stands on the north side of the river, insulated from the hills. The northern side has a partial growth of fir or pine. To the south, it rises in an unbroken precipice to the height of seven hundred feet, where it terminates in a sharp point, and may be seen at the distance of twenty miles. This rock may be considered as the point where tide-water commences.

April 19. — We formed our camp at the foot of the Long Narrows, a little above a settlement of Skilloots. Their dwellings were formed by sticks set in the ground, and covered with mats and straw, and so large, that each was the residence of several families.

The whole village was filled with rejoicing at having caught a salmon, which was considered as the harbinger of vast quantities that would arrive in a few days. In the belief that it would hasten their coming, the Indians, according to their custom, dressed the fish, and cut it into small pieces, one of which was given to every child in the village; and, in the good humor excited by this occurrence, they parted, though reluctantly, with four horses, for which we gave them two kettles, reserving to ourselves only one.

We resumed our route, and soon after halted on a hill, from the top of which we had a commanding view of the range of mountains in which Mount Hood stands, and which continued south as far as the eye could reach; their summits being covered with snow. Mount Hood bore south thirty degrees west; and another snowy summit, which we have called Mount Jefferson, south ten degrees west.

Capt. Clarke crossed the river, with nine men and a large part of the merchandise, to purchase, if possible, twelve horses to transport our baggage, and some pounded fish, as a reserve, on the passage across the mountains. He succeeded in purchasing only four horses, and those at double the price that had been paid to the Shoshonees.

April 20. — As it was much for our interest to preserve the good will of these people, we passed over several small thefts which they had committed; but this morning we learned that six tomahawks and a knife had been stolen during the night. We addressed ourselves to the chief, who seemed angry with his people; but we did not recover the articles: and soon afterwards two of our spoons were missing. We therefore ordered them all from the camp. They left us in ill-humor, and we therefore kept on our guard against any insult.

April 22. — We began our march at seven o'clock. We had just reached the top of a hill near the village, when the load of one of the horses turned; and the animal, taking fright at a robe which still adhered to him, ran furiously toward the village. Just as he came there, the robe fell, and an Indian made way with it. The horse was soon caught; but the robe was missing, and the Indians denied having seen it. These repeated acts of knavery had quite exhausted our patience; and Capt. Lewis set out for the village, determined to make them deliver up the robe, or to burn their houses to the ground. This retaliation was happily rendered unnecessary; for on his way he met two of our men, who had found the robe in one of the huts, hid behind some baggage.

April 24. — The Indians had promised to take our

canoes in exchange for horses; but, when they found that we were resolved on travelling by land, they refused giving us any thing for them, in hopes that we would be forced to leave them. Disgusted at this conduct, we determined rather to cut them in pieces than suffer these people to possess them; and actually began to do so, when they consented to give us several strands of beads for each canoe.

We had now a sufficient number of horses to carry our baggage, and therefore proceeded wholly by land. Passing between the hills and the northern shore of the river, we had a difficult and fatiguing march over a road alternately sandy and rocky.

The country through which we have passed for several days is of uniform character. The hills on both sides of the river are about two hundred and fifty feet high, in many places presenting a perpendicular face of black, solid rock. From the top of these hills, the country extends, in level plains, to a very great distance, and, though not as fertile as land near the falls, produces an abundant supply of low grass, which is an excellent food for horses. The grass must indeed be unusually nutritious: for even at this season of the year, after wintering on the dry grass of the plains, and being used with greater severity than is usual among the whites, many of the horses were perfectly fat; nor had we seen a single one that was really poor.

Having proceeded thirty-one miles, we halted for the night not far from some houses of the Wallawallas. Soon after stopping, we were joined by seven of that tribe, among whom we recognized a chief by the name of Yellept, who had visited us in October last, when we gave him a medal.

He appeared very much pleased at seeing us again, and invited us to remain at his village three or four days, during which he would supply us with such food as they had, and furnish us with horses for our journey. After the cold, inhospitable treatment we had lately received, this kind offer was peculiarly acceptable. After having made a hasty meal, we accompanied him to his village. Immediately on our arrival, Yellept, who proved to be a man of much influence, collected the inhabitants, and after having made an harangue to them, the object of which was to induce them to treat us hospitably, set them an example by bringing himself an armful of wood, and a platter containing three roasted mullets. They immediately followed the example by furnishing us with an abundance of the only sort of fuel they use, — the stems of shrubs growing in the plains. We then purchased four dogs, on which we supped heartily, having been on short allowance for two days previously.

We learned from these people, that, opposite to their village, there was a route which led to the mouth of the Kooskooskie; that the road was good, and passed over a level country well supplied with water and grass; and that we should meet with plenty of deer and antelope. We knew that a road in that direction would shorten our route eighty miles; and we concluded to adopt this route.

Fortunately there was among these Walla-wallas a prisoner belonging to a tribe of the Shoshonee Indians. Our Shoshonee woman, Sacajaweah, though she belonged to another tribe, spoke the same language as this prisoner; and by their means we were enabled to explain ourselves to the Indians, and to answer all their inquiries with respect to ourselves and the object of our journey. Our conversation inspired them with such confidence, that they soon brought several sick persons for whom they requested our assistance. We splintered the broken arm of one, gave some relief to another whose knee was contracted by rheumatism, and administered what we thought would be useful for ulcers and eruptions of the skin on various parts of the body, which are very common disorders among them. But our most valuable medicine was eye-water, which we distributed, and which, indeed, they very much required; for complaints of the eyes, occasioned by living so much on the water, and aggravated by the fine sand of the plains, were universal among them.

We were by no means dissatisfied at this new resource for obtaining subsistence, as the Indians would give us no provisions without merchandise, and our stock was very much reduced. We carefully abstained from giving them any thing but harmless medicines; and our prescriptions might be useful, and were therefore entitled to some remuneration.

May 5. — Almost the only instance of rudeness we encountered in our whole trip occurred here. We made our dinner on two dogs and a small quantity of roots. While we were eating, an Indian standing by, and looking with great derision at our eating dog's-flesh, threw a half-starved puppy almost into Capt. Lewis's plate, laughing heartily at the humor of it. Capt. Lewis took up the animal, and flung it back with great force into the fellow's face, and, seizing his tomahawk, threatened to cut him down if he dared to repeat such insolence. He went off, apparently much mortified; and we continued our dog-repast very quietly.

Here we met our old Chopunnish guide and his family; and soon afterward one of our horses, which had been separated from the others in the charge of Twisted-hair, was caught, and restored to us.

THE WALLA-WALLA.

We reached (May 1) a branch of the Walla-walla River. The hills of this creek are generally abrupt and rocky; but the narrow bottom bordering the stream is very fertile, and both possess twenty times as much timber as the Columbia itself. Indeed, we now find, for the first time since leaving Fort Clatsop, an abundance of fire-wood. The growth consists of cotton-wood, birch, the crimson haw, willow, choke-cherry, yellow currants, gooseberry, honeysuckle, rose-bushes, sumac, together with some corn-grass and rushes.

The advantage of a comfortable fire induced us, as the night was come, to halt at this place. We were soon supplied by Drewyer with a beaver and an otter; of which we took only a part of the beaver, and gave the rest to the Indians. The otter is a favorite food, though much inferior, in our estimation, to the dog, which they will not eat. The horse, too, is seldom eaten, and never except when absolute necessity compels. This fastidiousness does not, however, seem to proceed so much from any dislike to the food as from attachment to the animal; for many of them eat very freely of the horse-beef we give them.

There is very little difference in the general face of the country here from that of the plains on the Missouri, except that the latter are enlivened by vast herds of buffaloes, elks, and other animals, which are wanting here. Over these wide bottoms we continued, till, at the distance of twenty-six miles from our last encampment, we halted for the night.

We had scarcely encamped, when three young men from the Walla-walla village came in with a steel-trap, which we had inadvertently left behind, and which they had come a whole day's journey on purpose to restore. This act of integrity was the more pleasing because it corresponds perfectly with the general behavior of the Walla-wallas, among whom we had lost carelessly several knives, which were always returned as soon as found. We may, indeed, justly affirm, that, of all the Indians whom we have met, the Walla-wallas were the most hospitable, honest, and sincere.

TWISTED-HAIR.

On Wednesday, the 7th of May, we reached the Kooskooskee, and found it much more navigable than when we descended it last year. The water was risen, and covered the rocks and shoals. Here we found the chief, named Twisted-hair, in whose charge we had left our horses in our outward journey. We had suspicions that our horses, and especially our saddles, might not be easily recoverable after our long absence. The Twisted-hair was invited to come, and smoke with us. He accepted the invitation; and, as we smoked our pipes over the fire, informed us, that, according to his promise, he had collected the horses, and taken charge of them; but another chief, the Broken-arm, becoming jealous of him because the horses were confided to his care, was constantly quarrelling with him. At length, being an old man, and unwilling to live in perpetual disputes, he had given up the care of the horses, which had consequently become scattered. The greater part of them were, however, still in this neighborhood. He added, that on the rise of the river, in the spring, the earth had fallen from the door of the *cache,* and exposed the saddles, some of which had probably been lost; but, as soon as he was acquainted with the situation of them, he had had them buried in another place, where they were now. He promised that he would, on the morrow, send his young men, and collect such of the horses as were in the neighborhood. He kept his word. Next day, the Indians brought in twenty-one of the horses, the greater part of which were in excellent order; and the Twisted-hair restored about half the saddles we had left in the *cache,* and some powder and lead which were buried at the same place.

CHAPTER XVII.

THE ROCKY MOUNTAINS.

MAY 17.— The country along the Rocky Mountains, for several hundred miles in length and fifty in width, is a high level plain; in all its parts extremely fertile, and in many places covered with a growth of tall, long-leaved pine. Nearly the whole of this wide tract is covered with a profusion of grass and plants, which are at this time as high as the knee. Among these are a variety of esculent plants and roots, yielding a nutritious and agreeable food. The air is pure and dry; the climate as mild as that of the same latitudes in the Atlantic States, and must be equally healthy, since all the disorders which we have witnessed may fairly be imputed to other causes than the climate. Of course, the degrees of heat and cold obey the influence of situation. Thus the rains of the low grounds are snows in the high plains; and, while the sun shines with intense heat in the confined river-bottoms, the plains enjoy a much cooler air; and, at the foot of the mountains, the snows are even now many feet in depth.

CROSSING THE MOUNTAINS.

An attempt to cross the mountains in the early part of June failed on account of the snow, which still covered the track. It was plain we should have no chance of finding either grass or underwood for our horses. To proceed, therefore, would be to hazard the loss of our horses; in which case, if we should be so fortunate as to escape with our lives, we should be obliged to abandon our papers and collections. It was accordingly decided not to venture farther; to deposit here all the baggage and provisions for which we had no immediate use, and to return to some spot where we might live by hunting till the snow should have melted, or a guide be procured to conduct us. We submitted, June 17, to the mortification of retracing our steps three days' march.

On the 24th June, having been so fortunate as to engage three Indians to go with us to the falls of the Missouri for the compensation of two guns, we set out on our second attempt to cross the mountains. On reaching the place where we had left our baggage, we found our deposit perfectly safe. It required two hours to arrange our baggage, and prepare a hasty meal; after which the guides urged us to set off, as we had a long ride to make before we could reach a spot where there was grass for our horses. We mounted, and followed their steps; sometimes crossed abruptly steep hills, and then wound along their sides, near tremendous precipices, where, had our horses slipped, we should have been irrecoverably lost. Our route lay along the ridges which separate the waters of the Kooskooskie and Chopunnish, and above the heads of all the streams; so that we met no running water. Late in the evening, we reached a spot where we encamped near a good spring of water. It was on the steep side of a mountain, with no wood, and a fair southern aspect, from which the snow seemed to have disappeared for about ten days, and an abundant growth of young grass, like greensward, had sprung up. There was also a species of grass not unlike flag, with a broad succulent leaf, which is confined to the upper parts of the mountains. It is a favorite food with the horses; but it was then either covered with snow, or just making its appearance.

June 27. — We continued our route over the high

and steep hills of the same great ridge. At eight miles' distance, we reached an eminence where the Indians have raised a conical mound of stone six or eight feet high. From this spot we have a commanding view of the surrounding mountains, which so completely enclose us, that, although we have once passed them, we should despair of ever escaping from them without the assistance of the Indians; but our guides traverse this trackless region with a kind of instinctive sagacity. They never hesitate; they are never embarrassed; yet so undeviating is their step, that, wherever the snow has disappeared for even a hundred paces, we find the summer road. With their aid, the snow is scarcely a disadvantage; for although we are often obliged to slide down, yet the fallen timber and the rocks, which are now covered up, were much more troublesome when we passed in the autumn.

NOTE.

A later traveller through this region writes, "The mountains are indeed *rocky*. They are rocks heaped upon rocks, with no vegetation, excepting a few cedars growing out of the crevices near their base. Their tops are covered with perpetual snow. The main ridge of the mountains is of *gneiss* rock; yet, to-day, parallel ridges of a rock, nearly allied to *basalt*, have abounded. These ridges appear to be volcanic, forced up in

THE PARTY AGREE TO SEPARATE.

July 3, 1806. — It was agreed here that the expedition should be divided, to unite again at the confluence of the Missouri and the Yellowstone. The separation took place near the point where Clarke's River is crossed by the forty-seventh parallel of latitude. Capt. Lewis, with nine men, was to cross the mountains in a direction as nearly due east as possible, expecting to find some tributary of the Missouri, by following which he might reach that river, and by it retrace his way homeward. Capt. Clarke, with the remainder of the party, was to seek the head waters of the Yellowstone, and follow that stream to the proposed place of re-union.

In conformity with this arrangement, Capt. Lewis, under the guidance of friendly Indians, crossed the mountains by a route which led him, after travelling

---

dikes at different distances from each other, running from east-north-east to west-south-west. The strata are mostly vertical; but some are a little dipped to the south.

" Our encampment was near a small stream which runs through a volcanic chasm, which is more than a hundred feet deep, with perpendicular sides. Here was a passage made for the *water* by *fire*."

one hundred and four miles, to Medicine River, and by that river to the Missouri. He reached the falls of the Missouri on the 17th of July, and leaving there a portion of his party, under Sergt. Gass, to make preparations for transporting their baggage and canoes round the falls, set out, accompanied by Drewyer and the two brothers Fields, with six horses, to explore Maria's River, to ascertain its extent toward the north. From the 18th to the 26th, they were engaged in this exploration. On the eve of their return, an event occurred, which, being the only instance in which the expedition was engaged in any conflict with the Indians with loss of life, requires to be particularly related.

CONFLICT WITH THE INDIANS.

We were passing through a region frequented by the Minnetarees, a band of Indians noted for their thievish propensities and unfriendly dispositions. Capt. Lewis was therefore desirous to avoid meeting with them. Drewyer had been sent out for game, and Capt. Lewis ascended a hill to look over the country. Scarcely had he reached the top, when he saw, about a mile on his left, a collection of about thirty horses. By the aid of his spy-glass, he discovered that one-half of the horses were saddled, and that, on the eminence above the horses, several Indians were looking down towards the river, probably at Drewyer. This was a most unwelcome sight. Their probable numbers rendered any contest with them of doubtful issue. To attempt to escape would only invite pursuit; and our horses were so bad, that we must certainly be overtaken: besides which, Drewyer could not yet be aware that Indians were near; and, if we ran, he would most probably be sacrificed. We therefore determined to make the best of our situation, and advance towards them in a friendly manner. The flag which we had brought in case of such an emergency was therefore displayed, and we continued slowly our march towards them. Their whole attention was so engaged by Drewyer, that they did not immediately discover us. As soon as they did so, they appeared to be much alarmed, and ran about in confusion. When we came within a quarter of a mile, one of the Indians mounted, and rode towards us. When within a hundred paces of us, he halted; and Capt. Lewis, who had alighted to receive him, held out his hand, and beckoned him to approach: but he only looked at us, and then, without saying a word, returned to his companions.

The whole party now descended the hill, and rode towards us. As yet we saw only eight, but presumed that there must be more behind, as there were several more horses saddled. Capt. Lewis had with him but two men; and he told them his fears that these were Indians of the Minnetaree tribe, and that they would attempt to rob us, and advised them to be on the alert, should there appear any disposition to attack us.

When the two parties came within a hundred yards of each other, all the Indians, except one, halted. Capt. Lewis therefore ordered his two men to halt, while he advanced, and, after shaking hands with the Indian, went on and did the same with the others in the rear, while the Indian himself shook hands with our two men. They all now came up; and, after alighting, the Indians asked to smoke with us. Capt. Lewis, who was very anxious for Drewyer's safety, told them that the man who had gone down the river had the pipe, and requested, that, as they had seen him, one of them would accompany R. Fields to bring him back. To this they assented; and Fields went with a young man in search of Drewyer, who returned with them.

As it was growing late, Capt. Lewis proposed that they should encamp with us; for he was glad to see them, and had a great deal to say to them. They assented; and, being soon joined by Drewyer, the evening was spent in conversation with the Indians, in which Capt. Lewis endeavored to persuade them to cultivate peace with their neighbors. Finding them very fond of the pipe, Capt. Lewis, who was desirous of keeping a constant watch during the night, smoked with them to a late hour; and, as soon as they were all asleep, he woke R. Fields, and ordering him to rouse us all in case any Indian left the camp, as he feared they would attempt to steal our horses, he lay down by the side of Drewyer in the tent with the Indians, while the brothers Fields were stretched near the fire at the mouth of the tent.

At sunrise, the Indians got up, and crowded round the fire, near which J. Fields, who was then on watch, had carelessly left his rifle, near the head of his brother, who was asleep. One of the Indians slipped behind him, and, unperceived, took his brother's and his own rifle; while at the same time two others seized those of Drewyer and Capt. Lewis. As soon as Fields turned round, he saw the Indian running off with the rifles; and, instantly calling his brother, they pursued him for fifty or sixty yards; and just as they overtook him, in the scuffle for the rifles, R. Fields stabbed him through the heart with his knife. The Indian ran a few steps, and fell dead. They recovered their rifles, and ran back to the camp.

The moment the fellow touched his gun, Drewyer, who was awake, jumped up, and wrested it from him. The noise awoke Capt. Lewis, who instantly started from the ground, and reached to seize his gun, but found it gone, and, turning about, saw the Indian running off with it. He followed, and called to him to lay down the gun; which he did. By this time, the rest of the Indians were endeavoring to drive off our horses; and Capt. Lewis ordered his men to follow them, and fire upon the thieves if they did not release our horses. The result was, that we recovered four of our horses, and as many of theirs which they had left behind; so that we were rather gainers by the contest. Besides the Indian killed by Fields, one other was badly wounded.

We had no doubt but that we should be immediately pursued by a much larger party. Our only chance of safety was in rejoining our friends, who were many miles distant. We therefore pushed our horses as fast as we could; and, fortunately for us, the Indian horses proved very good. The plains were level, free from stones and prickly-pears, and in fine order for travelling over from the late rains. We commenced our ride in the early morning. At three o'clock, we had ridden, by estimate, sixty-three miles. We halted for an hour and a half to refresh our horses; then pursued our journey seventeen miles farther, when, as night came on, we killed a buffalo, and again stopped for two hours. The sky was now overclouded; but, as the moon gave light enough to show us the route, we continued for twenty miles farther, and then, exhausted with fatigue, halted at two in the morning. Next day, we rejoined the main body of our party in safety.

Capt. Lewis with his companions pursued their way down the Missouri, passing those points already noticed in their ascent. Our narrative, therefore, will leave them here, and attend the course of Capt. Clarke and his party down the Yellowstone.

CHAPTER XVIII.

CAPT. CLARKE'S ROUTE DOWN THE YELLOWSTONE.

JULY 3, 1806. — The party under Capt. Clarke, consisting of fifteen men, with fifty horses, set out through the valley of Clarke's River, along the western side of which they rode in a southern direction. The valley is from ten to fifteen miles in width, and is diversified by a number of small open plains, abounding with grass and a variety of sweet-scented plants, and watered by numerous streams rushing from the western mountains. These mountains were covered with snow about one-fifth of the way from the top; and some snow was still to be seen in the hollows of the mountains to the eastward.

July 7. — They reached Wisdom River, and stopped for dinner at a hot spring situated in the open plain. The bed of the spring is about fifteen yards in circumference, and composed of loose, hard, gritty stones, through which the water boils in large quantities. It is slightly impregnated with sulphur, and so hot, that a piece of meat, about the size of three fingers, was completely cooked in twenty-five minutes.

July 8. — They arrived at Jefferson's River, where they had deposited their goods in the month of August the year before. They found every thing safe, though some of the goods were a little damp, and one of the canoes had a hole in it. They had now crossed from Traveller's-Rest Creek to the head of Jefferson's River, which seems to form the best and shortest route over the mountains during almost the whole distance of one hundred and sixty-four miles. It is, in fact, an excellent road; and, by cutting down a few trees, it might be rendered a good route for wagons, with the exception of about four miles over one of the mountains, which would require a little levelling.

July 10. — The boats were now loaded, and Capt. Clarke divided his men into two bands. Sergt. Ordway, with nine men, in six canoes, was to descend the river; while Capt. Clarke, with the remaining ten, the wife and child of Chaboneau, and fifty horses, were to proceed by land to the Yellowstone. The latter party set out at five in the afternoon from the forks of the Missouri, in a direction nearly east. The plain was intersected by several great roads leading to a gap in the mountain about twenty miles distant, in a direction east-north-east; but the Indian woman, who was acquainted with the country, recommended another gap more to the south, through which Capt. Clarke determined to proceed.

They started early the next morning, and, pursuing the route recommended by the squaw, encamped in the evening at the entrance of the gap mentioned by her. Through this gap they passed next day, and, at the distance of six miles, reached the top of the dividing ridge which separates the waters of the Missouri from those of the Yellowstone. Nine miles from the summit, they reached the Yellowstone itself, about a mile and a half below where it issues from the Rocky Mountains. The distance from the head of the Missouri to this place is forty-eight miles, the greater part of which is through a level plain. They halted for three hours to rest their horses, and then pursued the Buffalo Road along the banks of the river.

Although but just emerging from a high, snowy mountain, the Yellowstone is here a bold, rapid, and deep stream, one hundred and twenty yards in width. They continued their course along the river till the 23d, when the party embarked on board of two canoes, each of which was twenty-eight feet long, sixteen or eighteen inches deep, and from sixteen to twenty-four inches wide. Sergt. Prior, with two men, was directed to take the horses to the Mandans for safe keeping until the re-union of the expedition.

July 24. — At eight o'clock, Capt. Clarke and the remainder of his party embarked, and proceeded very steadily down the river. They passed the mouths of several large rivers emptying into the Yellowstone; one of which was called the Big-horn, from the numbers of that remarkable species of sheep seen in its neighborhood. Next day, Capt. Clarke landed to examine a curious rock, situated in an extensive bottom on the right, about two hundred and fifty paces from the shore. It is nearly two hundred paces in circumference, two hundred feet high, and accessible only from the north-east; the other sides consisting of perpendicular cliffs, of a light-colored, gritty stone. The soil on the summit is five or six feet deep, of a good quality, and covered with short grass. From this height, the eye ranges over a wide extent of variegated country. On the south-west are the Rocky Mountains, covered with snow; on the north, a lower range, called the Little Wolf Mountains. The low grounds of the river extend nearly six miles to the southward, when they rise into plains, reaching to the mountains. The north side of the river is bounded by jutting, romantic cliffs, beyond which the plains are open and extensive, and the whole country enlivened by herds of buffaloes, elks, and wolves. After enjoying the prospect from this rock, to which Capt. Clarke gave the name of Pompey's Pillar, he descended, and continued his route. At the distance of six or seven miles, he stopped to secure two bighorns, which had been shot from the boat, and, while on shore, saw in the face of the cliff, about twenty feet above the water, a fragment of the rib of a fish, three feet long, and nearly three inches round, embedded in the rock itself.

BEAVERS, BUFFALOES, MOSQUITOES.

The beavers were in great numbers along the banks of the river, and through the night were flapping their tails in the water round the boats.

Aug. 1. — The buffaloes appeared in vast numbers. A herd happened to be on their way across the river. Such was the multitude of these animals, that although the river, including an island over which they passed, was a mile in width, the herd stretched, as thick as they could swim, completely from one side to the other. Our party, descending the river, was obliged to stop for an hour to let the procession pass. We consoled ourselves for the delay by killing four of the herd, and then proceeded, till, at the distance of forty-five miles, two other herds of buffaloes, as numerous as the first, crossed the river in like manner.

Aug. 4. — The camp became absolutely uninhabitable, in consequence of the multitude of mosquitoes. The men could not work in preparing skins for clothing, nor hunt in the low grounds : in short, there was no mode of escape, except by going on the sand-bars in the river, where, if the wind should blow, the insects do not venture. But when there is no wind, and particularly at night, when the men have no covering except their worn-out blankets, the pain they inflict is scarcely to be endured.

On one occasion, Capt. Clarke went on shore, and ascended a hill after one of the big-horns; but the mosquitoes were in such multitudes, that he could not keep them from the barrel of his rifle long enough to take aim.

This annoyance continued, till, on the 11th of September, they write, " We are no longer troubled with mosquitoes, which do not seem to frequent this part of the river; and, after having been persecuted with them during the whole route from the falls, it is a most happy exemption. Their noise was very agreeably exchanged for that of the wolves, which were howling in various directions all round us.

Aug. 12, 1806. — The party continued to descend the river. One of their canoes had, by accident, a small hole made in it; and they halted for the purpose of covering it with a piece of elk-skin. While there, about noon, they were overjoyed at seeing the boats of Capt. Lewis's party heave in sight. The whole expedition being now happily re-united, at about three o'clock all embarked on board the boats; but as the wind was high, accompanied with rain, we did not proceed far before we halted for the night.

THEY PART WITH SOME OF THEIR COMPANIONS.

On the 14th August, having now reached a part of the river where we occasionally met the boats of adventurous traders ascending the river, Capt. Lewis was applied to by one of the men, Colter, who was desirous of joining two trappers, who proposed to him to accompany them, and share their profits. The offer was an advantageous one; and as he had always performed his duty, and his services might be dispensed with, Capt. Lewis consented to his going, provided none of the rest would ask or expect a similar indulgence. To this they cheerfully answered, that they wished Colter every success, and would not apply for a discharge before we reached St. Louis. We therefore supplied him, as did his comrades also, with powder and lead, and a variety of articles which might be useful to him; and he left us the next day.

The example of this man shows how easily men may be weaned from the habits of civilized life, and brought to relish the manners of the woods. This hunter had now been absent many years from his country, and might naturally be presumed to have some desire to return to his native seats; yet, just at the moment when he is approaching the frontiers, he is tempted by a hunting-scheme to go back to the solitude of the woods.

A few days after this, Chaboneau, with his wife and child, concluded to follow us no longer, as he could be no longer useful to us. We offered to take him with us to the United States; but he said that he had there no acquaintance, and preferred remaining among the Indians. This man has been very serviceable to us, and his wife particularly so, among the Shoshonees. She has borne with a patience truly admirable the fatigues of our long journey, encumbered with the charge of an infant, which is now only nineteen months old. We paid him his wages, amounting to five hundred dollars and thirty-three cents, including the price of a horse and a lodge purchased of him, and pursued our journey without him.

THEY REACH HOME.

Sept. 8, 1806. — We reached Council Bluffs, and stopped for a short time to examine the situation of the place, and were confirmed in our belief that it would be a very eligible spot for a trading establishment.* Being anxious to reach the junction of the Platte River, we plied our oars so well, that by night we had made seventy-eight miles, and landed at our old encampment, on the ascent, twelve miles above that river. We had here occasion to remark the wonderful evaporation from the Missouri. The river does not appear to contain more water, nor is its channel wider, than at the distance of one thousand miles nearer its source, although within that space it receives about twenty rivers (some of them of considerable width), and a great number of smaller streams.

---

* Now the site of Omaha City.

A few days more brought us to the mouth of the Kansas River. About a mile below it, we landed to view the country. The low grounds are delightful, the whole country exhibiting a rich appearance; but the weather was oppressively warm. Descending as we had done from a high, open country, between the latitudes of forty-six and forty-nine degrees, to the wooded plains in thirty-eight and thirty-nine degrees, the heat would have been intolerable, had it not been for the constant winds from the south and the southwest.

On the 20th September, we reached the mouth of Osage River. A few miles lower down, we saw on the banks some cows feeding; and the whole party involuntarily raised a shout of joy at the sight of this evidence of civilization and domestic life.

We soon after reached the little French village of La Charette, which we saluted with a discharge of four guns and three hearty cheers. We landed, and were received with kindness by the inhabitants, as well as by some traders who were on their way to traffic with the Osages. They were all surprised and pleased at our arrival; for they had long since abandoned all hopes of ever seeing us return.

The third day after this, — viz., on Tuesday, the 23d

of September, 1806, — we arrived at St. Louis, and, having fired a salute, went on shore, and received the heartiest and most hospitable welcome from the whole village.

CONCLUSION.

The successful termination of the expedition was a source of surprise and delight to the whole country. The humblest of its citizens had taken a lively interest in the issue of this journey, and looked forward with impatience for the information it would furnish. Their anxieties, too, for the safety of the party, had been kept in a state of excitement by lugubrious rumors, circulated from time to time on uncertain authorities, and uncontradicted by letters or other direct information, from the time when the party left the Mandan towns, on their ascent up the river, in 1804, until their actual return to St. Louis.

The courage, perseverance, and discretion displayed by the commanders, and the fidelity and obedience of the men, were the theme of general approbation, and received the favorable notice of Government. A donation of lands was made to each member of the party; Capt. Lewis was appointed Governor of Louisiana, which, at that time, embraced the whole country west of the Mississippi, within the boundaries of the United States; and Capt. Clarke was made Superintendent of Indian Affairs.

It was not until some years after, however, that the world was put in possession of the detailed history of the expedition. Capt. Lewis, in the midst of other cares, devoted what time he could to the preparation of his journals for publication, and, in 1809, was on his way to Philadelphia for that purpose, but, at a village in Tennessee, was taken ill, and prevented from proceeding. Here the energetic mind, which had encountered so unfalteringly the perils and sufferings of the desert, gave way. Constitutional despondency overcame him: it is probable he lost his reason; for, in a rash moment, he applied a pistol to his head, and destroyed his life. His journals were published under the charge of Paul Allen of Philadelphia.

ELDORADO.

ELDORADO.

CHAPTER I.

THE DISCOVERY.

WHAT is meant by Eldorado? Is there such a country? and, if there be, where is it? The name literally means "The Golden Country," and was given to an unknown region in South America by the Spaniards, who had heard from the Indians marvellous tales of such a land lying in the interior of the continent, where gold and precious stones were as common as rocks and pebbles in other countries, and to be had for the trouble of picking them up. It was also a land of spices and aromatic gums. The first notion of this favored region was communicated by an Indian chief to Gonzalo Pizarro, brother of the conqueror of Peru, whose imagination was captivated by the account, and his ambition fired with a desire to add this, which promised to be the most brilliant of all, to the discoveries and conquests of his countrymen. He found no difficulty in awakening a kindred enthusiasm in the bosoms of his followers. In a short time, he mustered three hundred and fifty Spaniards, and four thousand Indians. One hundred and fifty of his company were mounted. The Indians were to carry the baggage and provisions, and perform the labors of the expedition.

A glance at the map of South America will give us a clear idea of the scene of the expedition. The River Amazon, the largest river of the globe, rises in the highest ranges of the Andes, and flows from west to east through nearly the whole breadth of the continent. Pizarro's expedition started in the year 1540 from Quito, near the sources of the great river, and, marching east, soon became entangled in the deep and intricate passes of the mountains. As they rose into the more elevated regions, the icy winds that swept down the sides of the Cordilleras benumbed their limbs, and many of the natives found a wintry grave in the wilderness. On descending the eastern slope, the climate changed; and, as they came to a lower level, the fierce cold was succeeded by a suffocating heat, while tempests of thunder and lightning poured on them with scarcely any intermission day or night. For more than six weeks, the deluge continued unabated; and the forlorn wanderers, wet, and weary with incessant toil, were scarcely able to drag their limbs along the soil, broken up as it was, and saturated with the moisture. After months of toilsome travel, they reached the region where grew the spice-trees. Their produce resembled the cinnamon of the East in taste, but was of inferior quality. They saw the trees bearing the precious bark spreading out into broad forests; yet, however valuable it might be for future commerce, it was of but little worth to them. But, from the savages whom they occasionally met, they learned, that at ten days' distance was a rich and fruitful land, abounding with gold, and inhabited by populous nations. The Spaniards were so convinced of the existence of such a country, that if the natives, on being questioned, professed their ignorance of it, they were supposed to be desirous of concealing the fact, and were put to the most horrible tortures, and even burnt alive, to compel them to confess. It is no wonder, therefore, if they told, in many instances, such stories as the Spaniards wished to hear, which would also have the effect of ridding their own territories of their troublesome guests by inducing them to advance farther. Pizarro had already reached the limit originally proposed for the expedition; but these accounts induced him to continue on.

As they advanced, the country spread out into broad plains, terminated by forests, which seemed to stretch on every side as far as the eye could reach. The wood was thickly matted with creepers and climbing plants, and at every step of the way they had to hew open a passage with their axes; while their garments, rotting from the effects of the drenching rains, caught in every bush, and hung about them in shreds. Their provisions failed, and they had only for sustenance such herbs and roots as they could gather in the forest, and such wild animals as, with their inadequate means, they could capture.

At length they came to a broad expanse of water, from whence flowed a stream, — one of those which discharge their waters into the great River Amazon. The sight gladdened their hearts, as they hoped to find a safer and more practicable route by keeping along its banks. After following the stream a considerable distance, the party came within hearing of a rushing noise, that seemed like thunder issuing from the bowels of the earth. The river tumbled along over rapids with frightful velocity, and then discharged itself in a magnificent cataract, which they describe as twelve hundred feet high. Doubtless this estimate must be taken with some allowance for the excited feelings of the Spaniards, keenly alive to impressions of the sublime and the terrible.

For some distance above and below the falls, the bed of the river contracted; so that its width did not exceed twenty feet. They determined to cross, in hopes of finding a country that might afford them better sustenance. A frail bridge was constructed by throwing trunks of trees across the chasm, where the cliffs, as if split asunder by some convulsion of Nature, descended sheer down a perpendicular depth of several hundred feet. Over this airy causeway, the men and horses succeeded in effecting their passage; though one Spaniard, made giddy by heedlessly looking down, lost his footing, and fell into the boiling surges below. They gained little by the exchange. The country wore the same unpromising aspect: the Indians whom they occasionally met in the pathless wilderness were fierce and unfriendly, and the Spaniards were engaged in perpetual conflict with them. From these they learned that a fruitful country was to be found down the river, at the distance of only a few days' journey; and the Spaniards held on their weary way, still hoping, and still deceived, as the promised land flitted before them, like the rainbow, receding as they advanced.

At length, spent with toil and suffering, Pizarro resolved to construct a bark large enough to transport the weaker part of his company and his baggage. The forests furnished him with timber; the shoes of the horses, which had died on the road, or been slaughtered for food, were converted into nails; gum, distilled from the trees, took the place of pitch; and the tattered garments of the soldiers served for oakum. At the end of two months, the vessel was ready, and the command given to Francisco Orellana. The troops now moved forward through the wilderness, following the course of the river; the vessel carrying the feebler soldiers. Every scrap of provisions had long since been consumed. The last of their horses had been devoured; and they greedily fed upon toads, serpents, and even insects, which that country, teeming with the lower forms of animal life, abundantly supplied.

The natives still told of a rich district, inhabited by a populous nation. It was, as usual, at the distance of several days' journey; and Pizarro resolved to halt where he was, and send Orellana down in his brigantine to procure a stock of provisions, with which he might return, and put the main body in condition to resume their march. Orellana, with fifty of the adventurers, pushed off into the middle of the river, where the stream ran swiftly; and his bark, taken by the current, shot forward as with the speed of an arrow, and was soon out of sight.

Days and weeks passed away, yet the vessel did not return; and no speck was to be seen on the waters as the Spaniards strained their eyes to the farthest point, till the banks closed in, and shut the view. Detachments were sent out, and, though absent several days, came back without intelligence of their comrades. Weary of suspense, Pizarro determined to continue their march down the river, which they did, with incredible suffering, for two months longer, till their doubts were dispelled by the appearance of a white man, wandering, half naked, in the woods, in whose famine-stricken countenance they recognized the features of one of their countrymen. Orellana had passed swiftly down the river to the point of its confluence with the Amazon, where he had been led to expect that he should find supplies for the wants of himself and his companions, but found none. Nor was it possible to return as he had come, and make head against the current of the river. In this dilemma, a thought flashed across his mind: it was, to leave the party under Pizarro to their fate, and to pursue his course down the great river on which he had entered; to explore Eldorado for himself, and make the best of his way home to Spain to claim the glory and reward of discovery. His reckless companions readily consented to this course, with the exception of the individual whom Pizarro found; and him, when he remonstrated, they put ashore, and left to shift for himself.

Pizarro and his party, deserted in the wilderness, unable to advance farther, had no alternative but to remain, or retrace their miserable way to Quito, the place they had started from more than a year before. They chose the latter, and commenced their return march with heavy hearts. They took a more northerly route than that by which they had approached the Amazon; and, though it was attended with fewer difficulties, they experienced yet greater distresses, from their greater inability to overcome them. Their only food was such scanty fare as they could pick up in the forest, or happily meet with in some forsaken Indian settlement, or wring by violence from the natives. Some sickened and sank down by the way, and perished where they fell; for there was none to help them. Intense misery had made them selfish; and many a poor wretch was abandoned to his fate, to die alone in the wilderness, or, more probably, to be devoured, while living, by the wild animals which roamed over it.

It took them a year to measure back their way to Quito; and the miseries they had endured were testified to by their appearance when they arrived, in sadly reduced numbers, at the place of their starting. Their horses gone, their arms broken and rusted, the skins of wild animals their only clothes, their long and matted locks streaming wildly down their shoulders, their faces blackened by the tropical sun, their bodies wasted by famine and disfigured by scars, it seemed as if the charnel-house had given up its dead, as, with unsteady step, they crept slowly onwards. More than half of the four thousand Indians who had accompanied the expedition had perished; and of the Spaniards, only eighty, and many of these irretrievably broken in constitution, found their way back to Quito.

Meanwhile, Orellana glided down the stream, which then was nameless and unknown, but which has since been called by his name, though it is more generally known by a name derived from a story which Orellana told, in his account of his voyage, of a nation of Amazons inhabiting its banks. But an account of Orellana's adventures must be reserved for our next chapter.

CHAPTER II.

ORELLANA DESCENDS THE RIVER.

WHEN Orellana, in his ill-appointed bark, and with his crew enfeebled by famine, had reached the junction of the River Napo with the Amazon, and found no sources of supply which he had been led to expect, he had no difficulty in satisfying his companions that their only chance of preservation was in continuing their descent of the river, and leaving the party under Pizarro to their fate. He then formally renounced the commission which Pizarro had given him, and received the command anew from the election of his men, that so he might make discoveries for himself, and not, holding a deputed authority, in the name of another. It was upon the last day of December, 1541, that this voyage was begun, — one of the most adventurous that has ever been undertaken. The little stock of provisions with which they had parted from the army was already exhausted, and they boiled their leathern girdles and the leather of their shoes with such herbs as seemed most likely to be nourishing and harmless; for it was only by experiment that they were able to distinguish the wholesome from the poisonous. On the 8th of January, being reduced almost to the last extremity with hunger, they heard before daylight an Indian drum,— a joyful sound; for be the natives what they would, friendly or hostile, this they knew, that it must be their own fault now if they should die of hunger. At daybreak, being eagerly upon the lookout, they perceived four canoes, which put back upon seeing the brigantine; and presently they saw a village where a great body of the natives were assembled, and appeared ready to defend it. The Spaniards were too hungry to negotiate. Orellana bade them land in good order, and stand by each other. They attacked the Indians like men who were famishing, and fought for food, put them speedily to the rout, and found an immediate supply. While they were enjoying the fruits of their victory, the Indians came near them, more to gratify curiosity than resentment. Orellana spoke to them in some Indian language which they partly understood. Some of them took courage, and approached him. He gave them a few European trifles, and asked for their chief, who came without hesitation, was well pleased with the presents which were given him, and offered them any thing which it was in his power to supply. Provisions were requested; and presently peacocks, partridges, fish, and other things, were brought in great abundance. The next day, thirteen chiefs came to see the strangers. They were gayly adorned with feathers and gold, and had plates of gold upon the breast. Orellana received them courteously, required them to acknowledge obedience to the crown of Castile, took advantage as usual of their ignorance to affirm that they consented, and took possession of their country in the emperor's name.

Such is Orellana's own account of this first interview. It was his object to create a high idea of the riches of the provinces which he had discovered. It is not probable that these tribes had any gold; for later discoveries showed that none of the tribes on the Amazon were so far advanced as to use it. It was here that they heard the first accounts of the rich and powerful nation composed wholly of women, whom, in recollection of the female warriors of classic antiquity, they called the Amazons. Here the Spaniards built a better brigantine than the frail one in which they were embarked. All fell to work, Orellana being the first at any exertion that was required. They calked it with cotton; the natives supplied pitch; and in thirty-five days the vessel was launched. On the 24th of April, they once more embarked. For eighty leagues, the banks were peopled with friendly tribes; then the course of the river lay between desert mountains, and they were fain to feed upon herbs and parched corn, not even finding a place where they could fish.

Thus far they seem to have found the natives friendly, or not actively hostile; but, as they descended, they came to a populous province, belonging to a chief called Omagua, if, as is conjectured, that is not rather the name of the tribe itself than of their chief. One morning, a fleet of canoes was seen advancing with hostile demonstrations. The Indians carried shields made of the skins of the alligator. They came on with beat of tambour and with war-cries, threatening to devour the strangers. The Spaniards brought their two vessels close together, that they might aid one another in the defence. But, when they came to use their powder, it was damp, and they had nothing but their cross-bows to trust to; and, plying these as well as they could, they continued to fall down the stream, fighting as they went. Presently they came to an Indian town. Half the Spaniards landed to attack it, leaving their companions to maintain the fight upon the water.

They won the town, and loaded themselves with provisions; but eighteen of the party were wounded, and one killed. They had neither surgeon nor any remedy for the wounded. Nothing could be done for them except "psalming;" that is, repeating some verses of the psalms over the wound. This mode of treatment was not unusual; and, as it was less absurd than the methods which were ordinarily in use at that day, it is no wonder if it proved more successful.

For two days and two nights after this, they were constantly annoyed by the canoes of the natives following, and endeavoring to board them. But the Spaniards had now dried some powder; and one of them, getting a steady mark at the chief of the Indians, shot him in the breast. His people gathered round him; and, while they were thus occupied, the brigantines shot ahead.

Thus they proceeded with alternate good and evil fortune, now finding the Indians friendly, and supplies of provisions abundant; and then encountering hostile tribes which assailed them with all their power, or long regions of unpeopled country, where they were reduced to the utmost straits for want of food. Six months had now been consumed on their voyage, and as yet no appearance of Eldorado; though, if their accounts may be trusted, they several times came upon populous places, which had many streets, all opening upon the river, and apparently leading to some greater city in the interior. On the 22d of June, on turning an angle of the river, they saw the country far before them, and great numbers of people collected, seemingly with hostile intentions. Orellana offered them trinkets, at which they scoffed; but he persisted in making towards the shore to get food, either by persuasion or force. A shower of arrows was discharged from the shore, which wounded five of the crew. They nevertheless landed, and, after a hot contest, repulsed the natives, killing some seven or eight of them. The historian of the voyage, who was one of the adventurers, affirms that ten or twelve Amazons fought at the head of these people, who were their subjects, and fought desperately; because any one who fled in battle would be beaten to death by these female tyrants. He describes the women as very tall and large-limbed, white of complexion, the hair long, platted, and banded round the head. It is amusing to observe how this story was magnified by later narrators, who learned it only by tradition. It is stated in these late accounts that Orellana fought on this occasion with a great army of women.

Of a prisoner whom they took, Orellana asked questions about Eldorado and the Amazons, and got, as usual, such answers as he expected. This may partly be set down to the score of self-deception, and partly to the fact that they conversed with these people by signs, and by means of the few words of their language which the Spaniards knew, or supposed they knew, the meaning of. He learned from the prisoner that the country was subject to women, who lived after the manner of the Amazons of the ancients, and who possessed gold and silver in abundance. There were in their dominions fine temples of the sun, all covered with plates of gold. Their houses were of stone, and their cities walled. We can hardly doubt that the desire to tempt adventurers to join him in his subsequent expedition to conquer and colonize those countries had its effect in magnifying these marvels.

Shortly after this, the Spaniards thought they perceived the *tide*. After another day's voyage, they came to some inhabited islands, and, to their infinite joy, saw that they had not been mistaken; for the marks of the tide here were certain. Here they lost another of their party in a skirmish with the natives. From this place the country was low; and they could never venture to land, except upon the islands, among which they sailed, as they supposed, about two hundred leagues; the tide coming up with great force. One day the smaller vessel struck upon a snag, which stove in one of her planks, and she filled. They, however, landed to seek for provisions; but the inhabitants attacked them with such force, that they were forced to retire; and, when they came to their vessels, they found that the tide had left the only serviceable one dry. Orellana ordered half his men to fight, and the other half to thrust the vessel into the water: that done, they righted the old brigantine, and fastened in a new plank, all which was completed in three hours, by which time the Indians were weary of fighting, and left them in peace. The next day they found a desert place, where Orellana halted to repair both vessels. This took them eighteen days, during which they suffered much from hunger.

As they drew near the sea, they halted again for fourteen days, to prepare for their sea-voyage; made cordage of herbs; and sewed the cloaks, on which they slept, into sails. On the 8th of August, they proceeded again, anchoring with stones when the tide turned, though it sometimes came in such strength as to drag these miserable anchors. Here the natives were happily of a milder mood than those whom they had lately dealt with. From them they procured roots and Indian corn; and, having laid in what store they could, they made ready to enter upon the sea in these frail vessels, with their miserable tackling, and with insufficient food, without pilot, compass, or any knowledge of the coast.

It was on the 26th of August that they sailed out of the river, passing between two islands, which were about four leagues asunder. The whole length of the voyage from the place where they had embarked to the sea they computed at eighteen hundred leagues. Thus far their weather had been always favorable, and it did not fail them now. They kept along the coast to the northward, just at safe distance. The two brigantines parted company in the night. They in the larger one got into the Gulf of Paria, from whence all their labor at the oar for seven days could not extricate them. During this time, they lived upon a sort of plum called " nogos," being the only food they could find. At length they were whirled through those tremendous channels which Columbus called the "Dragon's mouths," and, September the 11th, not knowing where they were, reached the Island of Cubagua, where they found a colony of their countrymen. The old brigantine had arrived at the same place two days before them. Here they were received with the welcome which their wonderful adventure deserved; and from hence Orellana proceeded to Spain, to give the king an account of his discoveries in person.

CHAPTER III.

ORELLANA'S ADVENTURE CONTINUED.

ORELLANA arrived safe in Spain, and was favorably received. His act of insubordination in leaving his commander was forgotten in the success of his achievement; for it had been successful, even if the naked facts only had been told, inasmuch as it was the first event which led to any certain knowledge of the immense regions that stretch eastward from the Andes to the ocean, besides being in itself one of the most brilliant adventures of that remarkable age. But Orellana's accounts went far beyond these limits, and confirming all previous tales of the wonderful Eldorado, with its temples roofed with gold, and its mountains composed of precious stones, drew to his standard numerous followers. Every thing promised fairly. The king granted him a commission to conquer the countries which he had explored. He raised funds for the expedition, and even found a wife who was willing to accompany him. In May, 1544, he set sail with four ships and four hundred men.

But the tide of Orellana's fortune had turned. He stopped three months at Teneriffe, and two at the Cape de Verde, where ninety-eight of his people died, and fifty were invalided. The expedition proceeded with three ships, and met with contrary winds, which detained them till their water was exhausted; and, had it not been for heavy rains, all must have perished. One ship put back in this distress, with seventy men and eleven horses on board, and was never heard of after. The remaining two reached the river. Having ascended about a hundred leagues, they stopped to build a brigantine. Provisions were scarce here, and fifty-seven more of his party died. These men were not, like his former comrades, seasoned to the climate, and habituated to the difficulties of the new world. One ship was broken up here for the materials: the other met with an accident, and became unserviceable; and they cut her up, and made a bark of the timbers.

Orellana meanwhile, in the brigantine, was endeavoring to discover the main branch of the river, which it had been easy to keep when carried down by the stream, but which he now sought in vain for thirty days among a labyrinth of channels. When he returned from this fruitless search, he was ill, and told his people that he would go back to Point St. Juan; and there he ordered them to seek him when they had got the bark ready. But he found his sickness increase upon him, and determined to abandon the expedition, and return to Europe. While he was seeking provisions for the voyage, the Indians killed seventeen of his men. What with vexation and disorder, he died in the river. This sealed the fate of the expedition. The survivors made no further exertions to reach Eldorado, but returned to their own country as they could. Such was the fate of Orellana, who, as a discoverer, surpassed all his countrymen; and though, as a conqueror, he was unfortunate, yet neither is he chargeable with any of those atrocities toward the unhappy natives which have left such a stain on the glories of Cortes and Pizarro.

The next attempt we read of to discover Eldorado was made a few years after, under Hernando de Ribera, by ascending the La Plata, or River of Paraguay. He sailed in a brigantine with eighty men, and encountered no hostility from the natives. They confirmed the stories of the Amazons with their golden city. "How could they get at them?" was the next question: "by land, or by water?"—"Only by land," was the reply. "But it was a two-months' journey; and to reach them now would be impossible, because the country was inundated." The Spaniards made light of this obstacle, but asked for Indians to carry their baggage. The chief gave Ribera twenty for himself, and five for each of his men; and these desperate adventurers set off on their march over a flooded country.

Eight days they travelled through water up to their knees, and sometimes up to their middle. By slinging their hammocks to trees, and by this means only, could they find dry positions for the night. Before they could make a fire to dress their food, they were obliged to raise a rude scaffolding; and this was unavoidably so insecure, that frequently the fire burned through, and food and all fell into the water. They reached another tribe, and were told that the Amazons' country was still nine days farther on; and then still another tribe, who told them it would take a month to reach them. Perhaps they would still have advanced; but here an insuperable obstacle met them. The locusts for two successive years had devoured every thing before them, and no food was to be had. The Spaniards had no alternative but to march back. On their way, they were reduced to great distress for want of food; and from this cause, and travelling so long half under water, the greater number fell sick, and many died. Of eighty men who accompanied Ribera upon this dreadful march, only thirty recovered from its effects.

This expedition added a few items to the story of Eldorado. Ribera declares under oath that the natives told him of a nation of women, governed by a woman, and so warlike as to be dreaded by all their neighbors. They possessed plenty of white and yellow metal: their seats, and all the utensils in their houses, were made of them. They lived on a large island, which was in a huge lake, which they called the "Mansion of the Sun," because the sun sank into it. The only way of accounting for these stories is, that the Spaniards furnished, in the shape of questions, the information which they fancied they received in reply; the Indians assenting to what they understood but imperfectly, or not at all.

MARTINEZ.

Another expedition, not long after Orellana's, was that conducted by Don Diego Ordaz, of which Sir

Walter Raleigh, in his "History of Guiana," gives an account. The expedition failed; Ordaz being slain in a mutiny of his men, and those who went with him being scattered. The only noticeable result was in the adventures of one Martinez, an officer of Ordaz, who had charge of the ammunition. We tell the story in the language of Sir Walter, slightly modernized: —

"It chanced, that while Ordaz, with his army, rested at the port of Morequito, by some negligence the whole store of powder provided for the service was set on fire; and Martinez, having the chief charge thereof, was condemned by the general to be executed forthwith. Martinez, being much favored by the soldiers, had all means possible employed to save his life; but it could not be obtained in other way but this, — that he should be set into a canoe alone, without any food, and so turned loose into the great river. But it pleased God that the canoe was carried down the stream, and that certain of the Guianians met it the same evening: and, not having at any time seen any European, they carried Martinez into the land to be wondered at; and so from town to town until he came to the great city of Manoa, the seat and residence of Inga, the emperor. The emperor, when he beheld him, knew him to be a Christian of those who had conquered the neighboring country of Peru, and caused him to be lodged in his palace, and well entertained. He lived seven months in Manoa, but was not suffered to wander into the country anywhere. He was also brought thither all the way blindfolded by the Indians, until he came to the entrance of Manoa itself. He avowed at his death that he entered the city at noon, and then they uncovered his face; and that he travelled all that day till night through the city, ere he came to the palace of Inga.

"After Martinez had lived seven months in Manoa, and began to understand the language of the country, Inga asked him whether he desired to return to his own country, or would willingly abide with him. Martinez, not desirous to stay, obtained permission of Inga to depart, who sent with him some Guianians to conduct him to the river of Orinoco, with as much gold as they could carry, which he gave to Martinez at his departure. But, when he arrived at the river's side, the natives, being at that time at war with Inga, robbed him and his Guianians of all his treasure, save only two bottles made of gourds, which were filled with beads of gold, which those people thought to contain his drink or food, with which he was at liberty to depart. So, in a canoe, he passed down by the river to Trinidad, and from thence to Porto Rico, where he died. In the time of his extreme sickness, and when he was without hope of life, receiving the sacrament at the hands of his confessor, he delivered this relation of his travels, and also called for his calabazas, or gourds of gold beads, which he gave to the church and the friars, to be prayed for.

"This Martinez was the one who christened the city of Manoa by the name 'Eldorado,' and upon this occasion. At the times of their solemn feasts, when the emperor carouses with his captains, tributaries, and governors, the manner is thus: All those that pledge him are first stripped naked, and their bodies anointed all over with a kind of white balsam very precious. When they are anointed all over, certain servants of the emperor, having prepared gold made into fine powder, blow it through hollow canes upon their naked bodies until they be all shining from the head to the foot. Upon this sight, and for the abundance of gold which he saw in the city, the images of gold in their temples, the plates, armors, and shields of gold which they use in the wars, he called it Eldorado."

Such is Sir Walter's narrative of one of the traditions which fired his enthusiasm to undertake the conquest of Eldorado. He asserts that he read it in "The Chancery of Saint Juan de Porto Rico," of which Berrio had a copy. It is pretty plainly tinctured with fable, but probably had an historical foundation.

After this, a good many years elapsed before any other expedition of note was fitted out in search of Eldorado. But the story grew, notwithstanding. An imaginary kingdom was shaped out. It was governed by a potentate who was called the Great Paytiti, sometimes the Great Moxu, sometimes the Enim, or Great Para. An impostor at Lima affirmed that he had been in his capital, the city of Manoa, where not fewer than three thousand workmen were employed in the silversmiths' street. He even produced a map of the country, in which he had marked a hill of gold, another of silver, and a third of salt. The columns of the palace were described as of porphyry and alabaster, the galleries of ebony and cedar: the throne was of ivory, and the ascent to it by steps of gold. The palace was built of white stone. At the entrance were two towers, and between them a column twenty-five feet in height. On its top was a large silver moon; and two living lions were fastened to its base with chains of gold. Having passed by these keepers, you came into a quadrangle planted with trees, and watered by a silver fountain, which spouted through four golden pipes. The gate of the palace was of copper, and its bolt was received in the solid rock. Within, a golden sun was placed upon an altar of silver; and four lamps were kept burning before it day and night.

It may surprise us that tales so palpably false as these should have deceived any, to such an extent as to lead them to get up costly and hazardous expeditions to go in search of the wonder; but we must remember, that what the Spaniards had already realized and demonstrated to the world in their conquests of Mexico and Peru was hardly less astonishing than these accounts. It is therefore no wonder that multitudes should be found willing to admit so much of the marvels of Eldorado as to see in them a sufficient inducement to justify the search; and others less credulous were perhaps willing to avail themselves of the credulity of the multitude to accomplish plans of conquest and ambition for themselves. Of the latter class, we may imagine the celebrated Sir Walter Raleigh to be one, who, at this time, undertook an expedition for the discovery and conquest of Eldorado.

CHAPTER IV.

SIR WALTER RALEIGH.

WALTER RALEIGH was born in the year 1552 in Devonshire, England, and received a good education, completed by a residence of two years at the University of Oxford. At the age of seventeen, he joined a volunteer corps of English to serve in France in aid of the Protestant cause. Afterwards he served five years in the Netherlands. In 1576, he accompanied his half-brother, Sir Humphrey Gilbert, on an expedition to colonize some part of North America; which expedition was unsuccessful. We next find him commanding a company of the royal troops in Ireland during the rebellion raised by the Earl of Desmond. In consequence of some serious differences which arose between him and his superior officer, he found it necessary to repair to court to justify himself. It was at this time that an incident occurred which recommended him to the notice of Queen Elizabeth, and was the foundation of his fortunes. Raleigh stood in the crowd one day where the queen passed on foot; and when she came to a spot of muddy ground, and hesitated for a moment where to step, he sprang forward, and, throwing from his shoulders his handsome cloak ("his clothes being then," says a quaint old writer, "a considerable part of his estate"), he spread it over the mud, so that the queen passed over dry-shod, doubtless giving an approving look to the handsome and quick-witted young officer. There is another story which is not less probable, because it is not less in character with both the parties. Finding some hopes of the queen's favor glancing on him, he wrote, on a window where it was likely to meet her eye, —

"Fain would I climb, but that I fear to fall."

And her majesty, espying it, wrote underneath, —

"If thy heart fail thee, wherefore climb at all?"

His progress in the queen's favor was enhanced by his demeanor when the matter in dispute between him and his superior officer was brought before the privy council, and each party was called upon to plead his own cause. "What advantage he had in the case in controversy," says a contemporary writer, "I know not; but he had much the better in the manner of telling his tale." The result was, that he became a man of "no slight mark;" "he had gotten the queen's ear in a trice;" "she took him for a kind of oracle," and "loved to hear his reasons to her demands," or, in more modern phrase, "his replies to her questions."

The reign of Queen Elizabeth has been called the heroic age of England. And, let us remember, the England of that day is ours as much as theirs who still bear the name of Englishmen. The men whose gallant deeds we now record were our ancestors, and their glory is our inheritance.

The Reformation in religion had awakened all the energies of the human mind. It had roused against England formidable enemies, among which Spain was the most powerful and the most intensely hostile. She fitted out the famous Armada to invade England; and England, on her part, sent various expeditions to annoy the Spaniards in their lately acquired possessions in South America. These expeditions were generally got up by private adventurers; the queen and her great nobles often taking a share in them. When there was nominal peace with Spain, such enterprises were professedly for discovery and colonization, though the adventurers could not always keep their hands off a rich prize of Spanish property that fell in their way; but, for the last fifteen years of Elizabeth's reign, there was open war between the two powers: and then these expeditions had for their first object the annoyance of Spain, and discovery and colonization for their second.

We find Raleigh, after fortune began to smile upon him, engaged in a second expedition, with Sir Humphrey Gilbert, for discovery and colonization in America. He furnished, from his own means, a ship called "The Raleigh," on board of which he embarked; but when a few days out, a contagious disease breaking out among the crew, he put back into port, and relinquished the expedition. Sir Humphrey, with the rest of the squadron, consisting of five vessels, reached Newfoundland without accident, took possession of the island, and left a colony there. He then set out exploring along the American coast to the south, he himself doing all the work in his little ten-ton cutter; the service being too dangerous for the larger vessels to venture on. He spent the summer in this labor till toward the end of August, when, in a violent storm, one of the larger vessels, "The Delight," was lost with all her crew. "The Golden Hind" and "Squirrel" were now left alone of the five ships. Their provisions were running short, and the season far advanced; and Sir Humphrey reluctantly concluded to lay his course for home. He still continued in the small vessel, though vehemently urged by his friends to remove to the larger one. "I will not forsake my little company, going homeward," said he, "with whom I have passed so many storms and perils." On the 9th of September, the weather was rough, and the cutter was with difficulty kept afloat, struggling with the violence of the waves. When the vessels came within hearing distance, Sir Humphrey cried out to his companions in "The Hind," "Be of good courage: we are as near to heaven by sea as by land." "That night, at about twelve o'clock," writes the historian of the voyage, who was himself one of the adventurers, "the cutter being ahead of us in 'The Golden Hind,' suddenly her lights were out, and the watch cried, 'The general is cast away!' which was too true." So perished a Christian hero. It was a fine end for a mortal man. Let us not call it sad or tragic, but heroic and sublime.

Raleigh, not discouraged by the ill success of this expedition, shortly after obtained letters-patent for another enterprise of the same kind, on the same terms as had been granted to Sir Humphrey. Two barks were sent to explore some undiscovered part of America north of Florida, and look out for a favorable situation for the proposed colony. This expedition landed on Roanoke Island, near the mouth of Albemarle Sound. Having taken formal possession of the country for the Queen of England and her servant Sir Walter Raleigh, they returned, and gave so favorable an account of the country, that her Majesty allowed it to be called Virginia, after herself, a virgin queen. The next year, Raleigh sent out a second expedition, and left a colony of a hundred men, which was the first colony planted by Englishmen on the continent of America. Soon after, Raleigh sent a third expedition with a hundred and fifty colonists; but having now expended forty thousand pounds upon these attempts, and being unable to persist further, or weary of waiting so long for profitable returns, he assigned over his patent to a company of merchants, and withdrew from further prosecution of the enterprise.

The years which followed were the busiest of Raleigh's adventurous life. He bore a distinguished part in the defeat of the Spanish Armada; and, in the triumphant procession to return thanks at St. Paul's for that great deliverance, he was conspicuous as commander of the queen's guard. He was a member of Parliament, yet engaged personally in two naval expeditions against the Spaniards, from which he reaped honor, but no profit; and was at the height of favor with the queen. But, during his absence at sea, the queen discovered that an intrigue existed between Raleigh and one of the maids of honor, which was an offence particularly displeasing to Elizabeth, who loved to fancy that all her handsome young courtiers were too much attached to herself to be capable of loving any other object. Raleigh, on his return, was committed a prisoner to the Tower, and, on being released after a short confinement, retired to his estate in Dorsetshire. It was during this retirement that he formed his scheme for the discovery and conquest of Eldorado. It had long been a subject of meditation to Raleigh, who declares in the dedication of his "History of Guiana," published after his return, that "many years since, he had knowledge, by relation, of that mighty, rich, and beautiful empire of Guiana, and of that great and golden city which the Spaniards call Eldorado, and the naturals Manoa." — "It is not possible," says one of the historians of these events, " that

Raleigh could have believed the existence of such a kingdom. Credulity was not the vice of his nature; but, having formed the project of colonizing Guiana, he employed these fables as baits for vulgar cupidity." Other writers judge him more favorably. It is probably true that he believed in the existence of such a country as Eldorado; but we can hardly suppose that he put faith in all the marvellous details which accompanied the main fact in popular narration.

CHAPTER V.

RALEIGH'S FIRST EXPEDITION.

AS the attempts of Pizarro and Orellana were made by the route of the river of the Amazons, and that of Ribera by the river of Paraguay, Raleigh's approach was by the Orinoco, a river second in size only to the Amazons, and which flows in a course somewhat parallel to that, and some five or ten degrees farther to the north. The region of country where this river discharges itself into the Atlantic was nominally in possession of the Spaniards, though they had but one settlement in what was called the province of Guiana, — the town of St. Joseph, then recently founded; and another on the island of Trinidad, which lies nearly opposite the mouth of the river. Raleigh, arriving at Trinidad, stopped some days to procure such intelligence as the Spaniards resident there could afford him respecting Guiana. He then proceeded to the main land, destroyed the town which the Spaniards had lately built there, and took the governor, Berrio, on board his own ship. He used his prisoner well, and "gathered from him," he says, "as much of Guiana as he knew." Berrio seems to have conversed willingly upon his own adventures in exploring the country, having no suspicion of Raleigh's views. He discouraged Raleigh's attempts to penetrate into the country, telling him that he would find the river unnavigable for his ships, and the nations hostile. These representations had little weight with Raleigh, as he attributed them to a very natural wish on Berrio's part to keep off foreigners from his province; but, on trying to find the entrance to the river, he discovered Berrio's account to be true, so far as related to the difficulties of the navigation. After a thorough search for a practicable entrance, he gave up all hopes of passing in any large vessel, and resolved to go with the boats. He took in his largest boat, with himself, sixty men, including his cousin, his nephew, and principal officers. Another boat carried twenty, and two others ten each. "We had no other means," he says in his account afterward published, "but to carry victual for a month in the same, and also to lodge therein as we could, and to boil and dress our meat."

The Orinoco, at nearly forty leagues from the sea, forms, like the Nile, a kind of fan, strewed over with a multitude of little islands, that divide it into numerous branches and channels, and force it to discharge itself through this labyrinth into the sea by an infinity of mouths, occupying an extent of more than sixty leagues. "The Indians who inhabit those islands," says Raleigh, "in the summer, have houses upon the ground, as in other places; in the winter they dwell upon the trees, where they build very artificial towns and villages: for, between May and September, the river rises to thirty feet upright, and then are those islands overflowed twenty feet high above the level of the ground; and for this cause they are enforced to live in this manner. They use the tops of palmitoes for bread; and kill deer, fish, and porks for the rest of their sustenance." Raleigh's account is confirmed by later travellers. Humboldt says, "The navigator, in proceeding along the channels of the delta of the Orinoco at night, sees with surprise the summits of the palm-trees illuminated by large fires. These are the habitations of the Guaraons, which are suspended from the trees. These tribes hang up mats in the air, which they fill with earth, and kindle, on a layer of moist clay, the fire necessary for their household wants."

Passing up with the flood, and anchoring during the ebb, Raleigh and his companions went on, till on the third day their galley grounded, and stuck so fast, that they feared their discovery must end there, and they be left to inhabit, like rooks upon trees, with these nations; but on the morrow, after casting out all her ballast, with tugging and hauling to and fro, they got her afloat. After four days more, they got beyond the influence of the tide, and were forced to row against a violent current, till they began to despair; the weather being excessively hot, and the river bordered with high trees, that kept away the air. Their provisions began to fail them; but some relief they found by shooting birds of all colors, — carnation, crimson, orange, purple, and of all other sorts, both simple and mixed. An old Indian whom they had pressed into their service was a faithful guide to them, and brought them to an Indian village, where they got a supply of bread, fish, and fowl. They were thus encouraged to persevere, and next day captured two canoes laden with bread, "and divers baskets of roots, which were excellent meat." Probably these roots were no other than potatoes;

for the mountains of Quito, to which Sir Walter was now approaching, were the native country of the potato, and the region from whence it was first introduced into Europe. The Spaniards and Portuguese introduced it earlier than the English; but to Raleigh belongs the credit of making it known to his countrymen. The story is, that Sir Walter, on his return home, had some of the roots planted in his garden at Youghal, in Ireland, and that his gardener was sadly disappointed in autumn on tasting the apples of the "fine American fruit," and proceeded to root up the "useless weeds," when he discovered the tubers.

Raleigh treated the natives with humanity, and, in turn, received friendly treatment from them. The chiefs told him fine stories about the gold-mines; but, unfortunately, the gold was not to be had without labor, and the adventurers were in no condition to undertake mining operations. What they wanted was to find a region like Mexico or Peru, only richer, where gold might be found, not in the rocks or the bowels of the earth, but in possession of the natives, in the form of barbaric ornaments that they would freely barter for European articles, or images of their gods, such as Christians might seize and carry away with an approving conscience.

Thus far, their search for such a region had been unsuccessful, and their only hope was of reaching it by farther explorations. But the river was rising daily, and the current flowed with such rapidity, that they saw clearly, if it went on to increase as it had done for some time past, it must soon debar all farther progress.

Raleigh found by talking with the chiefs that they were all hostile to the Spaniards, and willing enough to promise him their aid in driving them out of the country. He accordingly told them that he was sent by a great and virtuous queen to deliver them from the tyranny of the Spaniards. He also learned that the Indians with whom he was conversing were an oppressed race, having been conquered by a nation who dwelt beyond the mountains, — a nation who wore large coats, and hats of crimson color, and whose houses had many rooms, one over the other. They were called the Eperumei; and against them all the other tribes would gladly combine, for they were the general oppressors. Moreover, the country of these Eperumei abounded in gold and all other good things.

He continued to make daily efforts to ascend the river, and to explore the tributary streams, but found his progress debarred in some quarters by the rapid current of the swollen streams, and in others by falls in the rivers. The falls of one of the tributaries of the Orinoco, the Caroli, he describes as "a wonderful breach of waters, running in three parts; and there appeared some ten or twelve over-falls in sight, every one as high over the other as a church-tower." He was informed that the lake from which the river issued was above a day's journey for one of their canoes to cross, which he computed at about forty miles; that many rivers fall into it, and great store of grains of gold was found in those rivers. On one of these rivers, he was told, a nation of people dwell "whose heads appear not above their shoulders;" which, he says, "though it may be thought a mere fable, yet, for my own part, I am resolved it is true, because every child in those provinces affirm the same. They are reported to have their eyes in their shoulders, and their mouths in the middle of their breasts, and that a long train of hair groweth backward between their shoulders." Raleigh adds, "It was not my chance to hear of them till I was come away. If I had but spoken one word of it while I was there, I might have brought one of them with me to put the matter out of doubt." It might have been more satisfactory for the philosophers if he had done so; but his word was quite enough for the poets. One of that class, and the greatest of all, William Shakspeare, was, at that very time, writing plays for the gratification of Raleigh's gracious mistress and her subjects, and eagerly availed himself of this new-discovered tribe to introduce one of them in his play of "The Tempest," under the name of Caliban. He also makes Othello tell the gentle Desdemona "of most disastrous chances, and of the cannibals that each other eat'; the Anthropophagi, and men whose heads do grow beneath their shoulders." Nor are these the only instances in which we think we trace the influence of the romantic adventurer on the susceptible poet. The name of the divinity whom Caliban calls "my dam's God Setebos" occurs in Raleigh's narrative as the name of an Indian tribe; and Trinculo's plan of taking Caliban to England to make a show of him seems borrowed from this hint of Raleigh's. In his days of prosperity, Raleigh instituted a meeting of intellectual men at "The Mermaid," a celebrated tavern. To this club, Shakspeare, Beaumont, Fletcher, Jonson, Selden, Donne, and other distinguished literary men, were accustomed to repair; and here doubtless the adventures and discoveries of Sir Walter, set forth with that talent of which his writings furnish abundant proof, often engaged the listening group. Raleigh was then forty-eight, and Shakspeare thirty-six, years old. But, in justice to Raleigh, it should be added, that he did not invent these stories, and that later travellers and missionaries testify that such tales were current among the Indians, though as yet no specimen of the tribe has been seen by trustworthy narrators.

Raleigh now found that he must bring his westward progress to a conclusion: " for no half-day passed but the river began to rage and overflow very fearfully; and the rains came down in terrible showers, and gusts in great abundance, and men began to cry out for want of shift; for no man had place to bestow any other apparel than that which he wore on his back, and that was thoroughly washed on his body for the most part ten times a day; and we had now been near a month, every day passing to the westward, farther from our ships." They turned back, therefore, and, passing down the stream, went, without labor and against the wind, little less than one hundred miles a day. They stopped occasionally, both for provisions, and for conference with the natives. In particular, one old chief, with whom he had conferred formerly on his ascent, gave him the confidential communication, that the attempt to attack the city of Manoa, at that time, was desperate; for neither the time of the year was favorable, nor had he nearly a sufficient force. He advised, that, forbearing any further attempts at that time, Raleigh should rest satisfied with the information he had gained, and return to his own country for a larger force, with which to come again the next year, and unite all the tribes which were hostile to the Eperumei, or people of Manoa, and by their aid make an easy conquest of them. The old chief added, that, for his part and his people's, they wanted no share of the spoils of gold or precious stones: they only wanted to be avenged on their enemies, and to rescue from them their women whom the Eperumei had carried away in their frequent incursions; "so that, whereas they were wont to have ten or twelve wives apiece, they were now enforced to content themselves with three or four."

Raleigh met with no material misadventure in his way down the river; and, though a storm attacked them the same night, they anchored in the mouth of the river; so that, in spite of every shelter they could derive from the shores, the galley "had as much to do to live as could be, and there wanted little of her sinking, and all those in her:" yet next day they arrived safe at the Island of Trinidad, and found the ships at anchor, "than which," says Raleigh, "there was never to us a more joyful sight."

Raleigh was not favorably received by the queen on his return, nor was he welcomed with any popular applause; for he had brought home no booty, and his account of the riches of the land into which he had led the way was received with suspicion. He published it under this boastful title: "The Discovery of the large, rich, and beautiful Empire of Guiana; with a relation of the great and Golden City of Manoa, which the Spaniards call Eldorado. Performed by Sir Walter Raleigh." In spite of all the great promises which he held out, the acknowledgment that he had made a losing voyage tended to abate that spirit of cupidity and enterprise which he wished to excite.

Sir Walter's history of his expedition contains, besides the marvels already cited, numerous others, some of which have a basis of fact, others not. Of the former kind is his account of oysters growing on trees. He says, "We arrived at Trinidado the 22d of March, casting anchor at Port Curiapan. I left the ships, and kept by the shore in my barge, the better to understand the rivers, watering-places, and ports of the island. In the way, I passed divers little brooks of fresh water, and one salt river, that had store of oysters upon the branches of the trees. All their oysters grow upon those boughs and sprays, and not on the ground. The like is commonly seen in the West Indies and elsewhere."

Upon this narrative, Sir Robert Schomburgh, a late explorer, has the following remark: "The first accounts brought to Europe, of oysters growing on trees, raised as great astonishment as the relation of Eldorado itself; and to those who were unacquainted with the fact that these mollusks select the branches of the tree, on which they fix themselves during high water, when the branches are immersed, it may certainly sound strange, that shells, which we know live in Europe on banks in the depths of the sea, should be found in the West Indies on the branches of trees. They attach themselves chiefly to the mangrove-tree, which grows along the shore of the sea, and rivers of brackish water, and covers immense tracts of coast; rooting and vegetating in a manner peculiar to itself, even as far as low-water mark. The water flowing off during ebb leaves the branches, with the oysters attached to them, high and dry."

Respecting the Republic of Amazons, Sir Walter says, "I made inquiry among the most ancient and best travelled of the Orenoqueponi; and I was very desirous to understand the truth of those warlike women, because of some it is believed, of others not. I will set down what hath been delivered me for truth of those women; and I spake with a cacique, or lord of people, who said that he had been in the river, and beyond it also. The nations of those women are on the south side of the river, in the province of Topago; and their chiefest strengths and retreats are in the islands of said river. They accompany with men but once in a year, and for the time of one month, which, I gather from their relation, to be in April. At that time, all the kings of the borders assemble, and the queens of the Amazons; and, after the queens have chosen, the rest cast lots for their valentines. This one month they feast, dance, and drink of their wines in abundance; and, the moon being done, they all depart to their own provinces. If a son be born, they return him to the father; if a daughter, they nourish it and retain it, all being desirous to increase their own sex and kind. They carry on wars, and are very blood-thirsty and cruel."

Sir Robert Schomburgh, who explored these regions extensively between the years 1835 and 1844, says, in reference to this subject, "The result of this fatiguing and perilous journey has only strengthened our conviction that this republic of women was one of those inventions, designed merely to enhance the wonders, of which the new world was regarded as the seat. It would, however, be unjust to condemn Raleigh's proneness to a belief in their existence, when we find that Condamine believed in them; that Humboldt hesitated to decide against them; and that even Southey, the learned historian of Brazil, makes this remark, "Had we never heard of the Amazons of antiquity, I should, without hesitation, believe in those of America. Their existence is not the less likely for that reason; and yet it must be admitted, that the probable truth is made to appear suspicious by its resemblance to a known fable."

CHAPTER VI.

RALEIGH'S ADVENTURES CONTINUED.

WHEN Raleigh, on his first arrival, broke up the Spanish settlement in Trinidad, he took Berrio, the governor, prisoner, and carried him with him in his voyage up the river. Berrio seems to have borne his fate with good temper, and conciliated the good will of Raleigh; so that, when the expedition returned to the mouth of the river, he was set at liberty, and collected his little colony again. Berrio probably shared the same belief as Raleigh in the existence of the kingdom of Eldorado within the limits of his province, and was naturally desirous to avail himself of the respite which he gained by the termination of Raleigh's expedition, until it should return in greater force to penetrate to Eldorado, and take possession for himself and his countrymen. With these views, he sent an officer of his, Domingo de Vera, to Spain, to levy men; sending, according to Raleigh's account, "divers images, as well of men as of beasts, birds, and fishes, cunningly wrought in gold," in hopes to persuade the king to yield him some further help. This agent was more successful than Raleigh in obtaining belief. He is described as a man of great ability, and little scrupulous as to truth. Having been favorably received by the government, he attracted notice by appearing in a singular dress, which, as he was of great stature, and rode always a great horse, drew all eyes, and made him generally known as the Indian chief of Eldorado and the rich lands. Some trinkets in gold he displayed, of Indian workmanship, and some emeralds, which he had brought from America, and promised stores of both; and, by the aid of influential persons, he obtained seventy thousand dollars at Madrid, and five thousand afterwards at Seville, authority to raise any number of adventurers (though Berrio had asked only for three hundred men), and five good ships to carry them out. Adventurers flocked to him in Toledo, La Mancha, and Estremadura. The expedition was beyond example popular. Twenty captains of infantry, who had served in Italy and Flanders, joined it. Not only those who had their fortunes to seek were deluded: men of good birth and expectations left all to engage in the conquest of Eldorado; and fathers of families gave up their employments, and sold their goods, and embarked with their wives and children. Solicitations and bribes were made use of by eager volunteers. The whole expedition consisted of more than two thousand persons.

They reached Trinidad after a prosperous voyage, and took possession of the town. The little mischief which Raleigh had done had been easily repaired; for indeed there was little that he could do. The place did not contain thirty families, and the strangers were to find shelter as they could. Rations of biscuit and salt meat, pulse, or rice, were served out to them; but, to diminish the consumption as much as possible, detachments were sent off in canoes to the main land, where Berrio had founded the town of St. Thomas. Some flotillas effected their progress safely; but one, which consisted of six canoes, met with bad weather, and only three succeeded in entering the river, after throwing their cargoes overboard. The others made the nearest shore, where they were descried by the Caribs, a fierce tribe of natives, who slew them all, except a few women whom they carried away, and one soldier, who escaped to relate the fate of his companions.

The city of St. Thomas contained at that time four

hundred men, besides women and children. Berrio, to prepare the way for the discovery and conquest of Eldorado, sent out small parties of the new-comers under experienced persons, that they might be seasoned to the difficulties which they would have to undergo, and learn how to conduct themselves in their intercourse with the Indians. They were to spread the news that the king had sent out many Spaniards, and a large supply of axes, caps, hawk-bells, looking-glasses, combs, and such other articles of traffic as were in most request. They saw no appearance of those riches which Raleigh had heard of, nor of that plenty which he had found. The people with whom they met had but a scanty subsistence for themselves, and so little of gold or silver or any thing else to barter for the hatchets and trinkets of the Spaniards, that they were glad of the chance to labor as boatmen, or give their children, in exchange for them.

Berrio was not discouraged by the result of these journeys. Like Raleigh, he was persuaded that the great and golden city stood on the banks of a great lake, from which the River Caroli issued, about twelve leagues east of the mouth whereof his town was placed. A force of eight hundred men was now ordered on the discovery. The command was given to Correa, an officer accustomed to Indian warfare. Three Franciscan monks, and a lay brother of the same order, accompanied the expedition. Having reached a spot where the country was somewhat elevated, and the temperature cooler than in the region they had passed, they hutted themselves on a sort of prairie, and halted there in the hope that rest might restore those who began to feel the effect of an unwholesome climate. The natives not only abstained from any acts of hostility, but supplied them with fruits, and a sort of cassava (tapioca). This they did in sure knowledge that disease would soon subdue these new-come Spaniards to their hands. It was not long before a malignant fever broke out among the adventurers, which carried off a third part of their number. One comfort only was left them: the friars continued every day to perform mass in a place where all the sufferers could hear it; and no person died without performing and receiving all the offices which the Romish Church has enjoined. Correa himself sank under the disease. He might possibly have escaped it, acclimated as he was, if he had not overtasked himself when food was to be sought from a distance, and carried heavy loads to spare those who were less equal to the labor: for now the crafty Indians no longer brought supplies, but left the weakened Spaniards to provide for themselves as they could; and when Correa was dead, of whom, as a man accustomed to Indian war, they stood in fear, they collected their forces, and fell upon the Spaniards, who apprehended no danger, and were most of them incapable of making any defence. The plan appears to have been concerted with a young Indian chief who accompanied the Spaniards under pretence of friendship; and the women whom the Indians brought with them to carry home the spoils of their enemies bore their part with stones and stakes in the easy slaughter. The Spaniards who escaped the first attack fled with all speed, some without weapons, and some without strength to use them. The friars were the last to fly. With the soldiers to protect them, they brought off their portable altar, two crosses, and a crucifix. No attempt at resistance was made, except when a fugitive fell by the way. The word then passed for one of the fathers: some soldiers stood with their muskets to protect him while he hastily confessed and absolved the poor wretch, whom his countrymen then commended to God, and left to the mercy of the Indians.

In some places, the enemy set fire to the grass and

shrubbery, which in that climate grow with extreme luxuriance; by which means many of this miserable expedition perished. Not quite thirty out of the whole number got safe back to the town of St. Thomas. That place was in a deplorable state, suffering at once from a contagious disease and from a scarcity of provisions. To add to the distress, about a hundred persons more had just arrived from Trinidad. They came of necessity; for there were no longer supplies of food at Trinidad to sustain them. But they came with high-raised hopes, only repining at their ill luck in not having been in the first expedition, by which they supposed the first spoils of Eldorado had already been shared. They arrived like skeletons at a city of death. Not only were provisions scarce, but the supply of salt had altogether failed; and, without it, health in that climate cannot be preserved. To add to their misery, the shoes had all been consumed, and the country was infested by that insect (the chigua) which burrows in the feet, and attacks the flesh wherever the slightest wound gives it access. The torment occasioned by these insects was such, that the men willingly submitted to the only remedy they knew of, and had the sores cauterized with hot iron.

Among those who had come from Spain to enter

upon this land of promise, there was a "beata," or pious woman, who had been attached to a convent in Madrid, and accompanied a married daughter and her husband on this unhappy adventure, and devoted herself to the service of the sick. Some of the women, and she among them, looking upon the governor, Berrio, as the cause of their miseries, and thinking, that, as long as he lived, there was no hope of their escaping from this fatal place, resolved to murder him, and provided themselves with knives for the purpose. The indignation against him was so general, that they hesitated not to impart their design to one of the friars; and, luckily for Berrio, he interposed his influence to prevent it. One of the women who had sold her possessions in Spain to join the expedition made her way to the governor when the officers and friars were with him, and, emptying upon the ground before him a bag which contained one hundred and fifty doubloons, said, "Tyrant, take what is left, since you have brought us here to die." Berrio replied, with less of anger than of distress in his countenance, "I gave no orders to Domingo de Vera that he should bring more than three hundred men." He offered no opposition to the departure of such as would. Many who had strength or resolution enough trusted themselves to the river in such canoes as they could find, without boatmen or pilot, and endeavored to make their way back to Trinidad; some perishing by the hands of the natives, others by drowning, others by hunger, on the marshy shores which they reached. Vera soon died of a painful disease in Trinidad; and Berrio did not long survive him. Such was the issue of this great attempt for the conquest of the golden empire; " of which," says an old Spanish historian, " it may be said, that it was like Nebuchadnezzar's image, beginning in gold, but continuing through baser metal, till it ended in rude iron and base clay."

CHAPTER VII.

RALEIGH'S SECOND EXPEDITION.

RALEIGH'S first voyage disappointed every one but himself. He pretended to have obtained satisfactory evidence of the existence of Eldorado, and information of the place where it was; also proof of the existence of mines of gold; and to have conciliated the good will of the natives, and secured their co-operation with him in any future attempt. But he had brought home no gold; the shining stones which his followers had abundantly supplied themselves with were found to be worthless: and there was no evidence of the existence of a native sovereignty as far advanced in civilization and refinement as the Mexicans and Peruvians, the conquest of which would reflect as much glory upon the English name as the achievements of Cortez and Pizarro had reflected upon that of Spain. Raleigh's boastful representations, therefore, failed of effect. None of his countrymen were inclined to join with him in a further prosecution of the enterprise; and the subject was dropped for the time.

Raleigh was soon restored to favor, and employed in the naval expeditions against Spain which took place at this time. He greatly distinguished himself on several occasions, and was in high favor with Queen Elizabeth till her death; but, with the accession of James, his fortunes fell. He was accused (whether justly or not is still doubtful) of being concerned in treasonable plots against the king, and was brought to trial, found guilty, condemned to death, and committed prisoner to the Tower to await the execution of his sentence.

Raleigh, withdrawn from active labors by his imprisonment, was not idle. He turned to intellectual pursuits, and, with many minor pieces in prose and verse, executed his greatest work, "The History of the World," — a project of such vast extent, that the bare idea of his undertaking it excites our admiration. As an author, he stands on an eminence as high as that which he obtained in other paths. Hume says, "He is the best model of our ancient style;" and Hallam confirms the judgment. His imprisonment lasted thirteen years. At the expiration of that time, he had influence to have his sentence so far remitted as to allow him to go on a second expedition in search of Eldorado. Twenty years had elapsed since the former expedition; and the present was of a magnitude more like a national enterprise than a private one. Sir Walter's own ship, "The Destiny," carried thirty-six guns and two hundred men. There were six other vessels, carrying from twenty-five guns to three each. Raleigh embarked all his means in this expedition. His eldest son commanded one of the ships; and eighty of his companions were gentlemen volunteers and adventurers, many of them his relations.

Those who have thoughtfully considered Raleigh's career have seen reason to doubt whether he really believed the stories which he was so anxious to impress upon others. They have thought it more likely that his real object was to emulate the fame of Cortez and Pizarro; to dispossess Spain of some portion of her conquests in South America, and transfer them to his own country. This latter object was admissible at the time of his first expedition, because Spain and England were then at war; but was not so on the second, as the two nations were then at peace. But Raleigh had reason to think, that, if he could succeed in his object, there was no danger of his being called to very strict account respecting his measures.

He arrived off the coast of Guiana on the 12th of November, 1617; having had a long and disastrous voyage. One ship had left him, and returned home; another had foundered; forty-two of his men had died; many were suffering from sickness, and himself among the number. But he found the Indians friendly, and not forgetful of his former visit. He writes to his wife, "To tell you that I might be here king of the country were a vanity; but my name hath still lived among them here. They feed me with fresh meat, and all that the country yields. All offer to obey me."

Being too feeble from sickness to go himself, he sent forward an expedition, under Capt. Keymis, to enter the Orinoco, and take possession of the mines. Five companies of fifty men each, in five shallops, composed the expedition; Raleigh, with the remainder of his vessels, repairing to Trinidad to await the result.

Since Raleigh's former expedition, the Spaniards had made a settlement upon the main land, and founded a town to which they gave the name of St.

Thomas. The governor resided there, and there were in all about five hundred inhabitants. On the 12th of January, the English flotilla reached a part of the river twelve leagues from St. Thomas; and an Indian fisherman carried the alarm to that place. The governor, Palameque, mustered immediately the little force which he had at hand. This consisted of fifty-seven men only. Messengers were sent to summon those men who were at their farms, and two horsemen were sent out to watch the invaders' movements.

At eleven in the forenoon, the vessels anchored about a league from the town. The men landed, and the scouts hastened back with the intelligence. A Spanish officer, with ten men, was placed in ambush near the city. As soon as he was informed of the direction which the English were taking, he cut a match-cord in pieces, which he lighted at dark, and placed at intervals, where they might deceive the invaders by presenting the appearance of a greater force. The first discharge was from two pieces of cannon against the boats. The Spaniard, with his little band, then opened his fire upon the troops, and kept it up from the bushes as he retired before them. This skirmishing continued about an hour and a half, till he had fallen back to the place where the governor and his people were drawn up, at the entrance of the city, to make a stand. It was now nine at night. Raleigh says, in his account of the action, that some of the English, at the first charge, began to pause and recoil shamefully; whereupon his son, not tarrying for any musketeers, ran up at the head of a company of pikemen, and received a shot wound. Pressing then upon a Spanish captain with his sword, the Spaniard, taking the small end of his musket in his hand, struck him on the head with the stock, and felled him. His last words were, " Lord, have mercy upon me, and prosper the enterprise ! " and his death was instantly avenged by his sergeant, who thrust the Spaniard through with his halberd. In the heat of the fight, and in the confusion which the darkness occasioned, the Spanish commander was separated from his people, and slain. The Spaniards, however, had the advantage of knowing the ground; and, betaking themselves to the houses, they fired from them on the English, and killed many, till the assailants set fire to the houses; thus depriving themselves of that booty which was their main object. The English were now masters of the place; the remainder of the defendants, with the women and children, under the command of Grados, the officer who had deported himself so well in the first ambush, effecting their escape across the river. Grados stationed them at a place about ten miles distant from the town, where a few slight huts were erected for the women and children.

The captors searched in vain for gold in the city; but they had an idea that there was a rich gold-mine a short distance up the river. Accordingly, two launches, with twenty or thirty men in each, were despatched up the Orinoco. They came to the mouth of the creek, which led to the place where Grados had hutted the women and children; and the largest of the launches was about to enter, when Grados, who had posted nine of the invalids in ambush there, with about as many Indian bowmen, fired upon them so unexpectedly, and with such good aim, that only one of the crew is said to have escaped unhurt. The other launch also suffered some loss. Three days after, three launches were sent to take vengeance for this defeat; but Grados had removed his charge some two leagues into the country, and these vessels went up the river about a hundred leagues, treating with the Indians, to whom they made presents and larger promises, and after eighteen or twenty days returned, having effected nothing of importance.

The English had now been four weeks in the city, annoyed by the Spaniards and Indians, and losing many of their men, cut off in their foraging excursions by ambushes. After the unsuccessful attempt to discover the mine, no further effort was made for that purpose; Keymis alleging in his excuse, that "the Spaniards, being gone off in a whole body, lay in the woods between the mine and us, and it was impossible, except they had been beaten out of the country, to pass up the woods and craggy hills without the loss of the commanders, without whom the rest would easily be cut to pieces." The English, accordingly, retreated from the city, setting fire to the few houses that remained, and promising the Indians, as they went, that they would return next year, and complete the destruction of the Spaniards.

Raleigh was by no means satisfied with Keymis's excuses for his failure to discover the mine, and reproached him with so much severity, that Keymis, after the interview, retired to his cabin, and shot himself through the heart.

When Raleigh arrived in England, he found that the tidings of his attack on the Spaniards, and the utter failure of his expedition, had reached there before him. The Spanish ambassador was clamorous for punishment on what he called a piratical proceeding; and the king and the nation, who might have pardoned a successful adventurer, had no indulgence to extend to one so much the reverse. Finding a proclámation had been issued for his arrest, Raleigh endeavored to escape to France, but was taken in the attempt, and committed close prisoner to the Tower. He was made a victim to court intrigue. The weak king, James, was then negotiating a Spanish match for his son, and, to gratify the King of Spain and his court, sacrificed one of the noblest of his subjects. Without being put on trial for his late transactions, Raleigh's old sentence, which had been suspended sixteen years, was revived against him; and on the 29th of October, 1618, four months after his arrival, he was beheaded on the scaffold.

The fate of Raleigh caused a great sensation at the time, and has not yet ceased to excite emotion. The poet Thomson, in his " Summer," finely alludes to the various circumstances of his history, which we have briefly recorded: —

> "But who can speak
> The numerous worthies of the 'Maiden reign'?
> In Raleigh mark their every glory mixed, —
> Raleigh, the scourge of Spain, whose breast with all
> The sage, the patriot, and the hero, burned.

Nor sunk his vigor when a coward reign
The warrior fettered, and at last resigned
To glut the vengeance of a vanquished foe:
Then, active still and unrestrained, his mind
Explored the vast extent of ages past,
And with his prison-hours enriched the world;
Yet found no times in all the long research
So glorious or so base as those he proved
In which he conquered and in which he bled."

CHAPTER VIII.

THE FRENCH PHILOSOPHERS.

AFTER so many abortive attempts to reach the Golden Empire, the ardor of research greatly abated. No expeditions, composed of considerable numbers, have since embarked in the enterprise; but from time to time, for the century succeeding Raleigh's last attempt, private expeditions were undertaken and encouraged by provincial governors; and several hundred persons perished miserably in those fruitless endeavors.

The adventure we are now about to record was of an entirely different character in respect to its objects and the means employed; but it occupied the same field of action, and called into exercise the same qualities of courage and endurance.

In 1735, the French Academy of Science made arrangements for sending out two commissions of learned men to different and distant parts of the world to make measurements, with a view to determining the dimensions and figure of the earth. The great astronomer, Sir Isaac Newton, had deduced from theory, and ventured to maintain, that the earth was not a perfect globe, but a spheroid; that is, a globe flattened at the poles. For a long time after Newton's splendid discoveries in astronomy, a degree of national jealousy prevented the French philosophers from accepting his conclusions; and they were not displeased to find, when they could, facts opposed to them. Now, there were some supposed facts which were incompatible with this idea of Newton's, that the earth was flattened at the poles. The point was capable of being demonstrated by measurements, with instruments, on the surface; for, if his theory was true, a degree of latitude would be longer in the northern parts of the globe than in the regions about the equator.

We must not allow our story to become a scientific essay; and yet we should like to give our readers, if we could, some idea of the principle on which this process, which is called the measurement of an arc of the meridian, was expected to show the magnitude and form of the earth. We all know that geographical latitude means the position of places north or south of the equator, and is determined by reference to the north or pole star. A person south of the equator would not see the pole-star at all. One at the equator, looking at the pole-star, would see it, if no intervening object prevented, in the horizon. Advancing northward, he would see it apparently rise, and advance toward him. As he proceeded, it would continue to rise. When he had traversed half the distance to the pole, he would see the pole-star about as we see it in Boston; that is, nearly midway between the horizon and the zenith: and, when he had reached the pole, he would see the pole-star directly over his head. Dividing the quarter circle which the star has moved through into ninety parts, we say, when the star has ascended one-ninetieth part, that the observer has travelled over one degree of latitude. When the observer has reached Boston, he has passed over somewhat more than forty-two degrees, and, when he has reached the north-pole, ninety degrees, of latitude. Thus we measure our latitude over the earth's surface by reference to a circle in the heavens; and, because the portions into which we divide that circle are equal, we infer that the portions of the earth's surface which correspond to them are equal. This would be true if the earth were a perfect globe:

but if the earth be a spheroid, as Newton's theory requires it to be, it would *not* be true; for that portion of the earth's surface which is flattened will have less curvature than that which is not so, and less still than that portion which is protuberant. The degrees of least curvature will be longest, and those of greatest curvature shortest; that is, one would have to travel farther on the flattened part of the earth to see any difference in the position of the north-star than in those parts where the curvature is greater. So a degree of latitude near the pole, if determined by the position of the north-star, would be found, by actual measurement, to be longer than one similarly determined at the equator. It was to ascertain whether the fact was so that the two scientific expeditions were sent out.

The party which was sent to the northern regions travelled over snow and ice, swamps and morasses, to the arctic circle, and fixed their station at Tornea, in Lapland. The frozen surface of the river afforded them a convenient level for fixing what is called by surveyors the base line. The cold was so intense, that the glass froze to the mouth when they drank, and the metallic measuring rod to the hand. In spite, however, of perils and discomforts, they persevered in their task, and brought back careful measurements of a degree in latitude 66° north, to be compared with those made by the other party at the equator, whose movements we propose more particularly to follow.

Before we take leave of the northern commissioners, however, we will mention another method they took of demonstrating the same fact. If the earth be depressed at the poles, it must follow that bodies will weigh heavier there, because they are nearer the centre of the earth. But how could they test this fact, when all weights would be increased alike, — the pound of feathers and the pound of lead? The question was settled by observing the oscillation of a pendulum. The observers near the pole found that the pendulum vibrated faster than usual, because, being nearer the centre of the earth, the attracting power was increased. To balance this, they had to lengthen the pendulum; and the extent to which they had to do this measured the difference between the earth's diameter at the poles, and that in the latitude from which they came.

The commissioners who were sent to the equatorial regions were Messrs. Bouguer, La Condamine, and Godin, the last of whom was accompanied by his wife. Two Spanish officers, Messrs. Juan and De Ulloa, joined the commission. The party arrived at Quito in June, 1736, about two hundred years after Gonzalo Pizarro started from the same place in his search for Eldorado. In the interval, the country had become nominally Christian. The city was the seat of a bishopric, an audience royal, and other courts of justice; contained many churches and convents, and two colleges. But the population was almost entirely composed of Indians, who lived in a manner but very little different from that of their ancestors at the time of the conquest. Cuença was the place next in importance to the capital; and there, or in its neighborhood, the chief labors of the commission were transacted. They were conducted under difficulties as great as those of their colleagues in the frozen regions of the north, but of a different sort. The inhabitants of the country were jealous of the French commissioners, and supposed them to be either heretics or sorcerers, and to have come in search of gold-mines. Even persons connected with the administration employed themselves in stirring up the minds of the people, till at last, in a riotous assemblage at a bullfight, the surgeon of the French commissioners was killed. After tedious and troublesome legal proceedings, the perpetrators were let off with a nominal punishment. Notwithstanding every difficulty, the commissioners completed their work in a satisfactory manner, spending in all eight years in the task, including the voyages out and home.

The commissioners who had made the northern measurements reported the length of the degree at 66° north latitude to be 57.422 toises; Messrs. Bouguer and La Condamine, the equatorial degree, 56.753 toises; showing a difference of 669 toises, or $4,389\frac{3}{4}$ feet. The difference, as corrected by later measurements, is stated by recent authorities at 3,662 English feet; by which amount the polar degree exceeds the equatorial. Thus Newton's theory was confirmed.

His scientific labors having been finished, La Condamine conceived the idea of returning home by way of the Amazon River; though difficulties attended the project, which we who live in a land of mighty rivers, traversed by steamboats, can hardly imagine. The only means of navigating the upper waters of the river was by rafts or canoes; the latter capable of containing but one or two persons, besides a crew of seven or eight boatmen. The only persons who were in the habit of passing up and down the river were the Jesuit missionaries, who made their periodical visits to their stations along its banks. A young

Spanish gentleman, Don Pedro Maldonado, who at first eagerly caught at the idea of accompanying the French philosopher on his homeward route by way of the river, was almost discouraged by the dissuasives urged by his family and friends, and seemed inclined to withdraw from the enterprise; so dangerous was the untried route esteemed. It was, however, at length resolved that they should hazard the adventure; and a place of rendezvous was appointed at a village on the river. On the 4th of July, 1743, La Condamine commenced his descent of one of the streams which flow into the great river of the Amazons. The stream was too precipitous in its descent to be navigated by boats of any kind, and the only method used was by rafts. These are made of a light kind of wood, or rather cane, similar to the bamboo, the single pieces of which are fastened together by rushes, in such a manner, that they yield to every shock of moderate violence, and consequently are not subject to be separated even by the strongest. On such a conveyance, the French philosopher glided down the stream of the Chuchunga, occasionally stopping on its banks for a day or two at a time to allow the waters to abate, and admit of passing a dangerous rapid more safely; and sometimes getting fast on the shallows, and requiring to be drawn off by ropes by the Indian boatmen. It was not till the 19th of July that he entered the main river at Laguna, where he found his friend Maldonado, who had been waiting for him some weeks.

On the 23d of July, 1743, they embarked in two canoes of forty-two and forty-four feet long, each formed out of one single trunk of a tree, and each provided with a crew of eight rowers. They continued their course night and day, in hopes to reach, before their departure, the brigantines of the missionaries, in which they used to send once a year, to Pará, the cacao which they collected in their missions, and for which they got, in return, supplies of European articles of necessity.

On the 25th of July, La Condamine and his companion passed the village of a tribe of Indians lately brought under subjection, and in all the wildness of savage life: on the 27th, they reached another more advanced in civilization, yet not so far as to have abandoned their savage practices of artificially flattening their heads, and elongating their ears. The 1st of August, they landed at a missionary station, where they found numerous Indians assembled, and some tribes so entirely barbarous as to be destitute of clothing for either sex. "There are in the interior," the narration goes on to say, "some tribes which devour the prisoners taken in war; but there are none such on the banks of the river."

After leaving this station, they sailed day and night, equal to seven or eight days' journey, without seeing any habitation. On the 5th of August, they arrived at the first of the Portuguese missionary stations, where they procured larger and more commodious boats than those in which they had advanced hitherto. Here they began to see the first signs of the benefits of access to European sources of supply, by means of the vessel which went every year from Pará to Lisbon. They tarried six days at the last of the missionary stations, and again made a change of boats and of Indian crews. On the 28th August, being yet six hundred miles from the sea, they perceived the ebb and flow of the tide.

On the 19th September, they arrived at Pará, which La Condamine describes as a great and beautiful city, built of stone, and enjoying a commerce with Lisbon, which made it flourishing and increasing. He observes, "It is, perhaps, the only European settlement where silver does not pass for money; the whole currency being cocoa." He adds in a note, "Specie currency has been since introduced."

The Portuguese authorities received the philosophers with all the civilities and hospitalities due to persons honored with the special protection and countenance of two great nations,—France and Spain. The cannon were fired; and the soldiers of the garrison, with the governor of the province at their head, turned out to receive them. The governor had received orders from the home government to pay all their expenses, and to furnish them every thing requisite for their comfort and assistance in their researches. La Condamine remained three months at Pará; and then, declining the urgent request of the governor to embark in a Portuguese vessel for home by way of Lisbon, he embarked in a boat rowed by twenty-two Indians, under the command of a Portuguese officer, to coast along the shores of the continent to the French colony of Cayenne.

The city of Pará from whence he embarked is not situated upon the Amazon River, but upon what is called the River of Pará, which branches off from the Amazon near its mouth, and discharges itself into the sea at a distance of more than a hundred miles east of the Amazon. The intervening land is an island called Marajo, along the coast of which La Condamine and his party steered till they came to the place where the Amazon River discharges into the sea that vast bulk of waters which has been swelled by the contributions of numerous tributaries throughout a course of more than three thousand miles in length. It here meets the current which runs along the north-eastern coast of Brazil, and gives rise to that phenomenon which is called by the Indians Pororoca. The river and the current, having both great rapidity, and meeting nearly at right angles, come into contact with great violence, and raise a mountain of water to the height of one hundred and eighty feet. The shock is so dreadful, that it makes all the neighboring islands tremble; and fishermen and navigators fly from it in the utmost terror. The river and the ocean appear to contend for the empire of the waves: but they seem to come to a compromise; for the sea-current continues its way along the coast of Guiana to the Island of Trinidad, while the current of the river is still observable in the ocean at a distance of five hundred miles from the shore.

La Condamine passed this place of meeting in safety by waiting for a favorable course of tides, crossing the Amazon at its mouth, steering north;

and after many delays, caused by the timidity and bad seamanship of his Indian crew, arrived at last safe at Cayenne on the 26th February, 1744, having been eight months on his voyage, two of which were spent in his passage from Pará, a passage which he avers a French officer and crew, two years after him, accomplished in six days. La Condamine was received with all possible distinction at Cayenne, and in due time found passage home to France, where he arrived 25th February, 1745.

CHAPTER IX.

MADAME GODIN'S VOYAGE DOWN THE AMAZON.

ONE of the French commissioners, M. Godin, had taken with him on his scientific errand to Peru his wife; a lady for whom we bespeak the kind interest of our readers, for her name deserves honorable mention among the early navigators of the Amazon. The labors of the commission occupied several years; and when, in the year 1742, those labors were happily brought to a conclusion, M. Godin was prevented, by circumstances relating to himself individually, from accompanying his colleagues in their return to France. His detention was protracted from year to year, till at last, in 1749, he repaired alone to the Island of Cayenne to prepare every thing necessary for the homeward voyage of himself and his wife.

From Cayenne he wrote to Paris to the minister of marine, and requested that his government would procure for him the favorable interposition of the court of Portugal to supply him with the means of ascending the River Amazon to bring away his wife from Peru, and descend the stream with her to the Island of Cayenne. Thirteen years had rolled by since their arrival in the country, when at last Madame Godin saw her earnest wish to return home likely to be gratified. All that time, she had lived apart from her husband; she in Peru, he in the French colony of Cayenne. At last, M. Godin had the pleasure to see the arrival of a galiot (a small vessel having from sixteen to twenty oars on a side, and well adapted for rapid progress), which had been fitted out by the order of the King of Portugal, and despatched to Cayenne for the purpose of taking him on his long-wished-for journey. He immediately embarked; but, before he could reach the mouth of the Amazon River, he was attacked by so severe an illness, that he saw himself compelled to stop at Oyapoc, a station between Cayenne and the mouth of the river, and there to remain, and to send one Tristan, whom he thought his friend, in lieu of himself, up the river to seek Madame Godin, and escort her to him. He intrusted to him also, besides the needful money, various articles of merchandise to dispose of to the best advantage. The instructions which he gave him were as follows:—

The galiot had orders to convey him to Loreto, about half-way up the Amazon River, the first Spanish settlement. From there he was to go to Laguna, another Spanish town about twelve miles farther up, and to give Mr. Godin's letter, addressed to his wife, in charge to a certain ecclesiastic of that place, to be forwarded to the place of her residence. He himself was to wait at Laguna the arrival of Madame Godin.

The galiot sailed, and arrived safe at Loreto. But the faithless Tristan, instead of going himself to Laguna, or sending the letter there, contented himself with delivering the packet to a Spanish Jesuit, who was going to quite another region on some occasional purpose. Tristan himself, in the mean while, went round among the Portuguese settlements to sell his commodities. The result was, that M. Godin's letter, passing from hand to hand, failed to reach the place of its destination.

Meanwhile, by what means we know not, a blind rumor of the purpose and object of the Portuguese vessel lying at Loreto reached Peru, and came at last, but without any distinctness, to the ears of Madame Godin. She learned through this rumor that a letter from her husband was on the way to her; but all her efforts to get possession of it were fruitless. At last, she resolved to send a faithful negro servant, in company with an Indian, to the Amazon, to procure, if possible, more certain tidings. This faithful servant made his way boldly through all hinderances and difficulties which beset his journey, reached Loreto, talked with Tristan, and brought back intelligence that he, with the Portuguese vessel and all its equipments, were for her accommodation, and waited her orders.

Now, then, Madame Godin determined to undertake this most perilous and difficult journey. She was staying at the time at Riobamba, about one hundred and twenty miles south of Quito, where she had a house of her own with garden and grounds. These, with all other things that she could not take with her, she sold on the best terms she could. Her father, M. Grandmaison, and her two brothers, who had been living with her in Peru, were ready to accompany her. The former set out beforehand to a place the other side of the Cordilleras to make arrangements for his daughter's journey on her way to the ship.

Madame Godin received about this time a visit from a certain Mr. R., who gave himself out for a French physician, and asked permission to accompany her. He promised, moreover, to watch over her health, and to do all in his power to lighten the fatigues and discomforts of the arduous journey. She replied, that she had no authority over the vessel which was to carry her, and therefore could not answer for it that he could have a place in it. Mr. R., thereupon, applied to the brothers of Madame Godin; and they, thinking it very desirable that she should have a physician with her, persuaded their sister to consent to take him in her company.

So, then, she started from Riobamba, which had been her home till this time, the 1st of October, 1749, in company of the above-named persons, her black man, and three Indian women. Thirty Indians, to carry her baggage, completed her company. Had the luckless lady known what calamities, sufferings, and disappointments awaited her, she would have trembled at the prospect, and doubted of the possibility of living through it all, and reaching the wished-for goal of her journey.

The party went first across the mountains to Canelos, an Indian village, where they thought to embark on a little stream which discharges itself into the Amazon. The way thither was so wild and unbroken, that it was not even passable for mules, and must be travelled entirely on foot.

M. Grandmaison, who had set out a whole month

earlier, had stopped at Canelos no longer than was necessary to make needful preparations for his daughter and her attendants. Then he had immediately pushed on toward the vessel, to still keep in advance, and arrange matters for her convenience at the next station to which she would arrive. Hardly had he left Canelos, when the small-pox, a disease which in those regions is particularly fatal, broke out, and in one week swept off one-half of the inhabitants, and so alarmed the rest, that they deserted the place, and plunged into the wilderness. Consequently, when Madame Godin reached the place with her party, she found, to her dismay, only two Indians remaining, whom the fury of the plague had spared; and, moreover, not the slightest preparation either for her reception, or her furtherance on her journey. This was the first considerable mishap which befell her, and which might have served to forewarn her of the greater sufferings which she was to encounter.

A second followed shortly after. The thirty Indians who thus far had carried the baggage, and had received their pay in advance, suddenly absconded, whether from fear of the epidemic, or that they fancied, having never seen a vessel except at a distance, that they were to be compelled to go on board one, and be carried away. There stood, then, the deserted and disappointed company, overwhelmed, and knowing not what course to take, or how to help themselves. The safest course would have been to leave all their baggage to its fate, and return back the way they came; but the longing of Madame Godin for her beloved husband, from whom she had now been separated so many years, gave her courage to bid defiance to all the hinderances which lay in her way, and even to attempt impossibilities.

She set herself, therefore, to persuade the two Indians above mentioned to construct a boat, and, by means of it, to take her and her company to Andoas, another place about twelve days' journey distant. They willingly complied, receiving their pay in advance. The boat was got ready; and all the party embarked in it under the management of the two Indians.

After they had run safely two days' journey down the stream, they drew up to the bank to pass the night on shore. Here the treacherous Indians took the opportunity, while the weary company slept, to run away; and, when the travellers awoke next morning, they were nowhere to be found. This was a new and unforeseen calamity, by which their future progress was rendered greatly more hazardous.

Without a knowledge of the stream or the country, and without a guide, they again got on board their boat, and pushed on. The first day went by without any misadventure. The second, they came up with a boat which lay near the shore, alongside of an Indian hut built of branches of trees. They found there an Indian, just recovered from the sickness, and prevailed on him, by presents, to embark with them to take the helm. But fate envied them this relief: for, the next day, Mr. R.'s hat fell into the water; and the Indian, in endeavoring to recover it, fell overboard, and was drowned, not having strength to swim to the shore.

Now was the vessel again without a pilot, and steered by persons, not one of whom had the least knowledge of the course. Ere long, the vessel sprung a leak; and the unhappy company found themselves compelled to land, and build a hut to shelter them.

They were yet five or six days' journey from Andoas, the nearest place of destination. Mr. R. offered, for himself and another Frenchman his companion, to go thither, and make arrangements, that, within fourteen days, a boat from there should arrive and bring them off. His proposal was approved of. Madame Godin gave him her faithful black man to accompany him. He himself took good care that nothing of his property should be left behind.

Fourteen days were now elapsed; but in vain they strained their eyes to catch sight of the bark which Mr. R. had promised to send to their relief. They waited twelve days longer, but in vain. Their situation grew more painful every day.

At last, when all hope in this quarter was lost, they hewed trees, and fastened them together as well as they could, and made in this way a raft. When they had finished it, they put on their baggage, and seated themselves upon it, and suffered it to float down the stream. But even this frail bark required a steersman acquainted with navigation; but they had none such. In no long time, it struck against a sunken log, and broke to pieces. The people and their baggage were cast into the river. Great, however, as was the danger, no one was lost. Madame Godin sunk twice to the bottom, but was at last rescued by her brothers.

Wet through and through, exhausted, and half dead with fright, they at last all gained the shore. But only imagine their lamentable, almost desperate, condition! All their supplies lost; to make another raft impossible; even their stock of provisions gone! And where were they when all these difficulties overwhelmed them? In a horrid wilderness, so thick grown up with trees and bushes, that one could make a passage through it no other way than by axe and knife; inhabited only by fiercest tigers, and by the most formidable of serpents, — the rattlesnake. Moreover, they were without tools, without weapons! Could their situation be more deplorable?

CHAPTER X.

MADAME GODIN'S VOYAGE CONTINUED.

THE unfortunate travellers had now but the choice of two desperate expedients, — either to wait where they were the termination of their wretched existence, or try the almost impossible task of penetrating along the banks of the river, through the unbroken forest, till they might reach Andoas. They chose the latter, but first made their way back to their lately forsaken hut to take what little provisions they had there left. Having accomplished this, they set out on their most painful and dangerous journey. They observed, when they followed the shore of the river, that its windings lengthened their way. To avoid this, they endeavored, without leaving the course of the river, to keep a straight course. By this means, they lost themselves in the entangled forest; and every exertion to find their way was ineffect-'ual. Their clothes were torn to shreds, and hung dangling from their limbs; their bodies were sadly wounded by thorns and briers; and, as their scanty provision of food was almost gone, nothing seemed left to them but to sustain their wretched existence with wild fruit, seeds and buds of the palm-trees.

At last, they sank under their unremitted labor. Wearied with the hardships of such travel, torn and bleeding in every part of their bodies, and distracted with hunger, terror, and apprehensions, they lost the small remnant of their energy, and could do no more. They sat down, and had no power to rise again. In three or four days, one after another died at this stage of their journey. Madame Godin lay for the space of twenty-four hours by the side of her exhausted and helpless brothers and companions: she felt herself benumbed, stupefied, senseless, yet at the same time tormented by burning thirst. At last, Providence, on whom she relied, gave her courage and 'strength to rouse herself and seek for a rescue, which was in store for her, though she knew not where to look for it.

Around lay the dead bodies of her brothers and her other companions, — a sight which at another time would have broken her heart. She was almost naked. The scanty remnants of her clothing were so torn by the thorns as to be almost useless. She cut the shoes from her dead brothers' feet, bound the soles under her own, and plunged again into the thicket in search of something to allay her raging hunger and thirst. Terror at seeing herself so left alone in such a fearful wilderness, deserted by all the world, and apprehension of a dreadful death constantly hovering before her eyes, made such an impression upon her, that her hair turned gray.

It was not till the second day after she had resumed her wandering that she found water, and, a little while after, some wild fruit, and a few eggs of birds. But her throat was so contracted by long fasting, that she could hardly swallow. These served to keep life in her frame.

Eight long days she wandered in this manner hopelessly, and strove to sustain her wretched existence. If one should read in a work of fiction any thing equal to it, he would charge the author with exaggeration, and violation of probability. But it is history; and, however incredible her story may sound, it is rigidly conformed to the truth in all its circumstances, as it was afterwards taken down from the mouth of Madame Godin herself.

On the eighth day of her hopeless wandering, the hapless lady reached the banks of the Bobonosa, a stream which flows into the Amazon. At the break of day, she heard at a little distance a noise, and was alarmed at it. She would have fled, but at once reflected that nothing worse than her present circumstances could happen to her. She took courage, and went towards the place whence the sound proceeded; and here she found two Indians, who were occupied in shoving their boat into the water.

Madame Godin approached, and was kindly received by them. She told to them her desire to be conveyed to Andoas; and the good savages consented to carry her thither in their boat. They did so; and now behold her arrived at that place which the mean and infamous treachery of Mr. R. was the only cause of her not having reached long ago. This base fellow had, with unfeeling cruelty, thrown to the winds his promise to procure them a boat, and had gone on business of his own to Omaguas, a Spanish mission station, without in the least troubling himself about his pledged word, and the rescue of the unfortunates left behind. The honest negro was more true to duty, though he was born and bred a heathen, and the other a Christian.

While the civilized and polished Frenchman unfeelingly went away, and left his benefactress and her companions to languish in the depths of misery, the sable heathen ceased not his exertions till he had procured two Indians to go up the river with him, and bring away his deserted mistress and her companions. But, most unfortunately, he did not reach the hut where he had left them before they had carried into execution the unlucky determination to leave the hut, and seek their way through the wilderness. So he had the pain of failing to find her on his arrival.

Even then, the faithful creature did not feel as if all was done. He, with his Indian companions, followed the traces of the party till he came to the place where the bodies of the perished adventurers lay, which were already so decayed, that he could not distinguish one from the other. This pitiable sight led him to conclude that none of the company could have escaped death. He returned to the hut to take away some things of Madame Godin's which were left there, and carried them not only back with him to Andoas, but from thence (another touching proof of his fidelity) to Omaguas, that he might deposit the articles, some of which were of considerable value, in the hands of the unworthy Mr. R., to be by him delivered to the father of his lamented mistress.

And how did this unworthy Mr. R. behave when

he was apprised by the negro of the lamentable death of those whom he had so unscrupulously given over to destitution? Did he shudder at the magnitude and baseness of his crime? Oh, no! Like a heartless knave, he added dishonesty to cruelty, took the things into his keeping, and, to secure himself in the possession of them, sent the generous negro back to Quito. Joachim — for that was the name of this honest and noble black man — had unluckily set out on his journey back before Madame Godin arrived at Andoas. Thus he was lost to her; and her affliction at the loss of such a tried friend showed that the greatness of her past misfortunes had not made her incapable of feeling new distresses.

In Andoas she found a Christian priest, a Spanish missionary; and the behavior of this unchristian Christian contrasts with the conduct of her two Indian preservers, as that of the treacherous R. with that of the generous negro. For instance, when Madame Godin was in embarrassment how to show her gratitude to the good Indians who had saved her life, she remembered, that, according to the custom of the country, she wore around her neck a pair of gold chains, weighing about four ounces. These were her whole remaining property; but she hesitated not a moment, but took them off, and gave one to each of her benefactors. They were delighted beyond measure at such a gift; but the avaricious and dishonest priest took them away from them before the face of the generous giver, and gave them instead some yards of coarse cotton cloth, which they call, in that country, Tukujo. And this man was one of those who were sent to spread Christianity among the heathen, and one from whom those same Indians whom he had treated so dishonestly would hear the lesson, "Thou shalt not covet thy neighbor's goods"!

Madame Godin felt, at seeing such unchristian and unmanly behavior, such deep disgust, that, as soon as she was somewhat recruited from the effects of so many sufferings, she longed for a sight of some boat to enable her to escape from the companionship of this unjust priest, and get to Laguna, one of the aforementioned Spanish mission stations. A kind Indian woman made her a petticoat of cotton cloth, though Madame Godin had nothing to give her in payment for it. But this petticoat was to her, afterwards, a sacred thing, that she would not have parted with for any price. She laid it carefully away with the slippers which she made of her brothers' shoes, and never could, in after-times, look at the two without experiencing a rush of sad and tender recollections.

At Laguna she had the good fortune to find a missionary of better disposition. This one received her with kindness and sympathy, and exerted himself every way he could to restore her health, shattered by so much suffering. He wrote also on her behalf to the Governor of Omaguas, to beg him to aid in expediting her journey. By this means, the elegant Mr. R. learned that she was still alive; and as she was not likely in future to be burdensome to him, while he might, through her means, get a passage in the Portuguese vessel, he failed not to call upon her at Laguna. He delivered to her there some few of the things which Joachim had left in his charge; but to the question, "What had become of the rest?" he had no other answer to make but "They were spoilt." The knave forgot, when he said this, that gold bracelets, snuff-boxes, ear-rings, and pearls, of which this property consisted, are not apt to spoil.

Madame Godin could not forbear making to him the well-merited reproach that he was the cause of her late sufferings, and guilty of the mournful death of her brothers and her other companions. She desired to know, moreover, why he had sent away her faithful servant, the good Joachim; and his unworthy reply was, he had apprehensions that he would murder him. To the question, how he could have such a suspicion against a man whose tried fidelity and honest disposition were known to him, he knew not what to answer.

The good missionary explained to Madame Godin, after she was somewhat recruited from her late sufferings, the frightful length of the way, and the labors and dangers of her journey yet to come, and tried hard to induce her to alter her intention, and return to Rio Bambas, her former residence, instead of setting forth to encounter a new series of disappointments and perils. He promised, in that case, to convey her safely and with comfort. But the heroic woman rejected the proposal with immovable firmness. "God, who had so wonderfully protected her so far," she said, "would have her in his keeping for the remainder of her way. She had but one wish remaining, and that was to be re-united to her husband; and she knew no danger terrible enough to induce her to give up this one ruling desire of her heart."

The missionary, therefore, had a boat got ready to carry her to the Portuguese vessel. The Governor of Omaguas furnished the boat, and supplied it well with provisions: and, that the commander of the Portuguese galiot might be informed of her approach, he sent a smaller boat with provisions, and two soldiers by land, along the banks of the river, and betook himself to Loreto, where the galiot had been so long lying; and there he waited till Madame Godin arrived.

She still suffered severely from the consequences of the injuries which she had sustained during her wanderings in the wilderness. Particularly, the thumb of one hand, in which she had thrust a thorn, which they had not been able to get out, was in a bad condition. The bone itself was become carious, and she found it necessary to have the flesh cut open to allow fragments of the bone to come out. As for the rest, she experienced from the commander of the Portuguese vessel all possible kindness, and reached the mouth of the Amazon River without any further misadventure.

Mr. Godin, who still continued at Oyapoc (the same place where on account of sickness he had been obliged to stop), was no sooner informed of the approach of his wife than he went on board a vessel, and coasted along the shore till he met the galiot. The joy of again meeting, after a separation of so many years, and after such calamities undergone, was, as may well be supposed, on both sides, indescribably great. Their re-union seemed like a resurrection from the dead, since both of them had more than once given up all hope of ever seeing the other in this life.

The happy husband now conveyed his wife to Oyapoc, and thence to Cayenne; whence they departed on their return to France, in company with the venerable Mr. De Grandmaison. Madame Godin remained, however, constantly sad, notwithstanding her present ample cause for joy; and every endeavor to raise her spirits was fruitless, so deep and inextinguishable an impression had the terrible sufferings she had undergone made upon her mind. She spoke unwillingly of all that she had suffered; and even her husband found out with difficulty, and by little and little, the circumstances which we have narrated, taken from accounts under his own hand. He thought he could thereby infer that she had kept to herself, to spare his feelings, many circumstances of a distressing nature, which she herself preferred to forget. Her heart, too, was, by reason of her sufferings, so attuned to pity and forbearance, that her compassion even extended to the base and wicked men who had treated her with such injustice. She would therefore add nothing to induce her husband to invoke the vengeance of the law against the faithless Tristan, the first cause of all her misfortunes, who had converted to his own use many thousand dollars' worth of property which had been intrusted to him. She had even allowed herself to be pursuaded to take on board the boat from Omaguas down, for a second time, the mean-souled Mr. R.

So true is it that adversity and suffering do fulfil the useful purpose of rendering the human heart tender, placable, and indulgent.

CHAPTER XI.

HERNDON'S EXPEDITION.

IN the month of August, 1850, Lieut. Herndon, of the United-States navy, being on board the frigate "Vandalia," then lying at anchor in the harbor of Valparaiso, received information that he was designated by the Secretary of the Navy to explore the Valley of the Amazon. On the 4th of April, being then at Lima, he received his orders, and, on the 21st of May, commenced his land journey to the highest point on the Amazon navigable for boats, which is about three hundred miles from its source; in which distance there are twenty-seven rapids, the last of which is called the Pongo (or falls) de Manseriche. Over these the water rushes with frightful rapidity; but they are passed, with great peril and difficulty, by means of rafts. From the Pongo de Manseriche, Lieut. Herndon states that an unbroken channel of eighteen feet in depth may be found to the

Atlantic Ocean, — a distance of three thousand miles.

The party consisted of Lieut. Herndon, commander; Passed-midshipman Gibbon; a young master's mate named Richards; a young Peruvian, who had made the voyage down the Amazon a few years before, who was employed as interpreter to the Indians; and Mauricio, an Indian servant. They were mounted on mules; and their baggage of all kinds, including looking-glasses, beads, and other trinkets for the Indians, and some supplies of provisions, were carried also on muleback, under the charge of an *arriero*, or muleteer, who was an Indian. The party were furnished with a tent, which often came in use for nightly shelter, as the roadside inns furnished none, and the haciendas, or farm-houses, which they sometimes availed themselves of, afforded but poor accommodation. The following picture of the lieutenant's first night's lodgings, not more than ten miles from Lima, is a specimen: " The house was built of *adobe*, or sun-dried bricks, and roofed with tiles. It had but one room, which was the general receptacle for all comers. A mud projection, of two feet high and three wide, stood out from the walls of the room all around, and served as a permanent bed-place for numbers. Others laid their blankets and cloaks, and stretched themselves, on the floor; so that, with whites, Indians, negroes, trunks, packages, horse-furniture, game-cocks, and guinea-pigs, we had quite a caravansera appearance."

The lieutenant found the general answer to his inquiry for provisions for his party, and of fodder for their animals, was, "No hay" (there is none). The refusal of the people to sell supplies of these indispensable articles was a source of continued inconvenience. It arose probably from their fear to have it known that they had possessions, lest the hand of authority should be laid upon them, and their property be taken without payment. The cultivators, it must be remembered, are native Indians, under the absolute control of their Spanish masters, and have no recognized rights protected by law. While this state of things continues, civilization is effectually debarred progress.

The usual day's travel was twelve to fifteen miles. The route ascended rapidly; and the River Rimac, along whose banks their road lay, was soon reduced to a mountain torrent, raging in foam over the fragments of the rocky cliffs which overhung its bed. The road occasionally widened out, and gave room for a little cultivation.

May 27. — They had now reached a height of ten thousand feet above the level of the sea. Here the traveller feels that he is lifted above the impurities of the lower regions of the atmosphere, and is breathing air free from taint. The stars sparkled with intense brilliancy. The temperature at night was getting cool, and the travellers found they required all their blankets. But by day the heat was oppressive until tempered by the sea-breeze, which set in about eleven o'clock in the morning.

The productions of the country are Indian corn, alfalfa (a species of lucern), and potatoes. The potato, in this its native country, is small, but very fine. They saw here a vegetable of the potato kind called *oca*. Boiled or roasted, it is very agreeable to the taste, in flavor resembling green corn.

Here they entered upon the mining region. "The Earth here shows her giant skeleton bare: mountains, rather than rocks, rear their gray heads to the skies; and proximity made the scene more striking and sublime." Lieut. Herndon had brought letters to the superintendent of the mines, who received the travellers kindly and hospitably. This establishment is managed by a superintendent and three assistants, and about forty working hands. The laborers are

Indians, — strong, hardy-looking fellows, though low in stature, and stupid in expression. The manner of getting the silver from the ore is this: The ore is broken into pieces of the size of an English walnut, and then ground to a fine powder. The ground ore is then mixed with salt, at the rate of fifty pounds of salt to every six hundred of ore, and taken to the ovens to be toasted. After being toasted, the ore is laid in piles of about six hundred pounds upon the stone floor. The piles are then moistened with water, and quicksilver is sprinkled on them through a woollen cloth. The mass is well mixed by treading with the feet, and working with hoes. A little calcined iron pyrites, called *magistral*, is also added. The pile is often examined to see if the amalgamation is going on well. It is left to stand for eight or nine days until the amalgamation is complete; then carried to an elevated platform, and thrown into a well, or cavity: a stream of water is turned on, and four or five men trample and wash it with their feet. The amalgam sinks to the bottom, and the mud and water are let off by an aperture in the lower part of the well. The amalgam is then put into conical bags of coarse linen, which are hung up; and the weight of the mass presses out a quantity of quicksilver, which oozes through the linen, and is caught in vessels below. The mass, now dry, and somewhat harder than putty, is carried to the ovens, where the remainder of the quicksilver is driven off by heat, and the residue is *plata pina*, or pure silver. The proportion of pure silver in the amalgam is about twenty-two per cent. This is an unusually rich mine.

Returning from the mine, the party met a drove of llamas on their way from the hacienda. This is quite an imposing sight, especially when the drove is encountered suddenly at a turn of the road. The leader, who is always selected on account of his superior height, has his head decorated with tufts of woollen fringe, hung with little bells; and his great height (often six feet), gallant and graceful carriage, pointed ear, restless eye, and quivering lip, as he faces you for a moment, make him as striking an object as one can well conceive. Upon pressing on him, he bounds aside either up or down the cliff, and is followed by the herd, scrambling over places that would be impassable for the mule or the ass. The llama travels not more than nine or ten miles a day, his load being about one hundred and thirty pounds. He will not carry more, and will be beaten to death rather than move when he is overloaded or tired. The males only are worked: they appear gentle and docile, but, when irritated, have a very savage look, and spit at the object of their resentment. The guanaco, or alpaca, is another species of this animal, and the vicunia a third. The guanaco is as large as the llama, and bears a fleece of long and coarse wool. The vicunia is much smaller, and its wool is short and fine: so valuable is it, that it brings at the port of shipment a dollar a pound. Our travellers saw no guanacos, but now and then, in crossing the mountains, caught a glimpse of the wild and shy vicunia. They go in herds of ten or fifteen females, accompanied by one male, who is ever on the alert. On the approach of danger, he gives warning by a shrill whistle; and his charge make off with the speed of the wind.

On the 31st of May, the thermometer stood at thirty-six degrees at five, A.M. This, it must be remembered, was in the torrid zone, in the same latitude as Congo in Africa, and Sumatra in Asia; yet how different the climate! This is owing to the elevation, which at this water-shed of the continent, which separates the rivers of the Atlantic from those of the Pacific, was about sixteen thousand feet above the level of the sea. The peaks of the Cordillera presented the appearance of a hilly country at home on a winter's day; while the lower ranges were dressed in bright green, with placid little lakes interspersed, giving an air of quiet beauty to the scene.

The travellers next arrived at Morococha, where they found copper-mining to be the prevailing occupation. The copper ore is calcined in the open air, in piles consisting of ore and coal, which burn for a month. The ore thus calcined is taken to the ovens; and sufficient heat is employed to melt the copper, which runs off into moulds below. The copper, in this state, is impure, containing fifty per cent of foreign matter; and is worth fifteen cents the pound in England, where it is refined. There is a mine of fine coal near the hacienda, which yields an abundant supply.

The travellers passed other mining districts, rich in silver and copper. A large portion of the silver which forms the circulation of the world is dug from the range of mountains which they were now crossing, and chiefly from that slope of them which is drained off into the Amazon.

Their descent, after leaving the mining country, was rapid. On June 6, we find them at the head of a ravine leading down to the Valley of Tarma. The height of this spot above the level of the sea was 11,270 feet. As they rode down the steep descent, the plants and flowers that they had left on the other side began to re-appear. First the short grass and small clover, then barley, lucern, Indian corn, beans, turnips, shrubs, bushes, trees, flowers, growing larger and gayer in their colors, till the pretty little city of Tarma, imbosomed among the hills, and enveloped in its covering of willows and fruit-trees, with its long lawns of *alfalfa* (the greenest of grasses) stretching out in front, broke upon their view. It is a place of seven thousand inhabitants, beautifully situated in an amphitheatre of mountains, which are clothed nearly to the top with waving fields of barley. The lieutenant gives an attractive description of this mountain city, whose natural productions extend from the apples and peaches of the temperate zone to the oranges and pine-apples of the tropics; and whose air is so temperate and pure, that there was but one physician to a district of twenty thousand people, and he was obliged to depend upon government for a part of his support.

The party left Tarma on the 16th of June, and resumed their descent of the mountains. The ride was the wildest they had yet had. The ascents and descents were nearly precipitous; and the scene was rugged, wild, and grand beyond description. At certain parts of the road, it is utterly impossible for two beasts to pass abreast, or for one to turn and retreat; and the only remedy, when they meet, is to tumble one off the precipice, or to drag him back by the tail until he reaches a place where the other can pass. They met with a considerable fright in this way one day. They were riding in single file along one of those narrow ascents where the road is cut out of the mountain-side, and the traveller has a perpendicular wall on one hand, and a sheer precipice of many hundreds of feet upon the other. Mr. Gibbon was riding ahead. Just as he was about to turn a sharp bend of the road, the head of a bull peered round it, on the descent. When the bull came in full view, he stopped; and the travellers could see the heads of other cattle clustering over his quarters, and hear the shouts of the cattle-drivers far behind, urging on their herd. The bull, with lowered crest, and savage, sullen look, came slowly on, and actually got his head between the perpendicular rock and the neck of Gibbon's mule. But the sagacious beast on which he was mounted, pressing her haunches hard against the wall, gathered her feet close under her, and turned as upon a pivot. This placed the bull on the outside (there was room to pass, though no one would have thought it); and he rushed by at the gallop, followed in single file by the rest of the herd. The lieutenant owns that he and his friend "felt frightened."

On the 18th of June, they arrived at the first hacienda, where they saw sugar-cane, yucca, pine-apples, and plantains. Besides these, cotton and coffee were soon after found in cultivation. The laborers are native Indians, nominally free, but, by the customs of the country, pretty closely held in subjection to their employers. Their nominal wages are half a dollar a day; but this is paid in articles necessary for their support, which are charged to them at such prices as to keep them always in debt. As debtors, the law will enforce the master's claim on them; and it is almost hopeless for them to desert; for, unless they get some distance off before they are recognized, they will be returned as debtors to their employers. Freedom, under such circumstances, is little better than slavery; but it *is* better, for this reason, — that it only requires some improvement in the intelligence and habits of the laborers to convert it into a system of free labor worthy of the name.

The *yucca* (cassava-root) is a plant of fifteen or

twenty feet in height. It is difficult to distinguish this plant from the *mandioc*, which is called "wild yucca;" and this, "sweet yucca." This may be eaten raw; but the other is poisonous until subjected to heat in cooking, and then is perfectly wholesome. The yucca answers the same purpose in Peru that the mandioc does in Brazil. It is the general substitute for bread, and, roasted or boiled, is very pleasant to the taste. The Indians also make from it an intoxicating drink. Each plant will give from twenty to twenty-five pounds of the eatable root, which grows in clusters like the potato, and some tubers of which are as long and thick as a man's arm.

CHAPTER XII.

HERNDON'S EXPEDITION CONTINUED.

ON the 4th of July, the travellers arrived at the great mining station of Cerro Pasco. The weather was so cold, that the lieutenant, not being quite well, sat by the fire all day, trying to keep himself warm. The town is a most curious-looking place, entirely honey-combed, and having the mouths of mines, some of them two or three yards in diameter, gaping everywhere. From the top of a hill, the best view is obtained of the whole. Vast pits, called Tajos, surround this hill, from which many millions of silver have been taken; and the miners are still burrowing, like so many rabbits, in their bottoms and sides. The hill is penetrated in every direction; and it would not be surprising if it should cave in, any day, and bury many in its ruins. The falling-in of mines is of frequent occurrence: one caved in, some years ago, and buried three hundred persons. An

English company undertook mining here in 1825, and failed. Vast sums have been spent in constructing tunnels, and employing steam machinery to drain the mines; and the parties still persevere, encouraged by discovering, that, the lower they penetrate, the richer are the ores. The yield of these mines is about two million dollars' worth a year, which is equal to the yield of all the other mines of Peru together.

The lieutenant found the leading people here, as well as at Tarma, enthusiastic on the subject of opening the Amazon to foreign commerce. It will be a great day for them, they say, when the Americans get near them with a steamer.

On the 14th of July, they arrived at a spot of marshy ground, from which trickled in tiny streams the waters, which, uniting with others, swell till they form the broad River Huallaga, one of the head tributaries of the Amazon. Their descent was now rapid; and the next day they found themselves on a sudden among fruit-trees, with a patch of sugar-cane, on the banks of the stream. The sudden transition from rugged mountain-peaks, where there was no cultivation, to a tropical vegetation, was marvellous. Two miles farther on, they came in sight of a pretty village, almost hidden in the luxuriant vegetation. The whole valley here becomes very beautiful. The land, which is a rich river-bottom, is laid off into alternate fields of sugar-cane and alfalfa. The blended green and yellow of this growth, divided by willows, interspersed with fruit-trees, and broken into wavy lines by the serpentine course of the river, presented a scene which filled them with pleasurable emotions, and indicated that they had exchanged a semi-barbarous for a civilized society.

The party had had no occasion to complain of want of hospitality in any part of their route; but here they seemed to have entered upon a country where that virtue flourished most vigorously, having at its command the means of gratifying it. The owner of the hacienda of Quicacan, an English gentleman named Dyer, received the lieutenant and his large party exactly as if it were a matter of course, and as if they had quite as much right to occupy his house as they had to enter an inn. The next day they had an opportunity to compare with the Englishman a fine specimen of the Peruvian country gentleman. Col. Lucar is thus described: " He is probably the richest and most influential man in the province. He seems to have been the father of husbandry in these parts, and is the very type of the old landed proprietor of

Virginia, who has always lived upon his estates, and attended personally to their cultivation. Seated at the head of his table, with his hat on to keep the draught from his head, and which he would insist upon removing unless I would wear mine; his chair surrounded by two or three little negro children, whom he fed with bits from his plate; and attending with patience and kindness to the clamorous wants of a pair of splendid peacocks, a couple of small parrots of brilliant and variegated plumage, and a beautiful and delicate monkey,—I thought I had never seen a more perfect pattern of the patriarch. His kindly and affectionate manner to his domestics, and to his little grand-children, a pair of sprightly boys, who came in the evening from the college, was also very pleasing." The mention of a college in a region in some respects so barbarous may surprise our readers; but such there is. It has a hundred pupils, an income of seventy-five thousand dollars yearly, chemical and philosophical apparatus, and one thousand specimens of European minerals.

Ijurra, our lieutenant's Peruvian companion, had written to the governor of the village of Tingo Maria, the head of canoe navigation on the Huallaga, to send

Indians to meet the travellers here, and take their luggage on to the place of embarkation.

July 30. — The Indians came shouting into the farm-yard, thirteen in number. They were young, slight, but muscular-looking fellows, and wanted to shoulder the trunks, and be off at once. The lieutenant, however, gave them some breakfast; and then the party set forward, and, after a walk of six miles, reached the river, and embarked in the canoe. Two Indian laborers, called *peons*, paddled the canoe, and managed it very well. The peons cooked their dinner of cheese and rice, and made them a good cup of coffee. They are lively, good-tempered fellows, and, properly treated, make good and serviceable travelling companions. The canoe was available only in parts of the river where the stream was free from rapids. Where these occur, the cargo must be landed, and carried round. Lieut. Herndon and his party were compelled to walk a good part of the distance to Tingo Maria, which was thirty-six miles from where they first took the canoe.

"I saw here," says our traveller, "the *lucernago*, or fire-fly of this country. It is a species of beetle, carrying two white lights in its eyes, or rather in the places where the eyes of insects generally are, and a red light between the scales of the belly; so that it reminded me somewhat of the ocean steamers. They are sometimes carried to Lima (enclosed in an apartment cut into a sugar-cane), where the ladies at balls or theatres put them in their hair for ornament."

At Tingo Maria, their arrival was celebrated with much festivity. The governor got up a ball for them, where there was more hilarity than ceremony. The next morning, the governor and his wife accompanied our friends to the port. The governor made a short address to the canoe-men, telling them that their passengers were " no common persons; that they were to have a special care of them; to be very obedient," &c. They then embarked, and stood off; the boatmen blowing their horns, and the party on shore waving their hats, and shouting their adieus.

The party had two canoes, about forty feet long by two and a half broad, each hollowed out of a single log. The rowers stand up to paddle, having one foot in the bottom of the boat, and the other on the gunwale. There is a man at the bow of the boat to look out for rocks or sunken trees ahead; and a steersman, who stands on a little platform at the stern of the boat, and guides her motions. When the river was smooth, and free from obstruction, they drifted with the current, the men sitting on the trunks and boxes, chatting and laughing with each other; but, when they approached a "bad place," their serious looks, and the firm position in which each one planted himself at his post, showed that work was to be done. When the bark had fairly entered the pass, the rapid gestures of the bow-man, indicating the channel; the graceful position of the steersman, holding his long paddle; and the desperate exertions of the rowers, the railroad rush of the canoes, and the wild screaming laugh of the Indians as the boat shot past the danger, — made a scene so exciting as to banish the sense of danger.

After this specimen of their travel, let us take a glimpse of their lodging. "At half-past five, we camped on the beach. The first business of the boatmen, when the canoe is secured, is to go off to the woods, and cut stakes and palm-branches to make a house for the 'commander.' By sticking long poles in the sand, chopping them half-way in two about five feet above the ground, and bending the upper parts together, they make in a few minutes the frame of a little shanty, which, thickly thatched with palm-leaves, will keep off the dew or an ordinary rain. Some bring the drift-wood that is lying about the beach, and make a fire. The provisions are cooked and eaten, the bedding laid down upon the leaves that cover the floor of the shanty, the mosquito nettings spread; and after a cup of coffee, a glass of grog, and a cigar (if they are to be had), everybody retires for the night by eight o'clock. The Indians sleep round the hut, each under his narrow mosquito curtain, which glisten in the moonlight like so many tombstones."

The Indians have very keen senses, and see and hear things that would escape more civilized travellers. One morning, they commenced paddling with great vigor; for they said they heard monkeys ahead. It was not till after paddling a mile that they reached the place. "When we came up to them," says the lieutenant, "we found a gang of large red monkeys in some tall trees by the river-side, making a noise like the grunting of a herd of hogs. We landed; and, in a few moments, I found myself beating my way through the thick undergrowth, and hunting monkeys with as much excitement as I had ever felt in hunting squirrels when a boy." They found the game hard to kill, and only got three, — the lieutenant, with his rifle, one; and the Indians, with their blow-guns, two. The Indians roasted and ate theirs, and Lieut.

Herndon tried to eat a piece; but it was so tough, that his teeth would make no impression upon it.

Aug. 19.— The party arrived at Tarapoto. It is a town of three thousand five hundred inhabitants, and the district of which it is the capital numbers six thousand. The principal productions are rice, cotton, and tobacco; and cotton-cloth, spun and woven by the women, with about as little aid from machinery as the women in Solomon's time, of whom we are told, "She layeth her hands to the spindle, and her hands hold the distaff." The little balls of cotton thread which the women spin in this way are used as currency (and this in a land of silver-mines), and pass for twenty-five cents apiece in exchange for other goods, or twelve and a half cents in money. Most of the trade is done by barter. A cow is sold for one hundred yards of cotton cloth; a fat hog, for sixty; a large sheep, twelve; twenty-five pounds of salt fish, for twelve; twenty-five pounds of coffee, six; a head of plantains, which will weigh from forty to fifty pounds, for three needles; and so forth. All transportation of merchandise by land is made upon the backs of Indians, for want of roads suitable for beasts of burden. The customary weight of a load is seventy-five pounds: the cost of transportation to

Moyobamba, seventy miles, is six yards of cloth. It is easy to obtain, in the term of six or eight days, fifty or sixty peons, or Indian laborers, for the transportation of cargoes, getting the order of the governor, and paying the above price, and supporting the peons on the way. The town is the most important in the province of Mainas. The inhabitants are called civilized, but have no idea of what we call comfort in their domestic arrangements. The houses are of mud, thatched with palm, and have uneven earth floors. The furniture consists of a grass hammock, a standing bed-place, a coarse table, and a stool or two. The governor of this populous district wore no shoes, and appeared to live pretty much like the rest of them.

Vessels of five feet draught of water may ascend the river, at the lowest stage of the water, to within eighteen miles of Tarapoto.

Our travellers accompanied a large fishing-party. They had four or five canoes, and a large quantity of barbasco; a root which has the property of stupefying, or intoxicating, the fish. The manner of fishing is to close up the mouth of an inlet of the river with a net-work made of reeds; and then, mashing the barbasco-root to a pulp, throw it into the water. This turns the water white, and poisons it; so that the fish soon begin rising to the surface, dead, and are taken into the canoes with small tridents, or pronged sticks. Almost at the moment of throwing the barbasco into the water, the smaller fish rise to the surface, and die in one or two minutes; the larger fish survive longer.

The salt fish, which constitutes an important article of food and also of barter trade, is brought from down the river in large pieces of about eight pounds each, cut from the *vaca marina*, or sea-cow, also found in our Florida streams, and there called *manatee*. It is found in great numbers in the Amazon and its principal tributaries. It is not, strictly speaking, a fish, but an animal of the whale kind, which nourishes its young at the breast. It is not able to leave the water; but, in feeding, it gets near the shore, and raises its head out. It is most often taken when feeding.

Our travellers met a canoe of Indians, one man and two women, going up the river for salt. They bought, with beads, some turtle-eggs, and proposed to buy a monkey they had; but one of the women clasped the little beast in her arms, and set up a great outcry, lest the man should sell it. The man wore a long cotton gown, with a hole in the neck for the head to come through, and short, wide sleeves. He had on his arm a bracelet of monkeys' teeth, and the women had nose-rings of white beads. Their dress was a cotton petticoat, tied round the waist; and all were filthy.

Sept. 1. — They arrived at Laguna. Here they found two travelling merchants, a Portuguese and a Brazilian. They had four large boats, of about eight tons each, and two or three canoes. Their cargo consisted of iron and iron implements, crockery-ware, wine, brandy, copper kettles, coarse short swords (a very common implement of the Indians), guns, ammunition, salt, fish, &c., which they expected to exchange for straw hats, cotton cloth, sugar, coffee, and money. They were also buying up all the sarsaparilla they could find, and despatching it back in canoes. They invited our travellers to breakfast; and the lieutenant says, "I thought that I never tasted any thing better than the *farinha*, which I saw now for the first time."

Farinha is a general substitute for bread in all the course of the Amazon below the Brazilian frontier. It is used by all classes; and the boatmen seemed always contented with plenty of salt fish and farinha. The women make it in this way: They soak the root of the *mandioc* in water till it is softened a little, when they scrape off the skin, and grate the root upon a board, which is made into a rude grater by being smeared with some of the adhesive gums of the forest, and then sprinkled with pebbles. The white grated pulp is put into a conical-shaped bag made of the coarse fibres of the palm. The bag is hung up to a peg driven into a post of the hut; a lever is put through a loop at the bottom of the bag; the short end of the lever is placed under a chock nailed to the post below; and the woman hangs her weight on the long end. This elongates the bag, and brings a heavy pressure upon the mass within, causing the juice to ooze out through the wicker-work of the bag. When sufficiently pressed, the mass is put on the floor of a mud oven; heat is applied, and it is stirred with a stick till it granulates into very irregular grains, and is sufficiently toasted to drive off all the poisonous qualities which it has in a crude state. It is then packed in baskets (lined and covered with palm-leaves) of about sixty-four pounds' weight, which are generally sold all along the river at from seventy-five cents to one dollar. The sediment of the juice is tapioca, and is used to make custards, puddings, starch, &c. It will surprise some of our readers to be told that the juice extracted in the preparation of these wholesome and nutritive substances is a powerful poison, and used by the Indians for poisoning the points of their arrows.

CHAPTER XIII.

HERNDON'S EXPEDITION CONTINUED.

THE Huallaga is navigable, for vessels drawing five feet depth of water, 285 miles; and forty miles farther for canoes. Our travellers had now arrived at its junction with the Amazon; and their first sight of its waters is thus described: " The march of the great river in its silent grandeur was sublime; but in the untamed might of its turbid waters, as they cut away its banks, tore down the gigantic denizens of the forest, and built up islands, it was awful. I was reminded of our Mississippi at its topmost flood; but this stream lacked the charm which the plantation upon the bank, the city upon the bluff, and the steamboat upon the waters, lend to its fellow of the North. But its capacities for trade and commerce are inconceivably great; and to the touch of steam, settlement, and cultivation, this majestic stream and its magnificent water-shed would start up in a display of industrial results that would make the Valley of the Amazon one of the most enchanting regions on the face of the earth."

Lieut. Herndon speaks of the Valley of the Amazon in language almost as enthusiastic as that of Sir Walter Raleigh: " From its mountains you may dig silver, iron, coal, copper, zinc, quicksilver, and tin; from the sands of its tributaries you may wash gold, diamonds, and precious stones; from its forests you may gather drugs of virtues the most rare, spices of aroma the most exquisite, gums and resins of the most varied and useful properties, dyes of hue the most brilliant, with cabinet and building woods of the finest polish and the most enduring texture. Its climate is an everlasting summer, and its harvest perennial."

Sept. 8. — The party encamped at night on an island near the middle of the river. " The Indians, cooking their big monkeys over a large fire on the beach, presented a savage and most picturesque scene. They looked more like devils roasting human beings, than any thing mortal." We ask ourselves, on reading this, whether some such scene may not have given rise to the stories of cannibalism which Raleigh and others record.

They arrived at Nauta, a village of a thousand inhabitants, mostly Indians. The governor of the district received them hospitably. Each district has its governor, and each town its lieutenant-governor. These are of European descent. The other authorities of a town are *curacas*, captains, alcades, and constables. All these are Indians. The office of curaca is hereditary, and is not generally interfered with by the white governor. The Indians treat their curaca with great respect, and submit to corporal punishment at his mandate.

Sarsaparilla is one of the chief articles of produce collected here. It is a vine of sufficient size to shoot up fifteen or twenty feet from the root without support. It thus embraces the surrounding trees, and spreads to a great distance. The main root sends out many tendrils, generally about the thickness of a straw, and five feet long. These are gathered, and tied up in bundles of about an *arroba*, or thirty-two pounds' weight. It is found on the banks of almost every river of the region; but many of these are not worked, on account of the savages living on them, who attack the parties that come to gather it. The price in Nauta is two dollars the arroba, and in Europe from forty to sixty dollars.

From Nauta, Lieut. Herndon ascended the Ucayali, a branch of the Amazon, stretching to the north-west in a direction somewhat parallel to the Huallaga. There is the essential difference between the two rivers, as avenues for commerce, that the Ucayali is still in the occupation of savage tribes, unchristianized except where under the immediate influence of the mission stations planted among them; while the population of the Huallaga is tolerably advanced in civilization. The following sentences will give a picture of the Indians of the Ucayali: "These people cannot count, and I can never get from them any accurate idea of numbers. They are very little removed above 'the beasts that perish.' They are filthy, and covered with sores. The houses are very large, between thirty and forty feet in length, and ten or fifteen in breadth. They consist of immense roofs of small poles and canes, thatched with palm, and supported by short stakes, four feet high, planted in the ground three or four feet apart, and having the spaces, except between two in front, filled in with cane. They have no idea of a future state, and worship nothing. But they can make bows and canoes; and their women weave a coarse cloth from cotton, and dye it. Their dress is a long cotton gown. They paint the face, and wear ornaments suspended from the nose and lower lip."

Next let us take a view of the means in operation to elevate these people to civilization and Christianity. Sarayacu is a missionary station, governed by four Franciscan friars, who are thus described: "Father Calvo, meek and humble in personal concerns, yet full of zeal and spirit for his office, clad in his long serge gown, belted with a cord, with bare feet and accurate tonsure, habitual stoop, and generally bearing upon his shoulder a beautiful and saucy bird of the parrot kind, was my beau-ideal of a missionary monk. Bregati is a young and handsome Italian, whom Father Calvo sometimes calls St. John. Lorente is a tall, grave, and cold-looking Catalan. A lay-brother named Maguin, who did the cooking, and who was unwearied in his attentions to us, made up the establishment. I was sick here, and think that I shall ever remember with gratitude the affectionate kindness of these pious and devoted friars of St. Francis."

The government is paternal. The Indians recognize in the "padre" the power to appoint and remove curacas, captains, and other officers; to inflict stripes, and to confine in the stocks. They obey the priests' orders readily, and seem tractable and docile. The Indian men are drunken and lazy: the women do most of the work; and their reward is to be mal-treated by their husbands, and, in their drunken frolics, to be cruelly beaten, and sometimes badly wounded.

Our party returned to the Amazon; and we find occurring in their narrative names which are familiar to us in the history of our previous adventurers. They touched at Omaguas, the port where Madame Godin found kind friends in the good missionary and the governor, and where she embarked on her way to the galiot at Loreto; and they passed the mouth of the Napo, which enters the Amazon from the north, — the river down which Orellana passed in the first adventure. The lieutenant says, "We spoke two canoes that had come from near Quito by the Napo. There are few Christianized towns on the Napo; and the rowers of the boats were a more savage-looking set than I had seen," — so slow has been the progress of civilization in three hundred years.

The Amazon seems to be the land of monkeys. Our traveller says, "I bought a young monkey of an Indian woman to-day. It had coarse gray and white hair; and that on the top of its head was stiff, like the quills of the porcupine, and smoothed down in front as if it had been combed. I offered the little fellow some plantain; but, finding he would not eat, the woman took him, and put him to her breast, when he sucked away manfully and with great gusto. She weaned him in a week, so that he would eat plantain mashed up, and put into his mouth in small bits; but the little beast died of mortification because I would not let him sleep with his arms around my neck."

They got from the Indians some of the milk from the cow-tree. This the Indians drink, when fresh; and, brought in a calabash, it had a foamy appearance, as if just drawn from the cow. It, however, coagulates very soon, and becomes as hard and tenacious as glue. It does not appear to be as important an article of subsistence as one would expect from the name.

Dec. 2. — They arrived at Loreto, the frontier town of the Peruvian territory, and which reminds us again of Madame Godin, who there joined the Portuguese galiot. Loreto is situated on an eminence on the left bank of the river, which is here three-fourths of a mile wide, and one hundred feet deep. There are three mercantile houses in Loreto, which do a business of about ten thousand dollars a year. The houses at Loreto are better built and better furnished than those of the towns on the river above. The population of the place is two hundred and fifty, made up of Brazilians, mulattoes, negroes, and a few Indians.

At the next town, Tabatinga, the lieutenant entered the territory of Brazil. When his boat, bearing the American flag, was descried at that place, the Brazilian flag was hoisted; and when the lieutenant landed, dressed in uniform, he was received by the commandant, also in uniform, to whom he presented his passport from the Brazilian minister at Washington. As soon as this document was perused, and the lieutenant's rank ascertained, a salute of seven guns was fired from the fort; and the commandant treated him with great civility, and entertained him at his table, giving him roast beef, which was a great treat.

It was quite pleasant, after coming from the Peruvian villages, which are all nearly hidden in the woods, to see that Tabatinga had the forest cleared away from about it; so that a space of forty or fifty acres was covered with green grass, and had a grove of orange-trees in its midst. The commandant told him that the trade of the river was increasing very fast; that, in 1849, scarce one thousand dollars' worth of goods passed up; in 1850, two thousand five hundred dollars; and this year, six thousand dollars.

The sarsaparilla seems thus far to have been the principal article of commerce; but here they find another becoming of importance, — *manteca*, or oil made of turtle-eggs. The season for making manteca generally ends by the 1st of November. A commandant is appointed every year to take care of the beaches, prevent disorder, and administer justice. Sentinels are placed at the beginning of August, when the turtles commence depositing their eggs. They see that no one wantonly interferes with the turtles, or destroys the eggs. The process of making the oil is very disgusting. The eggs are collected, thrown into a canoe, and trodden into a mass with the feet. Water is poured on, and the mass is left to stand in the sun for several days. The oil rises to the top, is skimmed off, and boiled in large copper boilers. It is then put in earthen pots of about forty-five pounds' weight. Each pot is worth, on the beach, one dollar and thirty cents; and at Para, from two and a half to three dollars. The beaches of the Amazon and its tributaries yield from five to six thousand pots annually. It is used for the same purposes as lard with us.

CHAPTER XIV.

HERNDON'S EXPEDITION CONCLUDED.

ON Jan. 4, at about the point of the junction of the Purus River with the Amazon, Lieut. Herndon remarks, "The banks of the river are now losing the character of savage and desolate solitude that characterizes them above, and begin to show signs of habitation and cultivation. We passed to-day several farms, with neatly framed and plastered houses, and a schooner-rigged vessel lying off several of them."

They arrived at the junction of the River Negro. This is one of the largest of the tributaries of the Amazon, and derives its name from the blackness of its waters. When taken up in a tumbler, the water is a light-red color, like a pale juniper-water, and is probably colored by some such berry. This river, opposite the town of Barra, is about a mile and a half wide, and very beautiful. It is navigable for almost any draughts to the Masaya, a distance of about four hundred miles: there the rapids commence, and the farther ascent must be made in boats. By this river, a communication exists with the Orinoco, by means of a remarkable stream, the Cassaquiare, which seems to have been formed for the sole purpose of connecting these two majestic rivers, and the future dwellers upon them, in the bonds of perpetual union. Humboldt, the great traveller and philosopher, thus speaks of it, "The Cassaquiare, as broad as the Rhine, and whose course is one hundred and eighty miles in length, will not much longer form in vain a navigable canal between two basins of rivers which have a surface of one hundred and ninety thousand square leagues. The grain of New Grenada will be carried to the banks of the Rio Negro; boats will descend from the sources of the Napo and the Ucayali, from the Andes of Quito and Upper Peru, to the mouths of the Orinoco. A country nine or ten times larger than Spain, and enriched with the most varied productions, is accessible in every direction by the medium of the natural canal of the Cassaquiare and the bifurcation of the rivers."

The greatest of all the tributaries of the Amazon is the Madeira, whose junction our travellers next reached. For four hundred and fifty miles from its mouth, there is good navigation: then occur cascades, which are navigable only for boats, and occupy three hundred and fifty miles, above which the river is navigable for large vessels, by its great tributaries, into Bolivia and Brazil.

They next entered the country where the cocoa is regularly cultivated; and the banks of the river present a much less desolate and savage appearance than they do above. The cocoa-trees have a yellow-colored leaf; and this, together with their regularity of size, distinguishes them from the surrounding forest. Lieut. Herndon says, " I do not know a prettier place than one of these plantations. The trees interlock their branches, and, with their large leaves, make a shade impenetrable to any ray of the sun; and the large, golden-colored fruits, hanging from branch and trunk, shine through the green with a most beautiful effect. This is the time of the harvest; and we found the people of every plantation engaged in the open space before the house in breaking open the shells of the fruit, and spreading the seed to dry in the sun. They make a pleasant drink for a hot day by pressing out the juice of the gelatinous pulp that envelops the seeds. It is called cocoa-wine: it is a white, viscid liquor, has an agreeable, acid taste, and is very refreshing."

We must hasten on, and pass without notice many spots of interest on the river; but, as we have now reached a comparatively civilized and known region, it is less necessary to be particular. The Tapajos River stretches its branches to the town of Diamantino, situated at the foot of the mountains, where diamonds are found. Lieut. Herndon saw some of the diamonds and gold-sand in the possession of a resident of Santarem, who had traded much on the river. The gold-dust appeared to him equal in quality to that he had seen from California. Gold and diamonds, which are always united in this region as in many others, are found especially in the numerous watercourses, and also throughout the whole country. After the rains, the children of Diamantino hunt for the gold contained in the earth even of the streets, and in the bed of the River Ouro, which passes through the city; and they often collect considerable quantities. It is stated that diamonds are sometimes found in the stomachs of the fowls. The quantity of diamonds found in a year varies from two hundred and fifty to five hundred *oitavas;* the oitava being about seventeen carats. The value depends upon the quality and size of the specimen, and can hardly be reduced to an estimate. It is seldom that a stone of over half an oitava is found; and such a one is worth from two to three hundred dollars.

As an offset to the gold and diamonds, we have this picture of the climate: "From the rising to the setting of the sun, clouds of stinging insects blind the traveller, and render him frantic by the torments they cause. Take a handful of the finest sand, and throw it above your head, and you would then have but a faint idea of the number of these demons who tear the skin to pieces. It is true, these insects disappear at night, but only to give place to others yet more formidable. Large bats (true, thirsty vampires) literally throng the forests, cling to the hammocks, and, finding a part of the body exposed, rest lightly there, and drain it of blood. The alligators are so numerous, and the noise they make so frightful, that it is impossible to sleep."

At Santarem they were told the tide was perceptible, but did not perceive it. At Gurupa it was very apparent. This point is about five hundred miles from the sea. About thirty-five miles below Gurupa commences the great estuary of the Amazon. The river suddenly flows out into an immense bay, which might appropriately be called the "bay of a thousand islands;" for it is cut up into innumerable channels. The travellers ran for days through channels varying from fifty to five hundred yards in width, between numberless islands. This is the India-rubber country. The shores are low: indeed, one seldom sees the land at all; the trees on the banks generally standing in the water. The party stopped at one of the establishments for making India-rubber. The house was built of light poles, and on piles, to keep it out of the water, which flowed under and around it. This was the store, and, rude as it was, was a palace compared to the hut of the laborer who gathers the India-rubber. The process is as follows: A longitudinal gash is made in the bark of the tree with a hatchet. A wedge of wood is inserted to keep the gash open; and a small clay cup is stuck to the tree, beneath the gash. The cups may be stuck as close together as possible around the tree. In four or five hours, the milk has ceased to run, and each wound has given from three to five table-spoonfuls. The gatherer then collects it from the cups, pours it into an earthen vessel, and commences the operation of forming it into shapes, and smoking it. This must be done at once, as the juice soon coagulates. A fire is made on the ground, and a rude funnel placed over it to collect the smoke. The maker of the rubber now takes his last, if he is making shoes, or his mould, which is fastened to the end of a stick, pours the milk over it with a cup, and passes it slowly several times through the smoke until it is dry. He then pours on the other coats until he has the required thickness, smoking each coating till it is dry. From twenty to forty coats make a shoe. The soles and heels are, of course, given more coats than the body of the shoe. The figures on the shoes are made by tracing them on the rubber, while soft, with a coarse needle, or bit of wire. This is done two days after the coating. In a week, the shoes are taken from the last. The coating occupies about twenty-five minutes.

The tree is tall, straight, and has a smooth bark. It sometimes reaches a diameter of thirteen inches or more. Each incision makes a rough wound on the tree, which, although it does not kill it, renders it useless, because a smooth place is wanted to which to attach the cups. The milk is white and tasteless, and may be taken into the stomach with impunity.

Our travellers arrived at Pará on the 12th of April, 1852, and were most hospitably and kindly received by Mr. Norris, the American consul.

The journey of our travellers ends here. Lieut. Herndon's book is full of instruction, conveyed in a pleasant style. He seems to have manifested throughout good judgment, good temper, energy, and industry. He had no collisions with the authorities or with individuals, and, on his part, seems to have met friendly feelings and good offices throughout his whole route.

WILLIAM LEWIS HERNDON was born in Fredericksburg, Va., on the 25th of October, 1813. He entered the navy at the age of fifteen; served in the Mexican war; and was afterwards engaged for three years, with his brother-in-law, Lieut. Maury, in the National Observatory at Washington. In 1851-2, he explored the Amazon River, under commission of the United-States Government. In 1857, he was commander of the steamer "Central America," which left Havana for New York on Sept. 8, having on board four hundred and seventy-four passengers and a crew of one hundred and five men, and about two million dollars of gold. On Sept. 11, during a violent gale from the north-east and a heavy sea, she sprung a leak, and sunk, on the evening of Sept. 12, near the outer edge of the Gulf Stream, in lat. 31° 44' N. Only one hundred and fifty of the persons on board were saved, including the women and children. The gallant commander of the steamer was seen standing upon the wheel-house at the time of her sinking.

In a former chapter, we have told the fate of Sir Humphrey Gilbert. How fair a counterpart of that heroic death is this of the gallant Herndon!

CHAPTER XV.

LATEST EXPLORATIONS.

IN the year 1845, an English gentleman, Henry Walter Bates, visited the region of the Amazon for the purpose of scientific exploration. He went prepared to spend years in the country, in order to study diligently its natural productions. His stay was protracted until 1859, during which time he resided successively at Pará, Santarem, Ega, Barra, and other places; making his abode for months, or even years, in each. His account of his observations and discoveries was published after his return, and affords us the best information we possess respecting the country, its inhabitants, and its productions, brought down almost to the present time. Our extracts relate to the cities, the river and its shores, the inhabitants civilized and savage, the great tributary rivers, the vegetation, and the animals of various kinds.

Before proceeding with our extracts, we will remark the various names of the river.

It is sometimes called, from the name of its discoverer, "Orellana." This name is appropriate and well-sounding, but is not in general use.

The name of "Marañon," pronounced Maranyon, is still often used. It is probably derived from the natives.

It is called "The River of the Amazons," from the fable of its former inhabitants.

This name is shortened into "The Amazons," and, without the plural sign, "The Amazon," in common use.

Above the junction of the River Negro, the river is designated as "The Upper Amazon," or "Solimoens."

PARÁ.

"On the morning of the 28th of May, 1848, we arrived at our destination. The appearance of the city at sunrise was pleasing in the highest degree. It is built on a low tract of land, having only one small rocky elevation at its southern extremity: it therefore affords no amphitheatral view from the river; but the white buildings roofed with red tiles, the numerous towers and cupolas of churches and convents, the crowns of palm-trees reared above the buildings, all sharply defined against the clear blue sky, give an appearance of lightness and cheerfulness which is most exhilarating. The perpetual forest hems the city in on all sides landwards; and, towards the suburbs, picturesque country-houses are seen scattered about, half buried in luxuriant foliage.

"The impressions received during our first walk can never wholly fade from my mind. After traversing the few streets of tall, gloomy, convent-looking buildings near the port, inhabited chiefly by merchants and shopkeepers; along which idle soldiers, dressed in shabby uniforms, carrying their muskets carelessly over their arms; priests; negresses with red water-jars on their heads; sad-looking Indian women, carrying their naked children astride on their hips; and other samples of the motley life of the place, — were seen; we passed down a long, narrow street leading to the suburbs. Beyond this, our road lay across a grassy common, into a picturesque lane leading to the virgin forest. The long street was inhabited by the poorer class of the population. The houses were mostly in a dilapidated condition; and signs of indolence and neglect were everywhere visible. But amidst all, and compensating every defect, rose the overpowering beauty of the vegetation. The massive dark crowns of shady mangoes were seen everywhere among the dwellings, amidst fragrant, blossoming orange, lemon, and other tropical fruit-trees, — some in flower, others in fruit at various stages of ripeness. Here and there, shooting above the more dome-like and sombre trees, were the smooth columnar stems of palms, bearing aloft their magnificent crowns of finely-cut fronds. On the boughs of the taller and more ordinary-looking trees sat tufts of curiously leaved parasites. Slender woody lianas hung in festoons from the branches, or were suspended in the form of cords and ribbons; while luxuriant creeping plants overran alike tree-trunks, roofs, and walls, or toppled over palings in copious profusion of foliage.

"As we continued our walk, the brief twilight commenced; and the sounds of multifarious life came from the vegetation around, — the whirring of cicadas; the shrill stridulation of a vast number of crickets and grasshoppers, each species sounding its peculiar note; the plaintive hooting of tree-frogs, all blended together in one continuous ringing sound, — the audible expression of the teeming profusion of Nature. This uproar of life, I afterwards found, never wholly ceased, night or day: in course of time, I became, like other residents, accustomed to it. After my return to England, the death-like stillness of summer days in the country appeared to me as strange as the ringing uproar did on my first arrival at Pará."

CAMETÁ.

"I staid at Cametá five weeks, and made a considerable collection of the natural productions of the neighborhood. The town, in 1849, was estimated to contain about five thousand inhabitants. The productions of the district are cacao, India-rubber, and Brazil nuts. The most remarkable feature in the social aspect of the place is the mixed nature of the population, — the amalgamation of the white and Indian races being here complete. The aborigines were originally very numerous on the western bank of the Tocantins; the principal tribe being the Cametás, from which the city takes its name. They were a superior nation, settled, and attached to agriculture, and received with open arms the white immigrants who were attracted to the district by its fertility, natural beauty, and the healthfulness of the climate. The Portuguese settlers were nearly all males. The Indian women were good-looking, and made excellent wives; so the natural result has been, in the course of two centuries, a complete blending of the two races.

"The town consists of three long streets running parallel to the river, with a few shorter ones crossing them at right angles. The houses are very plain; being built, as usual in this country, simply of a strong framework, filled up with mud, and coated with white plaster. A few of them are of two or three stories. There are three churches, and also a small theatre, where a company of native actors, at the time of my visit, were representing light Portuguese plays with considerable taste and ability. The people have a reputation all over the province for energy and perseverance; and it is often said that they are as keen in trade as the Portuguese. The lower classes are as indolent and sensual here as in other parts of the province, — a moral condition not to be wondered at, where perpetual summer reigns, and where the necessaries of life are so easily obtained. But they are light-hearted, quick-witted, communicative, and hospitable. I found here a native poet, who had written some pretty verses, showing an appreciation of the natural beauties of the country; and was told that the Archbishop of Bahia, the primate of Brazil, was a native of Cametá. It is interesting to find the mamelucos (half-breeds) displaying talent and enterprise; for it shows that degeneracy does not necessarily result from the mixture of white and Indian blood.

"The forest behind Cametá is traversed by several broad roads, which lead over undulating ground many miles into the interior. They pass generally under shade, and part of the way through groves of coffee and orange trees, fragrant plantations of cacao, and tracts of second-growth woods. The narrow, broad-watered valleys, with which the land is intersected, alone have remained clothed with primeval forest, at least near the town. The houses along these beautiful roads belong chiefly to mameluco, mulatto, and Indian families, each of which has its own small plantation. There are only a few planters with large establishments; and these have seldom more than a dozen slaves. Besides the main roads, there are endless by-paths, which thread the forest, and communicate with isolated houses. Along these the traveller may wander day after day, without leaving the shade, and everywhere meet with cheerful, simple, and hospitable people."

RIVERS AND CREEKS.

"We made many excursions down the Irritiri, and saw much of these creeks. The Magoary is a magnificent channel: the different branches form quite a labyrinth, and the land is everywhere of little elevation. All these smaller rivers throughout the Pará estuary are of the nature of creeks. The land is so level, that the short local rivers have no sources and downward currents, like rivers, as we understand them. They serve the purpose of draining the land; but, instead of having a constant current one way, they have a regular ebb and flow with the tide. The natives call them *igarapés*, or canoe-paths. They are characteristic of the country. The land is everywhere covered with impenetrable forests: the houses and villages are all on the water-side, and nearly all communication is by water. This semi-aquatic life of the people is one of the most interesting features of the country. For short excursions, and for fishing in still waters, a small boat, called *montaria*, is universally used. It is made of five planks,—a broad one for the bottom, bent into the proper shape by the action of heat, two narrow ones for the sides, and two triangular pieces for stem and stern. It has no rudder: the paddle serves for both steering and propelling. The montaria takes here the place of the horse, mule, or camel of other regions. Besides one or more montarias, almost every family has a larger canoe, called *igarité*. This is fitted with two masts, a rudder, and keel, and has an arched awning or cabin near the stern, made of a framework of tough *lianas*, thatched with palm-leaves. In the igarité, they will cross stormy rivers fifteen or twenty miles broad. The natives are all boat-builders. It is often remarked by white residents, that the Indian is a carpenter and shipwright by intuition. It is astonishing to see in what crazy vessels these people will risk themselves. I have seen Indians cross rivers in a leaky montaria when it required the nicest equilibrium to keep the leak just above water: a movement of a hair's-breadth would send all to the bottom; but they manage to cross in safety. If a squall overtakes them as they are crossing in a heavily-laden canoe, they all jump overboard, and swim about until the heavy sea subsides, when they re-embark."

JUNCTION OF THE MADEIRA.

"Our course lay through narrow channels between islands. We passed the last of these, and then beheld to the south a sea-like expanse of water, where the Madeira, the greatest tributary of the Amazons, after two thousand miles of course, blends its waters with those of the king of rivers. I was hardly prepared for a junction of waters on so vast a scale as this, now nearly nine hundred miles from the sea. While travelling week after week along the somewhat monotonous stream, often hemmed in between islands, and becoming thoroughly familiar with it, my sense of the magnitude of this vast water-system had become gradually deadened; but this noble sight renewed the first feelings of wonder. One is inclined, in such places as these, to think the Paraenses do not exaggerate much when they call the Amazons the Mediterranean of South America. Beyond the mouth of the Madeira, the Amazons sweeps down in a majestic reach, to all appearance not a whit less in breadth before than after this enormous addition to its waters. The Madeira does not ebb and flow simultaneously with the Amazons; it rises and sinks about two months earlier: so that it was now fuller than the main river. Its current, therefore, poured forth freely from its mouth, carrying with it a long line of floating trees, and patches of grass, which had been torn from its crumbly banks in the lower part of its course. The current, however, did not reach the middle of the main stream, but swept along nearer to the southern shore.

"The Madeira is navigable 480 miles from its mouth: a series of cataracts and rapids then commences, which extends, with some intervals of quiet water, about 160 miles, beyond which is another long stretch of navigable stream."

JUNCTION OF THE RIO NEGRO.

"A brisk wind from the east sprung up early in the morning of the 22d: we then hoisted all sail, and made for the mouth of the Rio Negro. This noble stream, at its junction with the Amazons, seems, from its position, to be a direct continuation of the main river; while the Solimoens, which joins it at an angle, and is somewhat narrower than its tributary, appears to be a branch, instead of the main trunk, of the vast water-system.

"The Rio Negro broadens considerably from its mouth upward, and presents the appearance of a great lake; its black-dyed waters having no current, and seeming to be dammed up by the impetuous flow of the yellow, turbid Solimoens, which here belches forth a continuous line of uprooted trees, and patches of grass, and forms a striking contrast with its tributary. In crossing, we passed the line a little more than half-way over, where the waters of the two rivers meet, and are sharply demarcated from each other. On reaching the opposite shore, we found a remarkable change. All our insect pests had disappeared, as if by magic, even from the hold of the canoe: the turmoil of an agitated, swiftly-flowing river, and its torn, perpendicular, earthy banks, had given place to tranquil water, and a coast indented with snug little bays, fringed with sloping, sandy beaches. The low shore, and vivid, light-green, endlessly varied foliage, which prevailed on the south side of the Amazons, were exchanged for a hilly country, clothed with a sombre, rounded, and monotonous forest. A light wind carried us gently along the coast to the city of Barra, which lies about seven or eight miles within the mouth of the river.

"The town of Barra is built on a tract of elevated but very uneven land, on the left bank of the Rio Negro, and contained, in 1850, about three thousand inhabitants. It is now the principal station for the lines of steamers which were established in 1853; and passengers and goods are trans-shipped here for the Solimoens and Peru. A steamer runs once a fortnight between Pará and Barra; and another as often between this place and Nauta, in the Peruvian territory."

MAMELUCOS, OR HALF-BREEDS.

"We landed at one of the cacao-plantations. The house was substantially built; the walls formed of strong, upright posts, lathed across, plastered with mud, and whitewashed; and the roof tiled. The family were Mamelucos, or offspring of the European and the Indian. They seemed to be an average sample of the poorer class of cacao-growers. All were loosely dressed, and barefooted. A broad veranda extended along one side of the house, the floor of which was simply the well-trodden earth; and here hammocks were slung between the bare upright supports, a large rush-mat being spread on the ground, upon which the stout, matron-like mistress, with a tame parrot perched upon her shoulder, sat sewing with two pretty-looking mulatto-girls. The master, coolly clad in shirt and drawers, the former loose about his neck, lay in his hammock, smoking a long gaudily painted wooden pipe. The household utensils—earthen-ware jars, water-pots, and sauce-pans — lay at one end, near which was a wood-fire, with the ever-ready coffee-pot simmering on the top of a clay tripod. A large shed stood a short distance off, embowered in a grove of banana, papaw, and mango trees; and under it were the troughs, ovens, sieves, and other apparatus, for the preparation of mandioc. The cleared space around the house was only a few yards in extent: beyond it lay the cacao-plantations, which stretched on each side parallel to the banks of the river. There was a path through the forest, which led to the mandioc-fields, and, several miles beyond, to other houses on the banks of an interior channel. We were kindly received, as is always the case when a stranger visits these out-of-the-way habitations; the people being invariably civil and hospitable. We had a long chat, took coffee; and, on departing, one of the daughters sent a basketful of oranges, for our use, down to the canoe."

MÚRA INDIANS.

"On the 9th of January, we arrived at Matari, a miserable little settlement of Múra Indians. Here we again anchored, and went ashore. The place consisted of about twenty slightly built mud-hovels, and had a most forlorn appearance, notwithstanding the luxuriant forest in its rear. The absence of the usual cultivated trees and plants gave the place a naked and poverty-stricken aspect. I entered one of the hovels, where several women were employed cooking a meal. Portions of a large fish were roasting over a fire made in the middle of the low chamber; and the entrails were scattered about the floor, on which the women, with their children, were squatted. These had a timid, distrustful expression of countenance; and their bodies were begrimed with black mud, which is smeared over the skin as a protection against musquitoes. The children were naked: the women wore petticoats of coarse cloth, stained in blotches with *murixi*, a dye made from the bark of a tree. One of them wore a necklace of monkey's teeth. There were scarcely any household utensils: the place was bare, with the exception of two dirty grass hammocks hung in the corners. I missed the usual mandioc-sheds behind the house, with their surrounding cotton, cacao, coffee, and lemon trees. Two or three young men of the tribe were lounging about the low, open doorway. They were stoutly-built fellows, but less well-proportioned than the semi-civilized Indians of the Lower Amazons generally are. The gloomy savagery, filth, and poverty of the people in this place made me feel quite melancholy; and I was glad to return to the canoe."

MARAUÁ TRIBE.

A pleasanter picture is presented by the Indians of the Marauá tribe. Our traveller thus describes a visit to them: —

"Our longest trip was to some Indian houses, a distance of fifteen or eighteen miles up the Sapó; a journey made with one Indian paddler, and occupying a whole day. The stream is not more than forty or fifty yards broad: its waters are dark in color, and flow, as in all these small rivers, partly under shade, between two lofty walls of forest. We passed, in ascending, seven habitations, most of them hidden in the luxuriant foliage of the banks; their sites being known only by small openings in the compact wall of forest, and the presence of a canoe or two tied up in little shady ports. The inhabitants are chiefly Indians of the Marauá tribe, whose original territory comprises all the by-streams lying between the Jutahí and the Juruá, near the mouths of both these great tributaries. They live in separate families, or small hordes; have no common chief; and are considered as a tribe little disposed to adopt civilized customs, or be friendly with the whites. One of the houses belonged to a Jurí family; and we saw the owner, an erect, noble-looking old fellow, tattooed, as customary with his tribe, in a large patch over the middle of his face, fishing, under the shade of a colossal tree, with hook and line. He saluted us in the usual grave and courteous manner of the better sort of Indians as we passed by.

"We reached the last house, or rather two houses, about ten o'clock, and spent there several hours during the heat of the day. The houses, which stood on a high, clayey bank, were of quadrangular shape, partly open, like sheds, and partly enclosed with rude, mud walls, forming one or two chambers. The inhabitants, a few families of Marauás, received us in a frank, smiling manner. None of them were tattooed: but the men had great holes pierced in their ear-lobes, in which they insert plugs of wood; and their lips were drilled with smaller holes. One of the younger men, a fine, strapping fellow, nearly six feet high, with a large aquiline nose, who seemed to wish to be particularly friendly to me, showed me the use of these lip-holes, by fixing a number of little sticks in them, and then twisting his mouth about, and going through a pantomime to represent defiance in the presence of an enemy.

"We left these friendly people about four o'clock in the afternoon, and, in descending the umbrageous river, stopped, about half-way down, at another house, built in one of the most charming situations I had yet seen in this country. A clean, narrow, sandy pathway led from the shady port to the house, through a tract of forest of indescribable luxuriance. The buildings stood on an eminence in the middle of a level, cleared space; the firm, sandy soil, smooth as a floor, forming a broad terrace round them. The owner was a semi-civilized Indian, named Manoel; a dull, taciturn fellow, who, together with his wife and children, seemed by no means pleased at being intruded on in their solitude. The family must have been very industrious; for the plantations were very extensive, and included a little of almost all kinds of cultivated tropical productions, — fruit-trees, vegetables, and even flowers for ornament. The silent old man had surely a fine appreciation of the beauties of Nature; for the site he had chosen commanded a view of surprising magnificence over the summits of the forest; and, to give a finish to the prospect, he had planted a large number of banana-trees in the foreground, thus concealing the charred and dead stumps which would otherwise have marred the effect of the rolling sea of greenery. The sun set over the tree-tops before we left this little Eden; and the remainder of our journey was made slowly and pleasantly, under the checkered shade of the river banks, by the light of the moon."

THE FOREST.

The following passage describes the scenery of one of the peculiar channels by which the waters of the Amazon communicate with those of the Pará River:—

"The forest wall under which we are now moving consists, besides palms, of a great variety of ordinary forest-trees. From the highest branches of these, down to the water, sweep ribbons of climbing-plants of the most diverse and ornamental foliage possible. Creeping convolvuli and others have made use of the slender lianas and hanging air-roots as ladders to climb by. Now and then appears a mimosa or other tree, having similar fine pinnate foliage; and thick masses of ingá border the water, from whose branches hang long bean-pods, of different shape and size according to the species, some of them a yard in length. Flowers there are very few. I see now and then a gorgeous crimson blossom on long spikes, ornamenting the sombre foliage towards the summits of the forest. I suppose it to belong to a climber of the Combretaceous order. There are also a few yellow and violet trumpet-flowers. The blossoms of the ingás, although not conspicuous, are delicately beautiful. The forest all along offers so dense a front, that one never obtains a glimpse into the interior of the wilderness."

THE LIANA.

"The plant which seems to the traveller most curious and singular is the liana, a kind of osier, which serves for cordage, and which is very abundant in all the hot parts of America. All the species of this genus have this in common, that they twine around the trees and shrubs in their way, and after progressively extending to the branches, sometimes to a prodigious height, throw out shoots, which, declining perpendicularly, strike root in the ground beneath, and rise again to repeat the same course of uncommon growth. Other filaments, again, driven obliquely by the winds, frequently attach themselves to contiguous trees, and form a confused spectacle of cord, some in suspension, and others stretched in every direction, not unfrequently resembling the rigging of a ship. Some of these lianas are as thick as the arm of a man; and some strangle and destroy the tree round which they twine, as the boa-constrictor does its victims. At times it happens that the tree dies at the root, and the trunk rots, and falls in powder, leaving nothing but the spirals of liana, in form of a tortuous column, insulated and open to the day. Thus Nature laughs to scorn and defies the imitations of Art."

CACAO.

"The Amazons region is the original home of the principal species of chocolate-tree,— the theobroma cacao; and it grows in abundance in the forests of the upper river. The forest here is cleared before planting, and the trees are grown in rows. The smaller cultivators are all very poor. Labor is scarce: one family generally manages its own small plantation of ten to fifteen thousand trees; but, at harvest-time, neighbors assist each other. It appeared to me to be an easy, pleasant life: the work is all done under shade, and occupies only a few weeks in the year.

"The cultivated crop appears to be a precarious one. Little or no care, however, is bestowed on the trees; and weeding is done very inefficiently. The plantations are generally old, and have been made on the low ground near the river, which renders them liable to inundation when this rises a few inches more than the average. There is plenty of higher land quite suitable to the tree; but it is uncleared: and the want of labor and enterprise prevents the establishment of new plantations."

THE COW-TREE.

"We had heard a good deal about this tree, and about its producing from its bark a copious supply of milk as pleasant to drink as that of the cow. We had also eaten of its fruit at Pará, where it is sold in the streets by negro market-women: we were glad, therefore, to see this wonderful tree growing in its native wilds. It is one of the largest of the forest-monarchs, and is peculiar in appearance, on account of its deeply-scored, reddish, and ragged bark. A decoction of the bark, I was told, is used as a red dye for cloth. A few days afterward, we tasted its milk, which was drawn from dry logs that had been standing many days in the hot sun at the saw-mills. It was pleasant with coffee, but had a slight rankness when drunk pure. It soon thickens to a glue, which is very tenacious, and is often used to cement broken crockery. I was told that it was not safe to drink much of it; for a slave had recently lost his life through taking it too freely.

"To our great disappointment, we saw no flowers, or only such as were insignificant in appearance. I believe it is now tolerably well ascertained that the majority of forest-trees in equatorial Brazil have small and inconspicuous flowers. Flower-frequenting insects are also rare in the forest. Of course, they would not be found where their favorite food was wanting. In the open country, on the Lower Amazons, flowering trees and bushes are more abundant; and there a large number of floral insects are attracted. The forest-bees in South America are more frequently seen feeding on the sweet sap which exudes from the trees than on flowers."

CHAPTER XVI.

THE NATURALIST ON THE AMAZON.

ON the 16th of January, the dry season came abruptly to an end. The sea-breezes, which had been increasing in force for some days, suddenly ceased, and the atmosphere became misty: at length, heavy clouds collected where a uniform blue sky had for many weeks prevailed, and down came a succession of heavy showers, the first of which lasted a whole day and night. This seemed to give a new stimulus to animal life. On the first night, there was a tremendous uproar,—tree-frogs, crickets, goat-suckers, and owls, all joining to perform a deafening concert. One kind of goat-sucker kept repeating at intervals, throughout the night, a phrase similar to the Portuguese words, 'Joao corta pao,'—'John, cut wood;' a phrase which forms the Brazilian name of the bird. An owl in one of the trees muttered now and then a succession of syllables resembling the word 'murucututu.' Sometimes the croaking and hooting of frogs and toads were so loud, that we could not hear one another's voices within doors. Swarms of dragon-flies appeared in the day-time about the pools of water created by the rain; and ants and termites came forth in great numbers."

ANTS.

This region is the very headquarters and metropolis of ants. There are numerous species, differing in character and habits, but all of them at war with man, and the different species with one another. Our author thus relates his observations of the saüba-ant:—

"In our first walks, we were puzzled to account for large mounds of earth, of a different color from the surrounding soil, which were thrown up in the plantations and woods. Some of them were very extensive, being forty yards in circumference, but not more than two feet in height. We soon ascertained that these were the work of the saübas, being the outworks, or domes, which overlie and protect the entrances to their vast subterranean galleries. On close examination, I found the earth of which they are composed to consist of very minute granules, agglomerated without cement, and forming many rows of little ridges and turrets. The difference of color from the superficial soil is owing to their being formed of the undersoil brought up from a considerable depth. It is very rarely that the ants are seen at work on these mounds. The entrances seem to be generally closed : only now and then, when some particular work is going on, are the galleries opened. In the larger hillocks, it would require a great amount of excavation to get at the main galleries ; but I succeeded in removing portions of the dome in smaller hillocks, and then I found that the minor entrances converged, at the depth of about two feet, to one broad, elaborately worked gallery, or mine, which was four or five inches in diameter.

"The habit of the saüba-ant, of clipping and carrying away immense quantities of leaves, has long been recorded in books of natural history; but it has not hitherto been shown satisfactorily to what use it applies the leaves. I discovered this only after much time spent in investigation. The leaves are used to thatch the domes which cover the entrances to their subterranean dwellings, thereby protecting from the deluging rains the young broods in the nests beneath. Small hillocks, covering entrances to the underground chambers, may be found in sheltered places; and these are always thatched with leaves, mingled with granules of earth. The heavily-laden workers, each carrying its segment of leaf vertically, the lower end secured by its mandibles, troop up, and cast their burthens on the hillock; another relay of laborers place the leaves in position, covering them with a layer of earthy granules, which are brought one by one from the soil beneath.

"It is a most interesting sight to see the vast host of busy, diminutive workers occupied on this work. Unfortunately, they choose cultivated trees for their purpose, such as the coffee and orange trees."

THE FIRE-ANT.

"Aveyros may be called the headquarters of the fire-ant, which might be fittingly termed the scourge of this fine river. It is found only on sandy soils, in open places, and seems to thrive most in the neighborhood of houses and weedy villages, such as Aveyros: it does not occur at all in the shades of the forest. Aveyros was deserted a few years before my visit, on account of this little tormentor; and the inhabitants had only recently returned to their houses, thinking its numbers had decreased. It is a small species, of a shining reddish color. The soil of the whole village is undermined by it. The houses are overrun with them: they dispute every fragment of food with the inhabitants, and destroy clothing for the sake of the starch. All eatables are obliged to be suspended in baskets from the rafters, and the cords well soaked with copaiba-balsam, which is the only thing known to prevent them from climbing. They seem to attack persons from sheer malice. If we stood for a few moments in the street, even at a distance from their nests, we were sure to be overrun, and severely punished; for, the moment an ant touched the flesh, he secured himself with his jaws, doubled in his tail, and stung with all his might. The sting is likened, by the Brazilians, to the puncture of a red-hot needle. When we were seated on chairs in the evenings, in front of the house, to enjoy a chat with our neighbors, we had stools to support our feet, the legs of which, as well as those of the chairs, were well anointed with the balsam. The cords of hammocks are obliged to be smeared in the same way, to prevent the ants from paying sleepers a visit."

BUTTERFLIES.

"At Villa Nova, I found a few species of butterflies which occurred nowhere else on the Amazons. In the broad alleys of the forest, several species of Morpho were common. One of these is a sister-form to the Morpho Hecuba, and has been described under the name of Morpho Cisseis. It is a grand sight to see these colossal butterflies by twos and threes floating at a great height in the still air of a tropical morning. They flap their wings only at long intervals; for I have noticed them to sail a very considerable distance without a stroke. Their wing-muscles, and the thorax to which they are attached, are very feeble in comparison with the wide extent and weight of the wings; but the large expanse of these members doubtless assists the insects in maintaining their aerial course. The largest specimens of Morpho Cisseis measure seven inches and a half in expanse. Another smaller kind, which I could not capture, was of a pale, silvery-blue color; and the polished surface of its wings flashed like a silver speculum, as the insect flapped its wings at a great elevation in the sunlight."

THE BIRD-CATCHING SPIDER.

"At Cametá, I chanced to verify a fact relating to the habits of a large, hairy spider of the genus Mygale, in a manner worth recording. The individual was nearly two inches in length of body; but the legs expanded seven inches, and the entire body and legs were covered with coarse gray and reddish hairs. I was attracted by a movement of the monster on a tree-trunk: it was close beneath a deep crevice in the tree, across which was stretched a dense white web. The lower part of the web was broken; and two small birds, finches, were entangled in the pieces. They were about the size of the English siskin; and I judged the two to be male and female. One of them was quite dead; the other lay under the body of the spider, not quite dead, and was smeared with the filthy liquor, or saliva, exuded by the monster. I drove away the spider, and took the birds; but the second one soon died. The fact of a species of mygale sallying forth at night, mounting trees, and sucking the eggs and young of humming-birds, has been recorded long ago by Madame Merian and Palisot de Beauvois; but, in the absence of any confirmation, it has come to be discredited. From the way the fact has been related, it would appear that it had been derived from the report of natives, and had not been witnessed by the narrators. I found the circumstance to be quite a novelty to the residents hereabouts.

"The mygales are quite common insects. Some species make their cells under stones; others form artificial tunnels in the earth; and some build their dens in the thatch of houses. The natives call them crab-spiders. The hairs with which they are clothed come off when touched, and cause a peculiar and almost maddening irritation. The first specimen that I killed and prepared was handled incautiously; and I suffered terribly for three days afterward. I think this is not owing to any poisonous quality residing in the hairs, but to their being short and hard, and thus getting into the fine creases of the skin. Some mygales are of immense size. One day, I saw the children belonging to an Indian family who collected for me with one of these monsters, secured by a cord round its waist, by which they were leading it about the house as they would a dog."

BATS.

"At Caripí, near Pará, I was much troubled by bats. The room where I slept had not been used for many months, and the roof was open to the tiles and rafters. I was aroused about midnight by the rushing noise made by vast hosts of bats sweeping about the room. The air was alive with them. They had put out the lamp; and, when I relighted it, the place appeared blackened with the impish multitudes that were whirling round and round. After I had laid about well with a stick for a few minutes, they disappeared among the tiles; but, when all was still again, they returned, and once more extinguished the light. I took no further notice of them, and went to sleep. The next night, several of them got into my hammock. I seized them as they were crawling over me, and dashed them against the wall. The next morning, I found a wound, evidently caused by a bat, on my hip. This was rather unpleasant: so I set to work with the negroes, and tried to exterminate them. I shot a great many as they hung from the rafters; and the negroes, having mounted with ladders to the roof outside, routed out from beneath the eaves many hundreds of them, including young broods. There were altogether four species. By far the greater number belonged to the Dysopes perotis, a species having very large ears, and measuring two feet from tip to tip of the wings. I was never attacked by bats, except on this occasion. The fact of their sucking the blood of persons sleeping, from wounds which they make in the toes, is now well established; but it is only a few persons who are subject to this blood-letting."

PARROTS.

"On recrossing the river in the evening, a pretty little parrot fell from a great height headlong into the water near the boat, having dropped from a flock which seemed to be fighting in the air. One of the Indians secured it for me; and I was surprised to find the bird uninjured. There had probably been a quarrel about mates, resulting in our little stranger being temporarily stunned by a blow on the head from the beak of a jealous comrade. It was of the species called by the natives Maracaná; the plumage green, with a patch of scarlet under the wings. I wished to keep the bird alive, and tame it; but all our efforts to reconcile it to captivity were vain: it refused food, bit every one who went near it, and damaged its plumage in its exertions to free itself. My friends in Aveyros said that this kind of parrot never became domesticated. After trying nearly a week, I was recommended to lend the intractable creature to an old Indian woman living in the village, who was said to be a skilful bird-tamer. In two days, she brought it back almost as tame as the familiar love-birds of our aviaries. I kept my little pet for upward of two years. It learned to talk pretty well, and was considered quite a wonder, as being a bird usually so difficult of domestication. I do not know what arts the old woman used. Capt. Antonio said she fed it with her saliva.

"Our maracaná used to accompany us sometimes in our rambles, one of the lads carrying it on his head. One day, in the middle of a long forest-road, it was missed, having clung probably to an overhanging bough, and escaped into the thicket without the boy perceiving it. Three hours afterwards, on our return by the same path, a voice greeted us in a colloquial tone as we passed, 'Maracaná!' We looked about for some time, but could not see any thing, until the word was repeated with emphasis, 'Maracaná!' when we espied the little truant half concealed in the foliage of a tree. He came down, and delivered himself up, evidently as much rejoiced at the meeting as we were."

TURTLE-EGGS AND OIL.

"I accompanied Cardozo in many wanderings on the Solimoens, or Upper Amazons, during which we visited the *praias* (sand-islands), the turtle-pools in the forests, and the by-streams and lakes in the great desert river. His object was mainly to superintend the business of digging up turtle-eggs on the sand-banks; having been elected *commandante* for the year of the *praia-real* (royal sand-island) of Shimuni, the one lying nearest to Ega. There are four of these royal praias within the district, all of which are visited annually by the Ega people, for the purpose of collecting eggs, and extracting oil from their yolks. Each has its commander, whose business is to make arrangements for securing to every inhabitant an equal chance in the egg-harvest, by placing sentinels to protect the turtles while laying. The turtles descend from the interior pools to the main river in July and August, before the outlets dry up, and then seek, in countless swarms, their favorite sand-islands; for it is only a few praias that are selected by them out of the great number existing.

"We left Ega, on our first trip to visit the sentinels while the turtles were yet laying, on the 26th of September. We found the two sentinels lodged in a corner of the praia, or sand-bank, where it commences, at the foot of the towering forest-wall of the island; having built for themselves a little rancho with poles and palm-leaves. Great preparations are obliged to be taken to avoid disturbing the sensitive turtles, who, previous to crawling ashore to lay, assemble in great shoals off the sand-bank. The men, during this time, take care not to show themselves, and warn off any fisherman who wishes to pass near the place. Their fires are made in a deep hollow near the borders of the forest, so that the smoke may not be visible. The passage of a boat through the shallow waters where the animals are congregated, or the sight of a man, or a fire on the sand-bank, would prevent the turtles from leaving the water that night to lay their eggs; and, if the causes of alarm were repeated once or twice, they would forsake the praia for some quieter place. Soon after we arrived, our men were sent with the net to catch a supply of fish for supper. In half an hour, four or five large basketsful were brought in. The sun set soon after our meal was cooked: we were then obliged to extinguish the fire, and remove our supper-materials to the sleeping-ground, a spit of land about a mile off; this course being necessary on account of the musquitoes, which swarm at night on the borders of the forest.

"I rose from my hammock at daylight, and found Cardozo and the men already up, watching the turtles. The sentinels had erected for this purpose a stage about fifty feet high, on a tall tree near their station, the ascent to which was by a roughly-made ladder of woody lianas. The turtles lay their eggs by night, leaving the water in vast crowds, and crawling to the central and highest part of the praia. These places are, of course, the last to go under water, when, in unusually wet seasons, the river rises before the eggs are hatched by the heat of the sand. One would almost believe from this that the animals used forethought in choosing a place; but it is simply one of those many instances in animals where unconscious habit has the same result as conscious prevision. The hours between midnight and dawn are the busiest. The turtles excavate, with their broad-webbed paws, deep holes in the fine sand; the first-comer, in each case, making a pit about three feet deep, laying its eggs (about a hundred and twenty in number), and covering them with sand; the next making its deposit at the top of that of its predecessor; and so on, until every pit is full. The whole body of turtles frequenting a praia does not finish laying in less than fourteen or fifteen days, even when there is no interruption. When all have done, the area over which they have excavated is distinguishable from the rest of the praia only by signs of the sand having been a little disturbed.

"On arriving at the edge of the forest, I mounted the sentinels' stage just in time to see the turtles retreating to the water on the opposite side of the sand-bank after having laid their eggs. The sight was well worth the trouble of ascending the shaky ladder. They were about a mile off; but the surface of the sand was blackened with the multitudes which were waddling towards the river. The margin of the praia was rather steep; and they all seemed to tumble, head-first, down the declivity, into the water."

When the turtles have finished depositing their eggs, the process of collecting them takes place, of which our author gives an account as follows:—

THE EGG-HARVEST.

"My next excursion was made in company of Senior Cardozo, in the season when all the population of the villages turns out to dig up turtle-eggs, and to revel on the praias. Placards were posted on the church-doors at Ega, announcing that the excavation on Shimuni would commence on the 17th October. We set out on the 16th, and passed on the way, in our well-manned igarité (or two-masted boat), a large number of people, men, women, and children, in canoes of all sizes, wending their way as if to a great holiday gathering. By the morning of the 17th, some four hundred persons were assembled on the borders of the sand-bank; each family having erected a rude temporary shed of poles and palm-leaves to protect themselves from the sun and rain. Large copper kettles to prepare the oil, and hundreds of red earthenware jars, were scattered about on the sand.

"The excavation of the *taboleiro*, collecting the eggs, and preparing the oil, occupied four days. The commandante first took down the names of all the masters of households, with the number of persons each intended to employ in digging. He then exacted a payment of about fourpence a head towards defraying the expense of sentinels. The whole were then allowed to go to the taboleiro. They ranged themselves round the circle, each person armed with a paddle, to be used as a spade; and then all began simultaneously to dig, on a signal being given — the roll of drums — by order of the commandante. It was an animating sight to behold the wide circle of rival diggers throwing up clouds of sand in their energetic labors, and working gradually toward the centre of the ring. A little rest was taken during the great heat of mid-day; and, in the evening, the eggs were carried to the huts in baskets. By the end of the second day, the tabolciro was exhausted: large mounds of eggs, some of them four or five feet in height, were then seen by the side of each hut, the produce of the labors of the family.

"When no more eggs are to be found, the mashing process begins. The egg, it may be mentioned, has a flexible or leathery shell: it is quite round, and somewhat larger than a hen's egg. The whole heap is thrown into an empty canoe, and mashed with wooden prongs; but sometimes naked Indians and children jump into the mass, and tread it down, besmearing themselves with the yolk, and making about as filthy a scene as can well be imagined. This being finished, water is poured into the canoe, and the fatty mass then left for a few hours to be heated by the sun, on which the oil separates, and rises to the surface. The floating oil is afterwards skimmed off with long spoons, made by tying large mussel-shells to the end of rods, and purified over the fire in copper-kettles. At least six thousand jars, holding each three gallons of the oil, are exported annually from the Upper Amazons and the Madeira to Pará, where it is used for lighting, frying fish, and other purposes."

ELECTRIC EELS.

"We walked over moderately elevated and dry ground for about a mile, and then descended three or four feet to the dry bed of another creek. This was pierced in the same way as the former watercourse, with round holes full of muddy water. They occurred at intervals of a few yards, and had the appearance of having been made by the hands of man. As we approached, I was startled at seeing a number of large serpent-like heads bobbing above the surface. They proved to be those of electric eels; and it now occurred to me that the round holes were made by these animals working constantly round and round in the moist, muddy soil. Their depth (some of them were at least eight feet deep) was doubtless due also to the movements of the eels in the soft soil, and accounted for their not drying up, in the fine season, with the rest of the creek. Thus, while alligators and turtles in this great inundated forest region retire to the larger pools during the dry season, the electric eels make for themselves little ponds in which to pass the season of drought.

"My companions now cut each a stout pole, and proceeded to eject the eels in order to get at the other fishes, with which they had discovered the ponds to abound. I amused them all very much by showing how the electric shock from the eels could pass from one person to another. We joined hands in a line, while I touched the biggest and freshest of the animals on the head with my hunting-knife. We found that this experiment did not succeed more than three times with the same eel, when out of the water; for, the fourth time, the shock was hardly perceptible."

CHAPTER XVII.

ANIMATED NATURE.

THE number and variety of climbing trees in the Amazons forests are interesting, taken in connection with the fact of the very general tendency of the animals also to become climbers. All the Amazonian, and in fact all South-American monkeys, are climbers. There is no group answering to the baboons of the Old World, which live on the ground. The gallinaceous birds of the country, the representatives of the fowls and pheasants of Asia and Africa, are all adapted, by the position of the toes, to perch on trees; and it is only on trees, at a great height, that they are to be seen. Many other similar instances could be enumerated."

MONKEYS.

"On the Upper Amazons, I once saw a tame individual of the Midas leoninus, a species first described by Humboldt, which was still more playful and intelligent than the more common M. ursulus. This rare and beautiful monkey is only seven inches in length, exclusive of the tail. It is named leoninus on account of the long, brown mane which hangs from the neck, and which gives it very much the appearance of a diminutive lion. In the house where it was kept, it was familiar with every one: its greatest pleasure seemed to be to climb about the bodies of different persons who entered. The first time I went in, it ran across the room straightway to the chair on which I had sat down, and climbed up to my shoulder: arrived there, it turned round, and looked into my face, showing its little teeth, and chattering, as though it would say, "Well, and how do *you* do?" M. de St. Hilaire relates of a species of this genus, that it distinguished between different objects depicted on an engraving. M. Ardouin showed it the portraits of a cat and a wasp: at these it became much terrified; whereas, at the sight of a figure of a grasshopper or beetle, it precipitated itself on the picture, as if to seize the objects there represented."

THE CAIARÁRA.

"The light-brown caiarára is pretty generally distributed over the forests of the level country. I saw it frequently on the banks of the Upper Amazons, where it was always a treat to watch a flock leaping amongst the trees; for it is the most wonderful performer in this line of the whole tribe. The troops consist of thirty or more individuals, which travel in single file. When the foremost of the flock reaches the outermost branch of an unusually lofty tree, he springs forth into the air without a moment's hesitation, and alights on the dome of yielding foliage belonging to the neighboring tree, maybe fifty feet beneath; all the rest following his example. They grasp, on falling, with hands and tail, right themselves in a moment, and then away they go, along branch and bough, to the next tree.

"The caiarára is very frequently kept as a pet in the houses of natives. I kept one myself for about a year, which accompanied me in my voyages, and became very familiar, coming to me always on wet nights to share my blanket. It keeps the house where it is kept in a perpetual uproar. When alarmed or hungry, or excited by envy, it screams piteously. It is always making some noise or other, often screwing up its mouth, and uttering a succession of loud notes resembling a whistle. Mine lost my favor at last by killing, in one of his jealous fits, another and much choicer pet, — the nocturnal, owl-faced monkey. Some one had given this a fruit which the other coveted: so the two got to quarrelling. The owl-faced fought only with his paws, clawing out, and hissing, like a cat: the other soon obtained the mastery, and, before I could interfere, finished his rival by cracking its skull with its teeth. Upon this I got rid of him."

THE COAITA.

"The coaita is a large, black monkey, covered with coarse hair, and having the prominent parts of the face of a tawny, flesh-colored hue. The coaitas are called by some French zoölogists spider-monkeys, on account of the length and slenderness of their body and limbs. In these apes, the tail, as a prehensile organ, reaches its highest degree of perfection; and, on this account, it would perhaps be correct to consider the coaita as the extreme development of the American type of apes.

"The tail of the coaita is endowed with a wonderful degree of flexibility. It is always in motion, coiling and uncoiling like the trunk of an elephant, and grasping whatever comes within reach.

"The flesh of this monkey is much esteemed by the natives in this part of the country; and the military commandant every week sends a negro hunter to shoot one for his table. One day I went on a coaita-hunt, with a negro-slave to show me the way. When in the deepest part of the ravine, we heard a rustling sound in the trees overhead; and Manoel soon pointed out a coaita to me. There was something human-like in its appearance, as the lean, shaggy creature moved deliberately among the branches at a great height. I fired, but, unfortunately, only wounded it. It fell, with a crash, headlong, about twenty or thirty feet, and then caught a bough with its tail, which grasped it instantaneously; and there the animal remained suspended in mid-air. Before I could reload, it recovered itself, and mounted nimbly to the topmost branches, out of the reach of a fowling-piece, where we could perceive the poor thing apparently probing the wound with its fingers."

THE TAME COAITA.

"I once saw a most ridiculously tame coaita. It was an old female, which accompanied its owner, a trader on the river, in all his voyages. By way of giving me a specimen of its intelligence and feeling, its master set to, and rated it soundly, calling it scamp, heathen, thief, and so forth, all through the copious Portuguese vocabulary of vituperation. The poor monkey, quietly seated on the ground, seemed to be in sore trouble at this display of anger. It began by looking earnestly at him; then it whined, and lastly rocked its body to and fro with emotion, crying piteously, and passing its long, gaunt arms continually over its forehead; for this was its habit when excited, and the front of the head was worn quite bald in consequence. At length, its master altered his tone. 'It's all a lie,' my old woman. 'You're an angel, a flower, a good, affectionate old creature,' and so forth. Immediately the poor monkey ceased its wailing, and soon after came over to where the man sat."

SCARLET-FACED MONKEY.

The most singular of the Simian family in Brazil are the scarlet-faced monkeys, called by the Indians

Uakari, of which there are two varieties, the white and red-haired. Mr. Bates first met with the white-haired variety under the following circumstances: —

"Early one sunny morning, in the year 1855, I saw in the streets of Ega a number of Indians carrying on their shoulders down to the port, to be embarked on the Upper Amazons steamer, a large cage made of strong lianas, some twelve feet in length, and five in height, containing a dozen monkeys of the most grotesque appearance. Their bodies (about eighteen inches in height, exclusive of limbs) were clothed from neck to tail with very long, straight, and shining whitish hair; their heads were nearly bald, owing to the very short crop of thin gray hairs; and their faces glowed with the most vivid scarlet hue. As a finish to their striking physiognomy, they had bushy whiskers of a sandy color, meeting under the chin, and reddish yellow eyes. They sat gravely and silently in a group, and altogether presented a strange spectacle."

Another interesting creature is the owl-faced night ape. These monkeys are not only owl-faced, but their habits are those of the moping bird.

"They sleep all day long in hollow trees, and come forth to prey on insects, and eat fruits, only in the night. They are of small size, the body being about a foot long, and the tail fourteen inches; and are clothed with soft gray and brown fur, similar in substance to that of the rabbit. Their physiognomy reminds one of an owl or·tiger-cat. The face is round, and encircled by a ruff of whitish fur; the muzzle is not at all prominent; the mouth and chin are small; the ears are very short, scarcely appearing above the hair of the head; and the eyes are large, and yellowish in color, imparting the staring expression of nocturnal animals of prey. The forehead is whitish, and decorated with three black stripes, which, in one of the species, continue to the crown, and in the other meet on the top of the forehead.

"These monkeys, although sleeping by day, are aroused by the least noise; so that, when a person passes by a tree in which a number of them are concealed, he is startled by the sudden apparition of a group of little striped faces crowding a hole in a trunk."

Mr. Bates had one of the Nyctipithæci for a pet, which was kept in a box containing a broad-mouthed glass jar, into which it would dive, head foremost, when any one entered the room, turning round inside, and thrusting forth its inquisitive face an instant afterward to stare at the intruder. The Nyctipithecus, when tamed, renders one very essential service to its owner: it clears the house of bats as well as of insect vermin.

The most diminutive of the Brazilian monkeys is the "Hapale pygmæus," only seven inches long in the body, with its little face adorned with long, brown whiskers, which are naturally brushed back over the ears. The general color of the animal is brownish-tawny; but the tail is elegantly barred with black.

Mr. Bates closes his account by stating that the total number of species of monkeys which he found inhabiting the margins of the Upper and Lower Amazons was thirty-eight, belonging to twelve different genera, forming two distinct families.

THE SLOTH.

"I once had an opportunity, in one of my excursions, of watching the movements of a sloth. Some travellers in South America have described the sloth as very nimble in its native woods, and have disputed the justness of the name which has been bestowed upon it. The inhabitants of the Amazons region, however, both Indians and descendants of the Portuguese, hold to the common opinion, and consider the sloth as the type of laziness. It is very common for one native to call to another, in reproaching him for idleness, 'Bicho do Embaüba' (beast of the cecropia-tree); the leaves of the cecropia being the food of the sloth. It is a strange sight to see the uncouth creature, fit production of these silent woods, lazily moving from branch to branch. Every movement betrays, not indolence exactly, but extreme caution. He never looses his hold from one branch without first securing himself to the next; and, when he does not immediately find a bough to grasp with the rigid hooks into which his paws are so curiously transformed, he raises his body, supported on his hind legs, and claws around in search of a fresh foothold. After watching the animal for about half an hour, I gave him a charge of shot: he fell with a terrific crash, but caught a bough in his descent with his powerful claws, and remained suspended. Two days afterward, I found the body of the sloth on the ground; the animal having dropped, on the relaxation of the muscles, a few hours after death. In one of our voyages, I saw a sloth swimming across a river at a place where it was probably three hundred yards broad. Our men caught the beast, and cooked and ate him."

"We had an unwelcome visitor while at anchor in the port. I was awakened a little after midnight, as I lay in my little cabin, by a heavy blow struck at the sides of the canoe close to my head, succeeded by the sound of a weighty body plunging in the water. I got up; but all was quiet again, except the cackle of fowls in our hen-coop, which hung over the side of the vessel, about three feet from the cabin-door. Next morning I found my poultry loose about the canoe, and a large rent in the bottom of the hen-coop, which was about two feet from the surface of the water. A couple of fowls were missing.

"Antonio said the depredator was the sucumjú, the Indian name for the anaconda, or great water-serpent, which had for months past been haunting this part of the river, and had carried off many ducks and fowls from the ports of various houses. I was inclined to doubt the fact of a serpent striking at its prey from the water, and thought an alligator more likely to be the culprit, although we had not yet met with alligators in the river. Some days afterward, the young men belonging to the different settlements agreed together to go in search of the serpents. They began in a systematic manner, forming two parties, each embarked in three or four canoes, and starting from points several miles apart, whence they gradually approximated, searching all the little inlets on both sides of the river. The reptile was found at last, sunning itself on a log at the mouth of a muddy rivulet, and despatched with harpoons. I saw it the day after it was killed. It was not a very large specimen, measuring only eighteen feet nine inches in length, and sixteen inches in circumference at the widest part of the body."

ALLIGATORS.

"Our rancho was a large one, and was erected in a line with the others, near the edge of the sand-bank, which sloped rather abruptly to the water. During the first week, the people were all more or less troubled by alligators. Some half-dozen full-grown ones were in attendance off the praia, floating about on the lazily-flowing, muddy water. The dryness of the weather had increased since we left Shimuni, the currents had slackened, and the heat in the middle of the day was almost insupportable. But no one could descend to bathe without being advanced upon by one or other of these hungry monsters. There was much offal cast into the river; and this, of course, attracted them to the place. Every day, these visitors became bolder: at length, they reached a pitch of impudence that was quite intolerable. Cardozo had a poodle-dog named Carlito, which some grateful traveller whom he had befriended had sent him from Rio Janeiro. He took great pride in this dog, keeping it well sheared, and preserving his coat as white as soap and water could make it. We slept in our rancho, in hammocks slung between the outer posts; a large wood fire (fed with a kind of wood abundant on the banks of the river, which keeps alight all night) being made in the middle, by the side of which slept Carlito on a little mat. One night, I was awoke by a great uproar. It was caused by Cardozo hurling burning firewood with loud curses at a huge cayman, which had crawled up the bank, and passed beneath my hammock (being nearest the water) towards the place where Carlito lay. The dog raised the alarm in time. The reptile backed out, and tumbled down the bank into the river; the sparks from the brands hurled at him flying from his bony hide. Cardozo threw a harpoon at him, but without doing him any harm."

THE PUMA.

"One day, I was searching for insects in the bark of a fallen tree, when I saw a large, cat-like animal advancing towards the spot. It came within a dozen yards before perceiving me. I had no weapon with me but an old chisel, and was getting ready to defend myself if it should make a spring; when it turned round hastily, and trotted off. I did not obtain a very distinct view of it; but I could see its color was that of the puma, or American lion, although it was rather too small for that species.

"The puma is not a common animal in the Amazons forests. I did not see altogether more than a dozen skins in the possession of the natives. The fur is of a fawn-color. The hunters are not at all afraid of it, and speak in disparaging terms of its courage. Of the jaguar they give a very different account."

THE GREAT ANT-EATER.

"The great ant-eater, *tamandua* of the natives, was not uncommon here. After the first few weeks of residence, I was short of fresh provisions. The people of the neighborhood had sold me all the fowls they could spare. I had not yet learned to eat the stale and stringy salt fish which is the staple food of these places; and for several days I had lived on rice-porridge, roasted bananas, and farinha. Florinda asked me whether I could eat tamandua. I told her almost any thing in the shape of flesh would be acceptable: so she went the next day with an old negro named Antonio, and the dogs, and, in the evening, brought one of the animals. The meat was stewed, and turned out very good, something like goose in flavor. The people of Caripi would not touch a morsel, saying it was not considered fit to eat in those parts. I had read, however, that it was an article of food in other countries of South America. During the next two or three weeks, whenever we were short of fresh meat, Antonio was always ready, for a small reward, to get me a tamandua.

"The habits of the animal are now pretty well known. It has an excessively long, slender muzzle, and a worm-like, extensile tongue. Its jaws are destitute of teeth. The claws are much elongated, and its gait is very awkward. It lives on the ground, and feeds on termites, or white ants; the long claws being employed to pull in pieces the solid hillocks made by the insects, and the long flexible tongue to lick them up from the crevices."

THE JAGUAR.

Our traveller, though he resided long and in various parts of the Amazon country, never saw there a jaguar. How near he came to seeing one appears in the following extract. This animal is the nearest approach which America presents to the leopards and tigers of the Old World.

"After walking about half a mile, we came upon a dry water-course, where we observed on the margin of a pond the fresh tracks of a jaguar. This discovery was hardly made, when a rush was heard amidst the bushes on the top of a sloping bank, on the opposite side of the dried creek. We bounded forward: it was, however, too late; for the animal had sped in a few minutes far out of our reach. It was clear we had disturbed on our approach the jaguar while quenching his thirst at the water-hole. A few steps farther on, we saw the mangled remains of an alligator. The head, fore-quarters, and bony shell, were all that remained: but the meat was quite fresh, and there were many footmarks of the jaguar around the carcass; so that there was no doubt this had formed the solid part of the animal's breakfast."

PARÁ.

"I arrived at Pará on the 17th of March, 1859, after an absence in the interior of seven years and a half. My old friends, English, American, and Brazilian, scarcely knew me again, but all gave me a very warm welcome. I found Pará greatly changed and improved. It was no longer the weedy, ruinous, village-looking place that it had appeared when I first knew it in 1848. The population had been increased to twenty thousand by an influx of Portuguese, Madeiran, and German immigrants; and, for many years past, the provincial government had spent their considerable surplus revenue in beautifying the city. The streets, formerly unpaved, or strewed with stones and sand, were now laid with concrete in a most complete manner: all the projecting masonry of the irregularly-built houses had been cleared away, and the buildings made more uniform. Most of the dilapidated houses were replaced by handsome new edifices, having long and elegant balconies fronting the first floors, at an elevation of several feet above the roadway. The large swampy squares had been drained, weeded, and planted with rows of almond and other trees; so that they were now a great ornament to the city, instead of an eye-sore as they formerly were. Sixty public vehicles, light cabriolets, some of them built in Pará, now plied in the streets, increasing much the animation of the beautified squares, streets, and avenues. I was glad to see several new book-sellers' shops; also a fine edifice devoted to a reading-room, supplied with periodicals, globes, and maps; and a circulating library. There were now many printing-offices, and four daily newspapers. The health of the place had greatly improved since 1850, — the year of the yellow-fever; and Pará was now considered no longer dangerous to new-comers.

"So much for the improvements visible in the place; and now for the dark side of the picture. The expenses of living had increased about fourfold; a natural consequence of the demand for labor and for native products of all kinds having augmented in greater ratio than the supply, in consequence of large arrivals of non-productive residents, and considerable importations of money, on account of the steamboat-company and foreign merchants.

"At length, on the 2d of June, I left Pará, — probably forever. I took a last view of the glorious forest for which I had so much love, and to explore which I had devoted so many years. The saddest hours I recollect ever to have spent were those of the succeeding night, when, the pilot having left us out of sight of land, though within the mouth of the river, waiting for a wind, I felt that the last link which connected me with the land of so many pleasing recollections was broken."

THE END.

Press of Geo. C. Rand & Avery, No. 3, Cornhill, Boston.

www.ingramcontent.com/pod-product-compliance
Lightning Source LLC
Chambersburg PA
CBHW051900300426
44117CB00006B/474